A PHONOLOGY AND PROSODY OF MODERN ENGLISH

A PHONOLOGY AND PROSODY
OF MODERN ENGLISH

by

HANS KURATH

ANN ARBOR · THE UNIVERSITY OF MICHIGAN PRESS

Printed in West Germany

PREFACE

The mounting interest in American English in Europe and in other parts of the world makes it desirable to treat the chief regional types of cultivated American pronunciation in comparison with Standard British English. This has become possible through the completion of the field survey of the Eastern United States (1930—1948), which has raised into relief the marked regional differences in cultivated usage in the coastal plain along the Atlantic Ocean, the seedbed of all varieties of English current farther west on the North American continent.

The findings of this survey are presented in considerable detail in Hans Kurath and Raven I. Mc David, Jr., *The Pronunciation of English in the Atlantic States* (1961) and furnish the data used in the present volume. The dialectal subdivisions of this area, extending for more than a thousand miles along the Atlantic, are shown on Figure 3 of Hans Kurath, *A Word Geography of the Eastern United States* (1949). The major subareas are: the NORTH (New England and New York State, with the distinctive enclave of Metropolitan New York), the MIDLAND (Pennsylvania and adjoining areas to the east, west, and southwest), and the South (including the distinctive focal areas of Virginia and South Carolina). Lacking a single dominant cultural center, the regional types of cultivated American English bid fair to survive for many years to come. In this respect North America differs fundamentally from Great Britain, France, and German-speaking Europe, where the usage of the cultured of a particular focal area or of a national cultural institution is generally accepted as an ideal national standard.

The cultivated speech of the burgeoning Middle West and Far West, often misleadingly called 'General American', is in the main derived from that of western New England and Pennsylvania. It is reliably recorded in John S. Kenyon and Thomas A. Knott, *A Pronouncing Dictionary of American English* (1944), to which I am greatly indebted.

The speech of the plantation country along the Gulf of Mexico (from Georgia to eastern Texas) is derived in the main from that of South Carolina and Virginia. It has not yet been systematically investigated.

All aspects of English phonology and prosody are here treated from a structural point of view. In accordance with American practice, phonemes and phonemically written words are given between slanting lines, allophones and regional diaphones of phonemes in brackets. It will be stated, for instance, that the phoneme /o/ of *road* has the regional diaphones [ou ~ ɜu ~ oˑ ~ oə].

All vowels of Modern English, whether short, prolonged, or diphthongal, are treated as phonemic units. Thus *bit, bet, bat, hot, hut, foot* as well as *beat, bait, bite, boil, bout, boat, boot, hurt* are said to have the same phonemic structure, each consisting of a consonant plus a vowel plus a consonant. My reasons for choosing this phonemic interpretation of the English vowel sounds are briefly stated in *The Pronunciation of English in the Atlantic States*, pp. 3—4.

Although my treatment of the English syllabics differs sharply from that adopted by some American scholars, it is in principle clearly within the tradition of American structuralism as represented by Edward Sapir (1925) and Leonard Bloomfield (1933), the pioneers of this approach to the analysis of pronunciation, and as developed and applied by such Neo-Bloomfieldians as Bernard Bloch, Charles F. Hocket, and George L. Trager.

With regard to British usage and its history, I have relied very largely on the work of such scholars as Albert C. Baugh, Karl Brunner, George O. Curme, Ferdinand Holthausen, Eilert Ekwall, Otto Jespersen, Richard Jordan, Daniel Jones, Helge Kökeritz, Karl Luick, Henry C. Wyld, and R. E. Zachrisson. The *Oxford English Dictionary* and the *Michigan Middle English Dictionary* have been my constant companions. I have also drawn upon the unpublished field records from the Southern and the South Midland counties of England made by Guy S. Lowman, Jr. (1937—8). They proved especially helpful in dealing with the adoption in Standard English of certain pronunciations from areas adjoining the Home Counties. The systematization of the vowel phonemes of current British English and the account of the history of this vowel system are, however, my own. The reader should have no difficulty in 'translating' Daniel Jones' notation system into the phonemic system that I have adopted.

The history of the Modern English phonemes and of the stress patterns of words is presented in retrospect. This historical perspective serves to throw light on the comparative regularity of phonemic and prosodic changes that have produced the modern system or systems and provides insight into the complexities of some of these changes. It calls attention to deviant and unsystematized features, and to features adopted from other regional dialects and from foreign languages. The structure of a living language is never without its oddities—relics of the past, incipient shifts, and unassimilated foreign items.

In giving the sources of Modern English phonemes, only Middle English is presented in a phonemic notation. Old English, Old Norse, Latin, Old French, etc., are cited in traditional spelling, with the usual diacritic for long vowels.

In my presentation of the prosodic features of English—intoning, stressing, and timing—I have to a large extent followed my own light. I emphasize the *patterns* of intonation and stress, their interplay, and their relations to syntax and morphology. Pitch levels and degrees of stress serve to describe prosodic patterns, but in my opinion they are not 'phonemes' in any sense of the word. Many valuable suggestions have come to me from the lively discussion carried on in the last thirty years, notably by Bernard Bloch, Dwight L. Bolinger, F. Daneš, Otto von Essen, J. R. Firth, W. Jassem, Daniel Jones, Ilse Lehiste, William G. Moulton, Stanley S. Newman, Kenneth L. Pike, Robert P. Stockwell, George L. Trager, and N. S. Trubetzkoy. I am indebted to all of them, whether I agree with them or use their views as a foil.

In view of the existing diversity in the structural interpretation of the rather easily observable prosodic data, it would be too much to hope that my presentation will meet with general approval. Nevertheless, I feel that my views, which I support with rather full documentation, may lead to a fruitful discussion of an aspect of English grammar that has only recently received the attention it deserves.

July 30, 1963 Hans Kurath

TABLE OF CONTENTS

Phonology

Part I: The Phonemic System

Phonology

Part II: The Phonemes

PHONOLOGY

PART I:
THE PHONEMIC SYSTEM AND ITS HISTORY; PHONOTACTICS; MORPHOPHONEMICS; GRAPHEMICS

1. The System of Consonants

labials	labiodentals	dentals	alveolars	prepalatals	palatals	velars	laryngeal			
p			t		č	k		vl. } plosives		} obstruents
b			d		ǧ	g		v.		
	f	θ		s	š		h	vl. } fricatives		
	v	ð		z	ž			v.		
m			n			ŋ		v. nasals		} resonants
			lr					v. laterals		
(w)					j	w		v. semivowels		

1.1 Types of Consonants

The consonants of English fall into two major groups: OBSTRUENTS and RESONANTS.

The OBSTRUENTS are articulated by blocking the outlet of the oral cavity and the entrance to the nasal cavity, building up breath pressure, and then releasing the contact to permit the breath to escape through the mouth; or by narrowing the breath channel in the mouth and forcing the breath through it. In either case the entrance to the nasal cavity is blocked by the velum. Obstruents formed by blocking the breath channel and then 'exploding' it are called PLOSIVES (or stops); those formed by narrowing the channel and forcing breath through it to produce audible friction are called FRICATIVES. To the former group belong /p, t, č, k/, as in *pin, tin, chin, kin,* and /b, d, ǧ, g/, as in *bin, den, gem, gum*; to the latter /f, θ, s, š/, as in *fin, thin, sin, shun,* and /v, ð, z, ž/, as in *veal, these, zeal, rouge.* The consonant /h/ differs from the other fricatives in that the narrowing of the breath channels occurs in the larynx.

In articulating the RESONANTS, the breath channel is more or less open, so that the vibrating air column escapes rather freely through the mouth or through the nose. Sounds articulated in this manner have greater natural loudness (sonority) than obstruents, and are therefore properly called resonants (or sonorants). The resonants are of three kinds: NASALS, LATERALS, and SEMIVOWELS.

In articulating the NASALS /m, n, ŋ/, as in *ham, hen, hang,* the oral cavity is blocked by the lips or the tongue, and the velum is lowered so that the vibrating breath passes out through the nose, the nasal cavity along with the oral cavity or part of it functioning as a resonance chamber.

The SEMIVOWELS /j, w/, as in *you, woo,* and BE /ə/, as in *fear, poor,* have a vowel-like articulation, i.e. the tongue is arched more or less as in the vowels /i, u, ə/ of *he, who, her,* respectively.

The LATERALS are formed by blocking or narrowing the breath channel with the tip of the tongue and letting the vibrating breath escape through the gaps between the sides of the tongue and the gums.

In articulating /l/, as in *lay, low, ill, all,* the tip of the tongue touches the upper gum and so diverts the breath over the sides of the tongue.

Prevocalic /r/, as in *read, ray, row,* is articulated by pointing the tip of the tongue at the gums without touching them. This narrowing of the breath channel in front diverts part of the breath over the sides of the tongue. For the intervocalic allophone of /r/ in BE, as in *merry,* and its postvocalic allophone in AE, as in *harp, orb,* see 11.2.

As far as the voiced consonants of English are concerned, one can say that natural sonority is controlled by the degree of openness of the breath channel: semivowels are louder than laterals, laterals louder than nasals, and nasals louder than obstruents. This fact underlies the normal clustering of consonants in morphemes and in words consisting of a single morpheme, as illustrated in the following examples: *blue, brew, beauty, mute, new,* BE *lute;* and *old,* AE *lord, hand, elm,* AE *arm.*

In these clusters, the resonant adjoins the vowel—the loudest sound type; the obstruent precedes the resonant initially and follows it finally. In final clusters of two resonants, the lateral precedes the nasal, as in *elm,* AE *arm;* in initial resonant clusters, the semivowel adjoins the vowel, as in *mute, new,* BE *lute.*

The same general rule obtains in the few current final clusters of obstruents shown in *fast, left,* where the fricative adjoins the vowel and the plosive follows. The only exception to this rule in the native vocabulary are the initial /s/ clusters of *spin, still, skin.*

The Obstruents

Three distinctive features, functioning singly or in combination, serve to contrast each obstruent with all the others: the place of articulation, the manner of articulation, and phonation.

The place of articulation distinguishes /p/ from /t, č, k/; /b/ from /d, ǧ, g/; /f/ from /θ, s, š/; and /v/ from /ð, z, ž/. The manner of articulation brings /p/ into contrast with /f/, /t/ with /θ/, /b/ with /v/, /d/ with /ð/, etc. Phonation distinguishes /p/ from /b/, /f/ from /v/, etc. Place and manner of articulation are involved in /p/ ≠ /θ/; place, manner, and phonation in /p/ ≠ /ð/; and so forth.

The four subsets of obstruents exhibit four places of articulation: the /p, t, č, k/ set is matched in this respect by /b, d, ǧ, g/, /f, θ, s, š/, and /v, ð, z, ž/. However, the two sets of plosives and the two sets of fricatives have noticeably different places of articulation: /p, b/ are bilabial, /f, v/ labio-dental; /t, d/ are alveolar, /θ, ð/ dental or interdental; /č, ǧ/ are fairly closely matched by /š, ž/; but the velar plosives /k, g/ are unparalleled by fricatives, and the fricatives /s, z/ have no plosive counterparts. And there is, of course, a fifth voiceless fricative, /h/, to disturb the rough parallelism.

The Resonants

The three sets of resonants—nasals, laterals, and semivowels—do not parallel each other as to the place of articulation. But the nasals /m, n, ŋ/ match the plosives /p, t, k/ and /b, d, g/ in this respect, differing from /b, d, g/ only in the position assumed by the velum.

1.2 History of the Consonant System

The consonant system of English has changed rather little since late Middle English (c1400). No consonant phonemes have been lost, but the occurrence of several of them has been positionally restricted, and the incidence of others has been somewhat increased or reduced.

Two new consonants have developed in all cultivated regional dialects, the /ŋ/ of *sing* and the /ž/ of *measure*. A third consonant has arisen in BE and some coastal varieties of AE, the semivowel /ǝ/, as in *fear, fair, four, poor*. All three of these new consonants are severely restricted in their distribution.

The velar nasal /ŋ/ is derived from the syllable-final cluster /-ng/ of ME, as in *long* /lɔŋ ~ lʋŋ/ from ME /long/, where the velar was a positional allophone of /n/ before the velar plosive /g/. The fusion of /ng/ in the sound [ŋ] brought the velar nasal into contrast with /n/, as in *sing* /sɪŋ/ ≠ *sin* /sɪn/. This phoneme now occurs morpheme-finally, as in *long, sing, sing-ing, sing-er* and before the velar plosives /g, k/, as in *finger, longer, longest, Congress* and *think, tinker, conquer.*

The voiced palatal fricative /ž/ resulted from the fusion of the medial sequence /zj/, which in turn either derived from earlier /zi/, as in *vision, lesion,* or developed in the sequence /ziu/, as in *measure, usual.* Except for some recently adopted French words, as *rouge, massage,* /ž/ occurs only between vowels. It is the only consonant of MnE that is not native to English, though it appears now in the speech of some Americans in such native phrases as *àll these yéars* /ðižírz/, *hère's your* /hɪ̀rž₃/ *hát.*

The mid-central semivowel /ǝ/, as in *fear, fair* /fɪǝ, fɛǝ/, is derived from postvocalic /r/, which before this change was probably articulated with elevation of the back of the tongue, as it still is in the western counties of England and in the greater part of North America. This change took place in BE during the latter part of the 18. century. In America, /ǝ/ is now established in four separate areas along the coast of the Atlantic and the Gulf of Mexico: New England, Metropolitan New York, Virginia, and the 'cotton belt' extending from South Carolina westward into Texas. It seems probable that these coastal subareas adopted /ǝ/ from BE shortly before the Revolution. Though expansive in the coastal plain, /ǝ/ has not replaced postvocalic /r/ in the upland and inland.

The new MnE consonant phonemes /ŋ/ and /ž/ were already current in BE when the first American colonies were established, and are, for that reason, in general use in all parts of North America. On the other hand, the late new-comer /ǝ/ has been adopted only in the coastal areas that had the most intimate contacts with England in the 18. century.

The phoneme /h/, which in ME occurred in all major positions, is now restricted to prevocalic position. In ME, /h/ had a prevocalic [h]-like allophone, which survives in all cultivated varieties of MnE, and a palato-velar postvocalic allophone [x] (written *h* in early ME, later *gh*), which survives in the folk speech of Scotland and some parts of England. This positional variant of /h/ was either lost in the BE standard language in early MnE times or replaced by /f/, as in *through, eight* and *laugh, cough.* It does not survive in any section of America. It was doubtless current for some time among the Ulster Scots of Pennsylvania, since Pennsylvania German families used *gh* for German *ch* in Anglicizing the spelling of such names as *Bach* /bɔx/ as *Baugh,* now pronounced /bɔ/.

The change of postvocalic /r/ to the semivowel /ǝ/ in BE and coastal AE eliminated /r/ in that position.

The loss of the obstruents /k, g/ before /n/, as in *know, gnaw;* of /w/ before /r/, as in *wring, wrong;* of /h/ before /w/ in BE, as in *wheat, whale;* and of /l/ in *talk, walk* changed the distribution and/or the incidence of these consonants. These and other minor distributional and incidental changes that came about during the MnE period are pointed out in the treatment of the several consonants.

2. The System of Syllabics (Vowels)

The system of vowels of MnE consists of a set of CHECKED vowels, a set of FREE vowels, and the unstressed vowel /ə/. All checked and free vowels occur under full-stress and half-stress, some of them also under weak stress and unstress.

Checked vowels do not occur at the end of morphemes; they are always followed by one or two consonants. Free vowels, on the other hand, appear both finally and before consonants. Distribution is, therefore, one of the distinctive features in the English vowel system.

The checked vowels /ɪ, ɛ, æ, ɑ ~ ɒ, ʌ, ʊ/, as in *bid, bed, bad, odd, bud, good*, are monophthongal in BE, monophthongal or ingliding in ΛE. Ingliding [ɪə, ɛə, ʌə, ʊə] are common in the American South, and not unknown in the North and the Midland, especially under full stress, as in *give, bed, love, good*. Prolongation of the low checked vowels is common in America, as in *it's too bád, this is ódd*.

The free vowels /i, e, ai/ and /u, o, au/, as in *bee, bay, buy* and *who, hoe, how*, are generally articulated as upgliding diphthongs. However, monophthongal variants of /i, e, u, o/ are current in some sections of America (regional diaphones), and elsewhere as positional or prosodic allophones before voiceless obstruents, as in *keep, case, shoot, coach, imitate*.

The free vowels /ɔ, ɜ, ɑ̹/ as in *law, fur, far*, are monophthongal in BE and rather generally so in AE. But upgliding /ɔ/ is common in parts of the American South, upgliding /ɜ/ in the Lower South and in Metropolitan New York, and upgliding /ɑ̹/ occurs in coastal Virginia.

In summary one can say that checked vowels tend to glide to mid-central position, free vowels to a higher position. But both subsets of the English vowel system occur also as monophthongs, whether regionally, positionally, or prosodically.

From the point of view outlined above, the vowels of English are distinguished from each other by three features: (1) the quality produced by the resonance of the oral-pharyngeal cavity as determined by the position of the tongue and the lips; (2) the drift in quality resulting from the shift in the position of the tongue and/or the lips during the articulation of the vowel; and (3) phonotactic behavior, i.e. free versus limited distribution in morphemes.

Some checked vowels are paired with phonically similar free vowels, others not.

In all varieties of cultivated English the checked vowels /ɪ, ɛ, ʊ/ are paired in quality with free /i, e, u/, as in *lid ≠ lead, let ≠ late, good ≠ food*. In addition, checked /ɒ/ is paired with free /ɔ/, and /ʌ/ with /ɑ̹/, in BE, as in *rod ≠ laud* and *cup ≠ carp*; checked /ɑ/ with free /ɑ̹/ in Metropolitan New York and the South, as in *rod ≠ lard*; and checked /ɵ/ with free /o/ in eastern New England, as in *whole ≠ hole*.

Though phonically similar, the checked and the free vowel of such pairs are never identical in quality. Thus quality alone is sufficient to distinguish them, if both are monophthongal.

When either one or the other is diphthongal, or if both are diphthongal, the checked vowel drifting inward and the free vowel upward, drift in quality becomes a second distinctive feature between phonically similar vowels. Thus the checked vowel /ɛ/ of *let* differs in some dialects from the free vowel /e/ of *lay, late* both in quality and in drift.

Length is not a distinctive feature in the vowel system of MnE. It is automatic in the sense that the actual length of any English vowel depends upon a variety of factors. In general, (1) both checked and free vowels are longer under full stress than under half-stress or weak stress; (2) low vowels are longer than mid-vowels, mid-vowels longer than high vowels; (3) free vowels are longer in free than in checked position; (4) both checked vowels and free vowels in checked position are longer before voiced consonants than before voiceless consonants.

The actual manifestation of these general rules governing the sub-phonemic length of vowels varies noticeably from dialect to dialect.

The vowel systems of BE and of the regional types of AE have very much in common. Each consists of a set of checked vowels, a set of free vowels, and the unique unstressed vowel /ə/. Differences in the set of free vowels are greater than in the set of checked vowels.

2.1 The Checked Vowels

British English				*American English (1)*			
Front		Back		Front		Back	
bit	ɪ	ʊ	*foot*	*bit*	ɪ	ʊ	*foot*
bet	ɛ	ʋ	*hot*	*bet*	ɛ	ʌ	*hut*
bat	æ	ʌ	*hut*	*bat*	æ	ɑ	*hot*

American English (2)			*American English (3)*	
Back			Back	
ʊ	*pull*		ʊ	*foot*
ɵ	*whole*		ʌ	*hut*
ʌ	*hull*			

Each regional type, except AE[3], has three front vowels and three back vowels, articulated on three levels: high, mid, and low. The three checked front vowels stand in the same relation to each other in all varieties of MnE, though differing phonically, and they occur largely in the same words. The relation between the three checked back vowels varies regionally, as indicated in the diagrams presented above. Type AE[1] is

current in the greater part of North America. AE² is peculiar to eastern
New England, but yielding ground to AE³ (see the phoneme /ə/, 13.8).
AE³, lacking a low-back vowel, is current in western Pennsylvania and
to some extent in the Midwest and the Northwest (here *tot* rimes with
taught, *shock* with *talk*).

2.2 The Free Vowels

British English and American English (3)

	Front	Central	Back	
beat	i		u	*boot*
bait	e	з	o	*boat*
			ɔ	*bought*
bite	ai	ɐ	au	*bout*
		hurt		
		heart		

American English (1)

	Front	Central	Back	
beat	i		u	*boot*
bait	e	з	o	*boat*
			ɔ	*bought*
bite	ai		au	*bout*
		hurt		

American English (2)

	Front	Central	Back	
beat	i		u	*boot*
bait	e	з	o	*boat*
heart	ɐ		ɔ	*bought, lot*
bite	ai		au	*bout*
		hurt		

There is less symmetry between the free front vowels and back vowels
than in the set of checked vowels: all regional types, except AE², have
three front vowels, but four back vowels.

AE³, current in Metropolitan New York and the coastal South, is
structurally identical with BE, though the units of this system may have
striking regional diaphones.

Type AE¹ is current in all areas in which postvocalic /r/ is preserved:
the North from the Connecticut River westward, the Midwest, and the
southern upland. Here *far*, *hard* contain the sequence /ar/ to correspond
to the /ɐ/ of BE and AE³.

Type AE², peculiar to eastern New England, consists of the same
units as that of BE and AE³, but the /ɐ/ of *heart*, articulated as a low-

front [ɑ], occupies a different position in the system, and the /ɔ/ occurs not only in *law, caught*, but also in *lot, cot*.

The phoneme /ɔi/ of *boy, join* occurs in all varieties of cultivated English. It is an odd unit that cannot be assigned a meaningful place in the vowel system and has therefore not been entered in the schemes of free vowels. As the only foreign vowel phoneme in English it has not been integrated into the system.

The sets of checked and free vowels constituting the vowel systems of the several types of MnE do not differ from each other to such an extent that intercommunication is seriously hindered. And yet, they do have different systems, since the loss or addition of a single phoneme changes the internal balance of a system. To set up a composite scheme by incorporating in it all the units of the several related systems may be convenient for certain procedural or pedagogical purposes, but such a scheme does not describe a system, even if it be dignified by the term 'overall system'. The composite table presented below is intended to exhibit the vowel phonemes shared by all varieties of cultivated Modern English and some that are peculiar to certain regional types.

Composite Table of Vowels

	Front		Central		Back	
	Checked	*: Free*	*Checked*	*: Free*	*Checked*	*: Free*
High	ɪ	: i			ʊ	: u
Mid	ɛ	: e	ɜ		ʌ	: o
Lower mid	æ				(ɒ)[1]	: ɔ
Low		ai	(ɑ)[2]	: (ɐ)[3]		au

Omitted from this table are: the foreign syllabic /ɔi/, though shared by all dialects; the checked vowel /ə/ of eastern New England; and the back-gliding diphthong /iu/ occurring as a relic in the American North.

2.3 History of the Vowel System

The checked vowels of MnE are chiefly derived from the ME short vowels, the free vowels from the long vowels and diphthongs of ME. These major lines of development are suggested in the following tables.

---

[1] Only in BE, as in *lot*.
[2] Only in AE, as in *lot*.
[3] Only in BE and in coastal AE, as in *far*.

Table I: Checked Vowels

ME	i	e	a	o	u
MnE	ɪ	ɛ	æ	ɒ ~ ɑ	ʌ ʊ
	sit	set	cat	lot	buck full

Table II: Free Vowels

ME	ī	ẹ̄	ę̄	ā	ai	au	ou	ǭ	ō	iu	ū
MnE	ai	i		e		ɔ		o		u	au
	lie	reed, read		tale, tail		law		know, no		do, rue	now

In addition to the vowels listed above, all varieties of cultivated MnE have the free vowel /ɔi/ from ME /oi/ and /ui/, as in *joy*, *boil*; and the free vowel /ɜ/ from the ME sequences /ir, ur, er/, as in *fir*, *fur*, *fern*. BE and coastal AE have, in addition, the free vowel /ɑ/ from the earlier sequence /ar/, as in *far*, *hard*. Free /iu/ from ME /iu/ and /eu/, as in *new*, *few*, and checked /ɵ/ from ME /ǭ/, as in *stone*, *whole*, both of them recessive, occur only in New England and, as relics, in the New England settlements to the west.

Owing to the realignment of allophones and to adoptions from regional folk speech, the incidence of the several vowels in the lexicon is either increased or decreased, as pointed out below.

Most of the phonic shifts and all of the mergers and splits indicated in the tables given above took place from the Middle English to the Elizabethan period, approximately between 1400 and 1550 or 1600. This chronology of the changes obviously accounts for the fact that AE differs so little from BE in its vowel system and even in the incidence of the vowels in the vocabulary. Continuous contact of the leading families in the American seaports with England and the constant influx of cultured Englishmen during the Colonial period, we may safely assume, served to establish later developments, such as the free vowel /ɑ/ in *far*, *hard*, along the Atlantic coast.

The 'Great Vowel Shift' affecting the ME long vowels and the merging of some ME long vowels with ME diphthongs by the time of Shakespeare have been treated in great detail by various scholars since the last decades of the 19. century. Inter-rimes between earlier distinct vowels, unconventional spellings (inverse spellings), and descriptions of the pronunciation of the vowels on the part of orthoepists have been exploited in these efforts. Though competent scholars still disagree in the interpretation of some of this evidence, there is nevertheless considerable agreement on the main lines of the development. Further clarification may be expected when the publication of the findings of the dialect survey of England by Harold Orton and his associates is completed. Since Standard British English itself rests upon regional usage of the London area, but adopts features from adjoining areas, this new evidence will be of the greatest importance. It will help to elucidate those features in which AE differs from BE or in which the regional types of AE exhibit diversity, not only in the phonic realization of shared vowels, but also in the incidence of the phonemes, and even in the system of vowels.

Many details in the history of the vowels are briefly dealt with, or at least referred to, under the several vowels. Here we shall present an outline of the history of the vowel system from Middle English to Modern English and give rough dates for the more important changes. The chief purpose of this sketch is to convey some idea of the complicated background of the somewhat divergent regional systems of the present and of the phonemic units in these systems.

2.4 The Checked Vowels

The stressed short vowels of ME occurred only in checked position. With the loss of phonemic quantity in early MnE, this positional restriction survives as one of the distinguishing features of the descendents of this set of vowels. The ME short vowels form a triangular set consisting of two high vowels, two mid-vowels, and one low vowel:

sitten	i	u	*buk(ke), ful*
setten	e	o	*lot, los*
	a		
	cat(te), bath		

During the early MnE period, the back vowels /u/ and /o/ tended to be lowered and unrounded, except in certain positions, so that /u/ came to have the positional allophones [ʌ ~ ʊ] and /o/ the allophones [ʋ ~ ɔ]. The low vowel /a/ also developed positional allophones, presumably [æ ~ ɑ]. The precise phonic quality of these allophones is of course not known, but by inference from later developments we can approximate their quality. These phonic changes do not by themselves alter the triangular set of checked vowels, which c1500—c1550 probably had the following character:

sit	/ɪ/	/ʌ/ = [ʌ ~ ʊ]	*buck ~ ful*
set	/ɛ/	/ʋ/ = [ʋ ~ ɔ]	*lot ~ loss*
		/æ/ = [æ ~ ɑ]	
		cat ~ bath	

During the Elizabethan period, c1550—c1600, the allophones [ʌ ~ ʊ] became separate phonemes owing to the replacement of free /u/ (from ME /ǭ/) by [ʊ] before certain consonants, as in *look, book, foot, good*, which produced contrasting /ʊ/ ≠ /ʌ/ in such pairs as *look* ≠ *luck, book* ≠ *buck, foot* ≠ *hut, good* ≠ *cud*. This phonemic split of ME short /u/ changed the old triangular system into a quadrangular system consisting of two high vowels, two mid-vowels, and two low vowels:

sit	/ɪ/	/ʊ/	*full, book*
set	/ɛ/	/ʌ/	*buck*
cat	/æ/	/ɒ/ or /ɑ/	*lot*

This system of six checked vowels—three front vowels and three back vowels—survives in nearly all varieties of MnE, but with more or less striking differences in the phonic character of the units and, owing to later phonic shifts, in the relative position of /ʌ/ and /ɒ ~ ɑ/ in the system.

The present system of checked vowels in BE and in most varieties of AE can be represented as follows:

		AE		BE	
sit	ɪ	ʊ	*look*	ʊ	*look*
set	ɛ	ʌ	*luck*	ɒ	*lock*
cat	æ	ɑ	*lock*	ʌ	*luck*

Other changes affecting the MnE derivatives of the ME short vowels have no bearing on the system of the MnE checked vowels. But they have their own importance.

The early MnE allophones [ɒ ~ ɔ] from ME short /o/, and [æ ~ a] from ME short /a/, are differently treated in BE and in AE, from which we may infer that before the planting of the American colonies they were still allophonic, and that in all probability there were marked regional differences in the incidence of the allophones in the mother country.

In BE, the allophone [a ~ a·] of /æ/ (from ME /a/) occurring before voiceless fricatives and /n/-clusters, as in *staff, bath, fast, aunt, dance*, was ultimately phonemicized as free /ɑ/. Aside from New England and scattered instances elsewhere, AE has /æ/ in such words. It seems probable that AE usage is in this respect based upon regional dialects of England in which /æ/ had no striking allophones.

In AE, the more rounded allophone [ɔ ~ ɔ·] of /ɒ/ (from ME /o/) occurring before voiceless fricatives, as in *off, moth, loss*, fell in with the free vowel /ɔ/ (from ME /au/); usually also before the voiced velars, as in *long, dog*. Though this usage is current to some extent in BE, such words usually have /ɒ/, the same phoneme as *lot, lock*, etc.

Of all the short vowels of ME, the low vowel /a/ was most influenced by adjoining consonants. Some of its positional allophones were ultimately aligned with various phonemes: before /r/ with /ɑ/, as in *far*; before /l/ with /ɔ/, as in *fall*; before voiceless fricatives and /n/-clusters with /ɒ/, as in BE *fast, dance*; after /w/ with /ɔ ~ ʋ ~ ɑ/, as in *water, wash*. In other positions it appears, of course, as /æ/, as in *lap, bad, man*.

ME short /i, u, e/ before tautosyllabic /r/ were merged in early MnE, so that Elizabethan poets could rime *first* with *cursed*, *bird* with *herd*, *mirth* with *earth*. The phonic character of the resulting vowel can be inferred from later developments. It was probably a mid-central allophone of /ʌ/, since with early loss of /r/, as in the folk pronunciation of *nurse* /nʌs/, *curse* /kʌs/, it appears as /ʌ/, while with preservation of /r/ the new sequence was fused into a mid-central free vowel, as in *nurse* /nɜs/, *bird* /bɜd/, *earth* /ɜθ/. The articulation of /ɜ/ still has striking regional diaphones in England as well as in America.

The substitution of checked vowels (from ME short vowels) for phonically similar free vowels (from ME long vowels) in checked position during the sixteenth and the seventeenth centuries is a peculiar phenomenon. These substitutions are rarely consistent—often rather sporadic—in the BE standard, and even more so in AE. They do not have the character of normal phonemic rules of change (sound laws), but point in their inconsistency to adoption from other dialects or from regional variants of the standard (dialect borrowing).

Thus (1) the early MnE free mid-front vowel /e/, from ME long open /ẹ̄/, now appears as free /i/ in *leaf, lead*, etc.; but owing to the replacement by the phonically similar checked vowel, as /ɛ/ in *deaf, red*, etc.

(2) Early MnE free /o/, from ME long open /ǭ/, usually appears as /o/, as in *boat, stone*, etc.; but owing to the replacement by the checked vowel in EMnE, as /ʋ/ in BE *hot, shone* and as /ɑ/ in AE *hot*.

(3) Early MnE free /u/, from ME long close /ọ̄/ or /ū/ before labials, now usually appears as such in *food, boot, hoop, hoof, broom*; but early substitution of checked /ʋ/ has produced /ʌ/, as in *flood, gum*, and regional *soot*, and later substitution has lead to /ʋ/, as in *good, foot*, and regional *hoop, hoof, room*. Whether the regular occurrence of /ʋ/ before /k/, as in *look, book, shook*, etc., results from a substitution or an internal phonic change is an open question.

2.5 The Free Vowels

The long vowels and the diphthongs of ME occurred both at the end of words and morphemes and in checked position. With the loss of phonemic quantity in early MnE, this freedom from positional restriction became one of the distinguishing features of the derivatives of the ME long vowels and diphthongs.

The ME long vowels were articulated on four levels—high, mid-close, mid-open, and low, the short vowels only on three:

	Long		Short	
	ī	ū	i	u
	ẹ̄	ǭ	e	o
	ę̄	ǫ	a	
		ā		

In both sets, front vowels and back vowels are matched as to tongue level.

The ME diphthongs /ai, au, ou/ and foreign (OF) /oi, ui/ were upgliding, but /iu, eu/ were back-gliding.

Sweeping changes in the ME long vowels and diphthongs—usually called the Great Vowel Shift—took place between c1350 and c1550, which produced the essential features of the MnE system of free vowels. After the Elizabethan period, only one unit in this system was lost. One was added in all varieties of MnE, the /ɜ/ of *fur*. A second addition, the /ɒ/ of *far*, is peculiar to BE and to some coastal dialects of AE.

The MnE derivatives of the ME long vowels and some diphthongs are shown schematically in the following tables, with MnE examples.

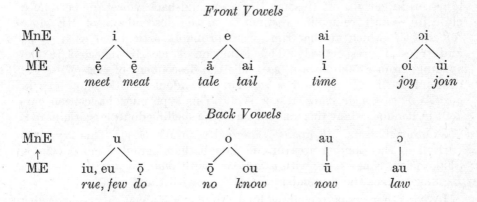

Front Vowels

Back Vowels

A striking feature of the changes that produced the MnE system of free vowels is the merging of some ME long vowels and upgliding diphthongs: /ā/ and /ai/, as in *tale* = *tail* /tel/, and /ǭ/ and /ou/, as in *no* = *know* /no/. These mergers antedate the Elizabethan period, as Shakespeare's rimes, such as *state* = *bait*, *frame* = *claim*, show. Since the ME diphthongs /ai/ and /ou/ now generally appear as upgliding diphthongs in the folk speech of the English Midland and the South (remaining largely distinct from the derivatives of ME /ā/ and /ǭ/ outside the Home Counties), it seems safe to assume that in standard BE the free vowels

/e/ and /o/ resulting from the mergers were upgliding diphthongs and not monophthongs, as is so often assumed.

It is generally agreed that the ME long high vowels /ī/ and /ū/ became upgliding diphthongs either in late ME or in early MnE. In Elizabethan English, they were probably pronounced [əi] and [əu], as in *lie, bite* and *now, out*; and they are still so sounded in some varieties of British and American English. At present, the American regional diaphones of /ai/ range all the way from [əi] to [aɨ] and [a·ə], and those of /au/ from [əu] to [ʌu] and [æʊ], while BE has [aɨ ~ ɑɨ] and [ʌu ~ ɑu], respectively. The lowered beginning of /ai/ and /au/ is apparently of rather recent date.

While the ME long high vowels /ī/ and /ū/ were shifted to /ai/ and /au/, the long close mid-vowels /ẹ̄/ and /ọ̄/ of ME were raised to high vowels, as in *see, meet* and *do, boot*. There is no immediate evidence to show whether the resulting free vowels /i/ and /e/ were monophthongal or diphthongal. Perhaps they had the regional diaphones [ɪi ~ i·] and]ʊu ~ u·], as at present.

The history of the ME long open mid-front vowel /ę̄/ is rather complicated. Its descendents appear in present English as the free vowel /i/ in *meat, leaf*, etc., as free /e/ in the words *great, break, steak*, and as checked /ɛ/ in *bread, deaf*, etc.

In some regional dialects, ME /ę̄/ became a close mid-front vowel [e· ~ ei] in early MnE (just as the open mid-back vowel /ǭ/ became a close [o· ~ ou]), remaining distinct from the descendents of ME close /ẹ̄/ and /ā/, which at that time were probably articulated as [i· ~ ɪi] and [ɛ· ~ ɛi], respectively. This situation is clearly reflected in the spelling: from c1500 onward, *ea* spells the descendent of ME /ę̄/, *ee* the descendent of ME /ẹ̄/, and *a, ai* the descendent of ME /ā, ai/, as in *meat* ≠ *meet* ≠ *mate, main*, respectively. This type must have been current in London, where this innovation in the spelling doubtless originated.

In other dialects, ME open /ę̄/ merged with ME /ā, ai/. This type was current in the London area in the Elizabethan period. Among others, Shakespeare rimes *speak* with *awake, sea* with *play, great* with *state*, etc. He never rimes the descendents of ME /ę̄/ with those of /ẹ̄/.

In yet other areas, including East Anglia, ME open /ę̄/ merged with close /ẹ̄/ in early MnE /i/, so that *meat* rimed with *meet*, but not with *mate*. This regional type became established in the BE standard in the course of the 17. century, as in *meat, lead, leak, leaf, breathe, bean, steal*, etc. But the /e/ of Shakespeare's time survives in *break, great, steak* and forms the basis of the checked /ɛ/ that was substituted for it in *sweat, red, deaf, breath* and numerous other words. This replacement of free /e/ by checked /ɛ/ must in all probability be attributed to the influence of the dialects spoken to the south and the west of the London area, where free /e/ was articulated as an ingliding [eə]. The triple descendents of

ME open /ę̄/, as in *beat* ≠ *great* ≠ *sweat*, point to dialect borrowing and preclude the common assumption of internal change.

Of the ME diphthongs, upgliding /ai/ merged with /ā/, as in *tail* = *tale*, and upgliding /ou/ with /ǭ/, as in *know* = *no*; upgliding /au/ became /ɔ/, as in *law, laud*; upgliding /oi/ and /ui/ merged in /ɔi/, as in *joy, join*; back-gliding /iu/ and /eu/ merged in /iu/, which later became the sequence /j + u/, the vowel merging with /u/ from ME /ǭ/, as in *new, true* and *few*.

Thus only ME /au/ and /oi, ui/ survive as separate phonemes, the former as /ɔ/, the latter as /ɔi/. With the exception of the shift of /iu/ to /ju/, all of these changes took place before the first American colonies were established; hence the general agreement of AE with BE.

The emergence of the free vowels /ɜ/ of *fur* and /ɑ/ of *far* is of later date.

The free vowel /ɜ/ is derived from the early MnE sequence /ʌr/ in which the ME sequences /ir, ur, er/ had been merged, as in *fir, fur, fern* /fɜ, fɜ, fɜn/. For a description of this development and the regional differences in articulation see under /ɜ/.

In the latter part of the 18. century, the free vowel /ɑ/ emerged in BE by fusion of the earlier sequence /ɑə/ from ME /ar/, as in *far, hard*. This change occurred much earlier in the speech of Essex and East Anglia and may have been current in the London area, at least in popular speech, long before it was noticed and approved by the orthoepists. In America, this phoneme is now current in the coastal plain along the Atlantic and the Gulf of Mexico, and must have been in use along the Atlantic before the Revolution. From the colonial seaports it spread westward into the Piedmont and was carried from there into the plantation country along the Gulf of Mexico in the 19. century. However, since this feature is fully established in rural Maine and New Hampshire, it seems probable that in New England, with its many early settlers from East Anglia, this phoneme is in part derived from English folk speech.

2.6 Vowels before /r/

The ME vowels, both short and long, suffered drastic changes before an /r/ of the same syllable, as in *fir, fern, far, for, fur, here, hare, more, poor*, and only less so before intersyllabic /r/, as in *spirit, merry, carry, borrow, furrow, hero, Mary, story, fury*. Only the major changes can be outlined here; details are presented under the several vowel phonemes of MnE.

The general effect of /r/ was to lower and to centralize the articulation of the vowel preceding it, especially if it belonged to the same syllable. From this effect it is safe to infer that postvocalic /r/ was velarized, as it still is in the west of England and in America. The lowering and centering of vowels produced various mergers and realignments of

allophones, and judging from the great regional differences in the incidence
of vowels before tautosyllabic /r/ or the derivative consonantal /ǝ/ in
America, there must have been marked regional differences in England
and probably also in standard English, though BE has now attained a
considerable degree of uniformity. Rather recent shifts must have taken
place both in England and in America, and some are still in progress.

To start with the short vowels of ME, we note that /i, u, e/ before
/r/ were merged in early MnE and that the resulting sequence /ʌr/ yielded
the new free vowel /ɜ/, as in *fir, fur, fern*. ME /a/ before /r/, which shifted
to /æ/ in other positions, either remained [a], or reverted to it, in early
MnE, as in *far, hard*. In AE, this [a] fell in with the /ɑ/ of *lot*; in BE the
sequence [ar], passing through [ɑǝ], became the new free vowel /ɑ/.
ME /o/ before /r/, as in *for*, remained rounded and fell in with the free
vowel /ɔ/ of *law, for* appearing as /fɔr/ in AE, as /fɔǝ ~ fɔ/ in BE.

The ME long vowels have, in the main, the same reflexes before /r/
as in other positions, but there is more merging.

ME /ī/ and /ū/ appear in MnE as /ai/ and /au/, as in *fire* and *power*.
In BE, the normal disyllabic pronunciation [faɪǝ, paʊǝ] is paralleled
by monosyllabic [fa·ǝ, pa·ǝ], especially in rapid speech; occasionally
also in some varieties of AE. This [a·] is an allophone of /ai/ and of /au/,
remaining distinct from the articulation of the /ɑ/ of *far, hard*. Thus
fire ≠ *far* and *power* ≠ *par*.

ME /ō, iu/ and /ǭ/ before /r/ remain distinct in most regional types
of AE, as in *poor* ≠ *pour, moor* ≠ *more, sure* ≠ *shore, cure* ≠ *core*. But
in BE /o ~ ɔ/ is common in place of /u ~ ʊ/ in *poor, moor, sure, cure*,
and also in the American South.

ME /ē̦/ is merged in part with ME /ē/, as in *hear* = *here* /hɪr ~ hɪǝ ~
hɪǝ/, and in part with ME /ā, ai/, as in *bear* = *bare* /bɛr ~ bɛǝ ~ bæǝ ~
beǝ/. In both cases the vowel varies regionally.

ME /a/ and /ai/ before /r/ are merged, as in other positions, but the
resulting vowel varies regionally, as in *fare* = *fair*.

The incidence of vowels before tautosyllabic /r/, or its derivative /ǝ/,
is severely restricted.

BE and some types of AE have in this position only six vowel phonemes, as shown in the table below:

	Front		Back	
here, hear	ɪ ~ i		ʊ ~ u	*poor, sure*
bear, fare, fair	ɛ ~ æ ~ e		o ~ ɔ	*pour, door*
fire	ai		au	*flower*

The American North and the South (but not the North Midland)
have, in addition, contrastive /o ≠ ɔ/, as in *four* ≠ *forty, hoarse* ≠ *horse*;
parts of the American South have contrastive /e ≠ æ/, as in *here* ≠ *hair*,

fear ≠ *fare*; and variants of AE in which postvocalic /r/ survives have /ɑ/, as in *far*, *hard*.

Before intersyllabic /r/ the number of contrastive vowels is somewhat greater. AE dialects with postvocalic /r/ have /ɪ/ in *spirit*, *hero*, /ɛ/ in *merry*, *Mary*, /æ/ in *carry*, /ɑ ~ ɔ/ in *borrow*, /ɜ/ in *furrow*, *furry*, /o/ in *story*, and /u/ in *fury*. BE has contrastive /ɪ ≠ ɛ ≠ æ ≠ ɒ ≠ ʌ ≠ ɜ/ in *spirit* ≠ *merry* ≠ *carry* ≠ *borrow* ≠ *furrow* ≠ *furry* and the contrastive sequences /ɪə ≠ ɛə ≠ ɔə ≠ uə/ in *hero* ≠ *Mary* ≠ *story* ≠ *fury*. Metropolitan New York is in substantial agreement with BE, but other dialects of AE lacking postvocalic /r/ have their own peculiarities, which are treated under the several vowels.

2.7 Concluding Remarks

The outline of the development of the English vowel system from ME to MnE presented above is of course subject to revision. The elimination of phonemic quantity in the vowels is a key problem. The early merging of some of the long vowels with upgliding diphthongs would seem to be the first step in the loss of phonemic quantity; and the introduction of upgliding free vowels contrasting with monophthongal or ingliding checked vowels, which is such a marked characteristic of MnE, completes the development.

The interpretations of the 'Great Vowel Shift' offered by K. Luick and O. Jespersen, and rather generally accepted, are hardly tenable. There is no evidence that the ME long high vowels /ī, ū/ were shifted earlier than the close mid-vowels /ē̦, ō̦/, or vice versa. Hence no reason for assuming that /ē̦, ō̦/ were 'sucked' into the positions vacated by /ī, ū/, or that the raising of /ē̦, ō̦/ 'pushed' /ī, ū/ out of their positions. It is much more probable that the entire set of the ME long vowels shifted simultaneously upward and in the process became upgliding diphthongs. The noteworthy facts are: (a) that, with all the shifting, all but one of the units of this set of vowels remained distinct, and (b) that ME /ā/ merged with /ai/ and /ǭ/ with /ou/, yielding upgliding vowels.

Further evidence for the sporadic replacement of free vowels by checked vowels in BE, as of /e/ by /ɛ/ in *red*, *sweat*, *deaf*, of /u/ by /ʊ/ in *foot*, *room*, of /o/ by /ɒ/ in BE *hot*, *shone*, may confidently be expected, when the findings of the English Dialect Survey of the Midland become available. These haphazard replacements cannot be accounted for by assuming internal realignments of positional allophones of /e, u, o/.

The origin of regional differences in the vowels of cultivated AE, whether systemic, phonic, or incidental, still offers many unsolved problems. We shall probably have to admit that BE of the seventeenth and the eighteenth century was less uniform than has generally been assumed. Apparently 'conflicting' opinions and prescriptions of the orthoepists may have to be reinterpreted in the light of the American evidence and recognized as observations of actually divided usage. The frequent attempts to 'reconcile' them may well be misguided.

3. The Phonemic Structure of Morphemes: Phonotactics

Phonemes are the units of speech that make up the morphemes. The sequence of phonemes constituting morphemes follows rather well defined rules in Modern English, which are briefly described below. Our examples will be words consisting of a single morpheme.

Such words as *met* ≠ *net* ≠ *let* ≠ *bet* ≠ *set* differ in that each contains a phoneme that contrasts with one phoneme in the other words. On the other hand, words like *ten* ≠ *net*, *pack* ≠ *cap*, *eat* ≠ *tea*, *own* ≠ *no*, *light* ≠ *tile*, which consist of the same phonemes, differ from each other in the sequence of phonemes. Both types have contrastive phonemic shapes. Hence the description of the phonemic structure of morphemes is concerned not only with the incidence of phonemes, but also with their sequence, i.e. with phonotactics.

English base morphemes and mono-morphemic words have a peak of loudness (sonoritiy) represented by a vowel (a syllabic). Any vowel can begin a word, as in *add, aid, odd, ode, out, ice*, etc. Some vowels—here called free vowels—can end a word, as in *tea, two, say, so, saw, fur, buy, boy, now*, BE *far*. Other vowels—here called checked vowels—never end a word, as those in *bit, bet, bat, hot, hut, foot*. Any vowel can be preceded and followed by a single consonant, as in *bit, beat, full, fool, bud, bite*, etc.

When a vowel is preceded or followed by two consonants, the more sonorous of the two—a resonant—adjoins the vowel, as in *play, pray, flow, free, few, slow, snow, sue, swell* and *help, hemp*, AE *harp, blind, prank*. Initial consonant clusters thus consist largely of an obstruent (a plosive or fricative) plus a resonant (a lateral, nasal, or semivowel), final clusters of a resonant followed by an obstruent.

The final consonant clusters /sp, st, sk, ft/, as in *gasp, fast, ask, left*, consisting of a fricative followed by a plosive, may be regarded as following the rule that the more sonorous consonant adjoins the vowel; perhaps also the final clusters consisting of a lateral and a nasal resonant, as in *elm, kiln* and AE *arm, barn*.

In the native vocabulary and in words from Old Norse, the only exceptions to the rule stated above are the /s/-clusters: initial /sp, st, sk/, as in *spin, still, skin*, and final /ks/, as in *fox, ox*, which consist of two obstruents. /s/ also precedes the normal /p, t, k/ clusters, as in *split, spring, stream, stew, scrub*, forming the only native clusters consisting of more than two consonants. Other abnormal /s/-clusters occur only in such foreign words as *skew, square, sphere, sthenic* and *lapse, Fitz, Fritz.*

It is of interest to observe that in Old and Middle English verse the abnormal initial clusters /sp, st, sk/ do not alliterate with /s/ followed by a vowel, but that the normal clusters /sm, sn, sl, sw/ do. The poets must have felt that the clusters /sp, st, sk/, each of which alliterates only with its like, were somehow peculiar.

Initial clusters foreign to the native vocabulary of English are rare, and except for the /sf/ of *sphere, atmosphere, hemisphere* have only regional currency, as /šl, šm, šw/ in Midwestern *Schlitz* (beer), *Schmidt, Schweizer*; or they are used only by the learned, as /sθ, tm/ in *sthenic, tmesis*. In other foreign clusters, the first consonant is dropped, as in *mnemonic, pneumatic, psychic, phthisic* /tízɪk/, *xenophobia*. Final clusters foreign to native words are /pt, kt/, as in *apt, inept, act, fact.*

Word-initial and word-final clusters consisting of a nasal and a plosive were reduced to a nasal in early MnE, as in *knee, know, gnat, gnaw* and in *long, sing, lamb, dumb*; but final /-nd/ survives, as in *land, find*. The rare initial /fn-/ of OE was replaced in early ME by /sn-/ in *sneeze*.

In morphologically complex words, any morpheme-final consonant or consonant cluster can, of course, be followed by any morpheme-initial consonant or consonant cluster, as in *hat-pin, mad-house, bath-towel, tail-light*; *friend-ship, wis-dom, man-hood, love-ly, watch-ful, dep-th*; *fif-th*; *land-lord, land-scape, wild-cat, help-mate*. Such composite medial clusters are sometimes reduced by dropping the middle member of a sequence of three (or four) consonants, as in *Christmas, lamppost, handsome, landscape*. Some speakers also omit the /f/ in *fifth* and the /d/ in *width*.

Sequences of word-final and word-initial consonants and consonant clusters within an utterance phrase are of course the rule, as in *this morning, cold water, he thanked me*. Occasionally such sequences are simplified, as in *àll these yéars* /ðižírz/, *lèt me sée/* lèmi sí/, especially in rapid informal speech.

Composite clusters containing sequences of consonants that do not occur as morpheme-initial or morpheme-final clusters indirectly signal breaks between morphemes and between the words of an utterance phrase. This indirect function of phonotactics—often interpreted as a 'phoneme of open juncture'—is discussed in the *Prosody* (24).

4. The Alternation of Phonemes: Morphophonemics

Most morphemes of Modern English have an invariable phonemic shape in one and the same regional dialect, as *home, love, good, out, mother, apple, country, open, able, again*. They consist of certain phonemes arranged in a fixed order.

But in some morphemes one or two of the phonemes alternate. Though rather numerous, these alternations are so varied in MnE that they often do not fall into obvious patterns. Some alternations have grammatical functions, others not.

Vowel alternations in morphemes without grammatical function are recorded under the several vowels, including those that distinguish word classes, as in *food ~ feed, bond ~ bind, seat ~ sit*. They may be said to be lexical in character.

Alternations of vowels that distinguish the plural of nouns from the singular, and the stem of the past tense and the past participle of verbs from the stem of the present, are primarily the concern of morphology. They are grammatically contrastive. They are not listed under the several phonemes, but will be briefly outlined here.

Grammatically functional vowel alternation in the noun is rare in MnE. It distinguishes the plural from the singular in the following cases: *goose ≠ geese, tooth ≠ teeth, foot ≠ feet, louse ≠ lice, mouse ≠ mice, man ≠ men, woman ≠ women*.

In all instances except the last, the plural form has a vowel derived from that of the singular by palatal mutation in early Old English.

In the verb, functional vowel alternations are rather numerous. Some go back to vowel gradation (ablaut) in the Indo-European parent language as in *write ≠ wrote ≠ writt-en, sing ≠ sang ≠ sung*; others result from palatal mutation (umlaut) in Old English, as in *tell ≠ tol-d*; others again descend from the shortening of /ȩ̄/ and /ę̄/ before consonant cluster to /e/ in early ME, as in *feed ≠ fed* (ME *fed-de*), *keep ≠ kep-t* (ME *kep-te*).

In verb stems with ancient gradation—historically the so-called strong verbs—a great variety of alternations occur in MnE. Placing the vowel of the present stem first and that of the past tense and/or the past participle after it, the alternations are:

(1) /ɪ ≠ æ/ in *begin, bid, drink, shrink, sing, sink, sit, spring, stink, swim*, BE *spin*; /ɪ ≠ ʌ/ in *begin, cling, dig, drink, fling, shrink, sing, sink, sling, spin, spring, stick, sting, stink, string, swim, swing, win, wring*; /ɪ ≠ e/ in *give*.

(2) /ɛ ≠ ɒ, ɑ/ in *get, tread*; /ɛ ≠ o, ɔ/ in *swell, bear, swear, tear*.

(3) /æ ≠ ʌ/ in *hang*; /æ ≠ ʊ/ in *stand*.

(4) /ʌ ≠ æ/ in *run*; /ʌ ≠ e/ in *come*.

(5) /i ≠ o/ in *cleave, freeze, heave, speak, steal, weave*; /i ≠ ɔ/ in *see*; /i ≠ e, ɛ/ in *eat*; /i ≠ ɪ/ in AE *be ≠ been*.

(6) /e ≠ o/ in *break, stave in, wake*; /e ≠ ʊ/ in *forsake, shake, take*; /e ≠ u/ in *slay*.

(7) /ai ≠ o/ in *drive, ride, rise, smite, stride, strive, write*, AE *dive*, AE *shine*, BE *thrive*; /ai ≠ ɪ/ in *bite, chide, drive, hide, slide, smite*; *write*;

/ai ≠ ʌu/ in *bind, find, grind, wind*; /ai ≠ e/ in *lie*; ai ≠ u/ in *fly*; /ai ≠ ʌ/ in *strike*; /ai ≠ ɔ/ in *fight*; /ai ≠ ʋ/ in BE *shine*.

(8) /ɔ ≠ u/ in *draw*; /ɔ ≠ ɛ/ in *fall*.

(9) /o ≠ u/ in *blow, grow, know, throw*; /o ≠ ɛ/ in *hold*: /o ≠ ɔ, ʋ/ in *go ≠ gone*.

(10) /u ≠ o/ in *chose*; /u ≠ ʌ/ in *do ≠ done*; /u ≠ ʋ, α/ in *shoot*; /u ≠ ɪ/ in *do ≠ did*.

In verbs that had the ME alternation /ē, ę̄ ≠ e/ in the stem of the present vs. the stem of the past and the past participle, MnE has the alternation /i ≠ ɛ/. Thus (a) without suffix: *bleed, breed, feed, lead, meet, read, speed*; (b) with suffix /-t/: *bereave, cleave, creep, deal, dream, feel, keep, kneel, leave, mean, sleep, sweep, weep*; (c) with suffix /-d/: *flee*.

Isolated grammatical alternations of varying background occur in *bring ≠ brough-t, buy ≠ bough-t, catch ≠ caugh-t, seek ≠ sough-t, beseech ≠ besough-t, think ≠ though-t, teach ≠ taugh-t, work ≠ wrough-t, owe ≠ ough-t, sell ≠ sol-d, tell ≠ tol-d, hear ≠ hear-d, say ≠ sai-d, clothe ≠ clad, shoe ≠ sho-d, lose ≠ los-t ≠ for-lor-n*.

Rather full, though not exhaustive, lists of words exhibiting purely lexical alternations of phonemes are given under the several phonemes. These alternations have synchronic as well as historical significance.

Some types of lexical alternations occur in a sufficiently large number of instances to constitute patterns, as the following.

(1) The alternations of the voiceless fricatives /f, θ, s/ with the corresponding voiced fricatives /v, ð, z/ at the end of morphemes, as in *leaf ~ leave-s, proof ~ prove, give ~ gif-t, breath ~ breathe, worth ~ worth-y, glass ~ glaze*. In all such cases, /v, ð, z/ were followed by /ə/ in ME, as in *lēves, brēthen, glāsen*, which was lost in MnE.

(2) Vowel alternations that seem extraordinary in MnE because of the phonic remoteness of the alternants are derived from the ME alternation of phonemically long and short vowels of similar quality, the latter appearing before consonant clusters and in trisyllabics. Thus the ME alternant /ī ~ i/ has yielded MnE /ai ~ ɪ/ in *five ~ fifth, wise ~ wis-dom, bile ~ bil-eous*; ME /ū ~ u/ has become /ʌu ~ ʌ/ in *south ~ south-ern, house ~ husband, abound ~ abund-ant*; ME /ē ~ e/ appears as /i ~ ɛ/ in *deep ~ dep-th, zeal ~ zeal-ous, sheep ~ shep-herd*; ME /ǭ ~ o/ as /u ~ ʋ, α/ in *food ~ fodd-er, bloom ~ bloss-om*; ME /ǭ ~ o/ as /o ~ ʋ, α/ in *holy ~ holi-day, joke ~ joc-ular*; ME /ā ~ a/ as /e ~ æ/ in *shade ~ shadow*.

(3) The alternation of various stressed vowels with the unstressed vowel /ə/ is a characteristic feature of MnE. This alternation is partly a reflex of varying ME stress patterns, as in *súbject ~ subjéct, cónvert ~ convért, mágic ~ magícian, nátive ~ natívity*; partly the result of varying stress in MnE, as in the auxilliary verbs (*have, was, can, could*, etc.), the articles, and some pronouns, prepositions and conjunctions.

(4) In BE, the loss of /r/ after vowels and its preservation between vowels has produced alternants without and with /r/, as in *star ~ starry*, *fur ~ furry*, *dear ~ dearest*, *care ~ caring*, *bear ~ bear it*; and the splitting of early MnE /æ/ has resulted in the alternation /ɐ ~ æ/, as in *pass ~ pass-age*, *class ~ class-ify*.

(5) The systematic alternation /-əz, -ɪz ~ -z ~ -s/ in the suffix of the plural of nouns and of the 3. singular present of verbs is derived from ME /-əs, -is/. In this unstressed suffix, the /s/ became voiced in early MnE. The vowel survived after /s, z, š, č, ǧ/, as in *pass-es, ris-es, blush-es, preach-es, judg-es*; was lost after all other sounds, yielding the alternant /-z/, as in *see-s, beg-s*, etc., and with unvoicing after voiceless consonants, the alternant /-s/, as in *keep-s, laugh-s*, etc.

(6) The alternants of the suffix /-əd, -ɪd ~ -d ~ -t/ of the past tense and the past participle of certain verbs have a similar history. ME /-əd, -id/ retained the vowel after /t, d/, as in *hat-ed, blind-ed*; was reduced to /d/ in other positions, as in *bann-ed, rais-ed, sow-ed*; and the /d/ was unvoiced after voiceless consonants as in *lick-ed, pass-ed, pas-t*. However, the alternant /-t/ is largely derived from the ME variant suffix /-tə/, as in *kep-t*. Moreover, there is a 'zero' alternant of this suffix in MnE, as in *rid, hit, shut, set*, derived from ME /-də, -tə/ following a base ending in /d/ or /t/.

Some isolated alternations go back to OE, as /k ~ č/ in *speak ~ speech*, *wreck ~ wretch*, *cool ~ chill*, and those appearing in *long ~ leng-th*, *broad ~ bread-th*, *old ~ eld-est*; some to ME, as /n ~ m/ in the prefixes *con- ~ com-, syn- ~ sym-*.

Others result from phonemic changes in modern times, as /s ~ š/, from /s ~ sj/, in *grace ~ graci-ous*, *con-fess ~ con-fessi-on*; /z ~ ž/, from /z ~ zj/, in *please ~ pleas-ure*, *use ~ us-ual*; /t ~ č/, from /t ~ tj/, in *cult ~ cult-ure*; /t ~ š/, from /t ~ sj/, in *act ~ acti-on*, *convert ~ con-versi-on*.

When, in conclusion, we note that some alternations occur only in scattered foreign words, as in *defend ~ defense*, *expand ~ expansi-on*, *leg-al ~ leg-islate*; and in historically connected morphemes whose status in MnE is at best tenuous, as in *con-ceive ~ concep-tion, suspec-t ~ suspici-on*, the complexities and the vagaries of the alternation of phonemes in the shapes of English morphemes are clearly demonstrated.

5. Homophony

English tolerates a large number of homophonous words. Most of them, to be sure, belong to different word classes and therefore appear in different constructions. Thus the syntax distinguishes the nouns *bear*, *rain, steel, toe, weight* from the homophonous verbs *bear, reign, steal, tow, wait,* and the nouns *light, week* from the adjectives *light, weak.*

Nevertheless, the number of homophonous nouns is rather large, e.g. *beach = beech, doe = dough, fair = fare, fir = fur, knight = night, might = mite, sail = sale, son = sun, tail = tale, waist = waste.* These are tolerated because the lexical context almost invariably makes it clear which word is intended. Indeed, it requires considerable ingenuity to construct a sentence in which the word intended would remain ambiguous. And when the lexical context leaves the choice open, as in *Whàt a brìght* /sʌn/! or *I hàve a dáte,* the situation in which the utterance occurs usually clarifies the speaker's intention. Only occasionally has one of two homophonous nouns been eliminated in English because it gave rise to misunderstandings or to unpleasant associations. Thus when ME *quẹne* 'woman, loose woman, harlot' became homophonous with *quẹn* 'queen' in early MnE, it was given up in literary English.

Most of the homophones of MnE result from the loss of inflectional endings, the merging of vowel phonemes, the realignment of allophones, and the loss of consonants during modern times. In the majority of the cases, the present spelling of homophonous pairs is a reliable clue to the underlying phonological changes.

The list of homophones given under the phonemes are not exhaustive, but most of the more widely current instances will be found there. The historical background is usually briefly pointed out.

6. Spelling: Graphemics

The spelling of Modern English is in a large measure a heritage of the late Middle Ages. With the emergence of English as a literary language in the 14. century, a system of spelling was devised to render the phonemes of the spoken language. At that time, the correlation between graphemes and phonemes was systematic, although not all of the vowel phonemes were distinguished in the spelling. The introduction of printing a century later (1475) served to standardize this spelling, though it was already out of step with the phonemic system, which had undergone remarkable changes between 1400 and 1500. During the last four centuries the two have drifted farther and farther apart.

The spelling system of late Middle English that stands back of the spelling of Modern English was devised by scholars who wrote and spoke Latin and French, the languages of scholarship and high society. In the main, they adapted the spelling of Latin to rendering the English phonemes, but French spellings were retained in words taken from that language and in a few instances carried over into native words.

The chief features of this system are:

(1) In accordance with Latin spelling practices, phonically similar short and long vowels, though phonemically distinct, are spelled alike. Thus the letter *i* represents ME /i/ and /ī/; *a* stands for /a/ and /ā/; etc.

(2) Owing to the paucity of letters for vowels in Latin, the long open and close mid-vowels are not differentiated, so that the letter *e* represents the three stressed vowels /e, ẹ, ę/ and the letter *o* the three stressed vowels /o, ọ, ǫ/.

(3) The ME diphthongs are represented by the digraphs *ai ~ ay, oi ~ oy, au ~ aw, ou ~ ow, iu ~ iw*, the variants in *y* and *w* later restricted to word-final and prevocalic position, as in *day, snow* and *laying, sowing*.

(4) Following Latin usage, long intervocalic consonants are written double, as in *sitten, fillen*.

(5) For the English consonants /š/ and /θ, ð/, without counterparts in Latin, the digraphs *sh* and *th* are introduced, replacing native *sc* and *þ ~ ð*; and *qu* takes the place of earlier *cw* /kw/.

(6) The long high-back vowel /ū/, earlier spelled *u*, is written *ou ~ ow* in accordance with French spelling.

(7) The long high-front vowel /ǖ/ in French words (later merged in native /iu/) retains the French spelling *u*.

(8) Whether the spelling of the unstressed vowel /ə/ with *e* is to be attributed to OF and/or continues a native tradition is not clear.

With the sweeping changes in the quality of the vowels from ME to early MnE, most of the vowel graphs came to have different values. The merging of vowels and diphthongs resulted in alternate spellings, as in *tale = tail, rode = rowed*, and the realignment of allophones caused further confusion. Only two noteworthy improvements were made. Early in the 16. century, the digraphs *ea* and *oa* were introduced to distinguish the descendents of ME open /ę̄/ and /ǭ/, as in *meat* and *boat*, from the descendents of ME close /ẹ̄/ and /ọ̄/, as in *meet* and *boot*.

As a result of certain phonemic changes, some graphic practices devised for the writing of ME came to have a new function.

(1) In ME, double consonant letters represented phonemically long consonants, which occurred only between a short stressed vowel and a following unstressed vowel, as in *sitten, fellen, bagges, dogge, bucke*. With the loss of phonemically long consonants by c1400, the writing of double letters was retained as a diacritic of vowel quantity. Since the short vowels of ME yield the checked vowels of MnE, the double letters now indicate checked vowels, as in *sitting, swimmer* and *fell, egg, staff, pass* (but finally, as in *sit, bid, beg*, etc., double letters are not always written).

(2) In disyllabic words containing a long vowel and ending in /ə/, spelled *e*, the graph *e* was retained after the loss of /ə/ (c1400) to mark the preceding long vowel. In MnE, the split digraphs consisting of a vowel letter and *e* indicate free vowels derived from ME long vowels, as in *bite, late, rode, mute.* The letter *e* also functions as a diacritic in *toe, lie.*

These adaptations of ME spellings to new uses, insofar as they are relatively systematic, have radically changed the relation between sound and symbol in MnE. Double consonant letters and *e* now function as diacritics of vowel types, i.e. of checked vowels and of free vowels, respectively, whereas in ME double letters represented long consonant phonemes and the letter *e* spelled the phoneme /ə/.

A characteristic feature of MnE spelling is the retention of the spelling of the sequences that were merged into free vowels in modern times. Thus /ɜ/ continues to be spelled *ir ~ ur ~ er ~ ear*, as in *fir, fur, fern, learn*, and BE /ɑ/ is written with the digraphs *ar, ear, er*, as in *hard, hearth, clerk.*

After the loss of consonants, the letter is usually kept. Sometimes it comes to be part of a digraph for a vowel, as the *l* in *talk, folk*; sometimes it is simply a nuisance, as *gh* in *though*, BE *plough.*

The conservatism of English spelling in the face of merged phonemes and of innumerable instances of realigned positional allophones has produced an amazing variety of spellings for some of the vowel phonemes, which are of historical interest. One can safely say that the number of variant spellings of an English phoneme is a fair index to the number of sources that have contributed to it. This may delight the historian; but to the person who must learn to match the spellings with the sounds he has used since childhood, mastering English spelling is a time-consuming and frustrating task.

The spelling of each phoneme is treated in relation to its history in the proper section of the Phonology (8 to 15).

PHONOLOGY

PART II: THE PHONEMES

7. Preliminary Remarks

The treatment of each phoneme includes a brief discussion of the following topics:

(1) *Articulation*, with comments on allophones and regional diaphones.

(2) *Distribution:* occurrence in the several positions within morphemes and words; clustering of consonants; peculiarities as between the native and the foreign vocabulary.

(3) *Regionalisms:* regional differences in distribution and in lexical incidence.

(4) *Alternation* with other phonemes in morphemes and words.

(5) *Homophones* resulting from the merging of phonemes and other phonemic changes.

(6) *History:* the Middle English sources, both native and foreign.

(7) *Spelling* in its relation to the native and the foreign sources of the phoneme.

8. The Plosive Consonants

8.1 The Plosive /p/
Articulation

The voiceless bilabial plosive /p/ is articulated by putting the lower against the upper lip and then releasing the contact. The velum shuts the entrance to the nasal cavity and the vocal lips are open.

The /p/ has rather marked positional allophones. Before a stressed vowel, whether alone or followed by a consonant, it is aspirated, [pʰ], as in *pin, plead, proud, pure,* in BE also in the cluster /sp/, as in *spin, spew,* though not as strongly. In all other positions it is unaspirated. Final /p/ is sometimes unexploded, as in *give up,* before an initial /p/, as in *lamp-post,* always so; before an /m/, as in *lamp-maker,* the /p/ is exploded into the nasal cavity, the lips remaining closed. Between voiced sounds, as in *pepper and salt,* a *couple of days,* the /p/ is sometimes voiced in AE.

Distribution

The voiceless bilabial plosive consonant /p/ occurs initially, finally, and medially, as in *path, port, top, hope, open, supper*. Initially it can be followed by the resonants /l, r, j/, as in *plight, plea, prod, proof, pew, pure*, and preceded by /s/, as in *spin, split, spring, spew*. At the end of a morpheme it can be preceded by the resonants /m, l, r/ as in *stamp, help*, AE *sharp* and by /s/, as in *rasp*. Rare final clusters containing /p/ occur in *apt, empty, glimpse*. In BE, the /p/ is usually dropped in *empty, glimpse*.

Regionalisms

Regional differences in the incidence of /p/ are rare. In *empty, glimpse*, AE usually has /p/, BE not. *Diphtheria, diphthong* often have /p/ in America, but the spelling pronunciation with /f/ is favored, especially in the North; in BE /p/ is uncommon.

Alternation

In *(un)-kemp-t ~ comb*, /p/ alternates with zero.

History

The phoneme /p/ is derived from ME /p/, in which OE short and long /pp/ had been merged. In the native vocabulary of ME, /p/ is not frequent, but it appears in numerous words adopted from Latin and Old French in the Middle Ages. In modern times many other foreign words containing /p/ have come into English. It goes without saying that the allophones of /p/ described above are wholly of English descent; e.g., the unaspirated /p/ of Old French was Anglicized as [pʰ] before stressed vowels.

In *pumpkin, empty, glimpse, dempster* 'judge', the original medial clusters /mk, mt, ms/ became /mpk, mpt, mps/ through premature raising of the velum. The /p/ occasionally appears also in *something*. *Lobster* (ME *lopester, lopster*) and *webster* 'weaver' (ME *webbestre, webster*) have /p/ before the voiceless cluster /st/. In the intervocalic clusters of *cobweb* (late ME *copweb*), *cupboard, raspberry*, AE *clapboard*, the original /p/ became /b/ in early MnE and was then lost in *cupboard, clapboard, raspberry*.

Spelling

The phoneme /p/ is spelled *p* in all positions, regularly so at the beginning and at the end of a word, as in *pan, plant, pray* and *cup, hemp, help, sharp*.

The spelling *pp* is used in two situations: (1) Between a stressed checked vowel and a following unstressed vowel or syllabic /l/, as in *pepper, dapper, copper, puppet, dipper, happy, stopping, upper, nipple, apple, stopple, supple,* where it indicated in ME that the vowel preceding /p/ was short. Note the alternate spellings of the morphemes *dip ~ dipp-er, stop ~ stopp-ing, up ~ upp-er,* etc. (2) In words taken from Latin or Old French, as in *appear, oppose, opposite, applaud, approve, oppress,* where the Latin spelling was retained or later introduced.

Rare spellings of /p/ appear in *lobster, Webster,* and in *hiccough,* a variant spelling of *hiccup* prompted by an erroneous association with *cough.*

In *cupboard, raspberry,* AE *clapboard,* the *p* is no longer pronounced. *Pneumonia, pneumatic, psychology, psalm, ptomaine, Ptolemy, receipt, corps, coup,* etc., retain the foreign spelling, although here the /p/ has never been pronounced in English.

8.2 The Plosive /b/

Articulation

The voiced bilabial plosive /b/ is articulated like /p/, except that the vocal lips vibrate.

In final position, the normally voiced plosive /b/ is often partially unvoiced and not always exploded. Unvoicing before a voiceless consonant occurs in *Webster* (cp. *web*).

Distribution

The plosive /b/ occurs singly in initial, final, and medial position, as in *bin, bid, book, boat, boy* and *rib, knob, robe, tribe* and *ribbon, habit, feeble, saber,* respectively. It is frequent after checked vowels, but rather uncommon after free vowels, where it occurs only in words taken from other languages, chiefly French and Latin.

The plosive /b/ enters into clusters with resonants. Initially it can be followed by /l, r, j/, as in *blind, blue, brain, brown, beauty, butte;* finally it can follow /l, r/, as in *bulb* and AE *barb, absorb;* medially it can follow /m, l, r/, as in *timber, tremble, bramble, humble, bombard, album, halberd,* AE *harbor, orbit.* The medial clusters /bj/ and /lbj/ occur in *fabulous, tabulate,* and *albumen,* respectively.

Homophones

Through the loss of final /b/, *climb, jamb, plumb* became homophonous with *clime, jam, plum.*

History

MnE /b/ descends from ME /b/ in all positions. In turn, ME /b/ is derived from OE /b/, as in *bind, blow, brew, ebb, rib,* or from OF and L /b/, as in *bawd, blue, brief, beauty, robe, tribe, barber, humble*. The postvocalic clusters /rb, lb/ of MnE, as in *barb, harbor, bulb*, and /b/ after free vowels, as in *daub, lobe, cube, bribe*, occur only in words taken from foreign languages, chiefly French and Latin.

The final /mb/ cluster in *climb, comb, dumb, bomb, jamb, plumb*, was reduced to /m/ before 1600, but the medial sequence /mb/ is preserved in *bombard, humble, timber*, because here the /b/ started the second syllable.

In *cobweb* the original /p/ became /b/ before the /w/. In *Webster, lobster* the unvoiced bilabial plosive preceding /st/ may belong to the /p/ phoneme rather than to /b/; cp. *dopester, Dempster*. In *thimble*, from earlier *thimel*, /b/ arose as a transition sound in the sequence /ml/.

Spelling

The spelling *b* occurs in all positions, regularly so initially and, except for *ebb*, also finally.

Intervocalic /b/ is written *b* after free vowels, as in *feeble, baby, sober, noble, ruby, ruble*. After checked vowels, the usual spelling is *bb*, as in *ribbon, pebble, rabbit, cobble, rubber, hubbub* and *ebbing, rubbing*, etc.; but in *habit, debutante, tabulate, ribald*, etc., the foreign spelling is retained.

In *climb, comb, womb* the *b* is no longer pronounced; *crumb, limb, numb, thumb*, which never had the /b/ phoneme, have spellings analogical to *climb, comb*. In *debt, doubt, subtle*, the *b* is a purely graphic Latinism.

8.3 The Plosive /t/

Articulation

The voiceless alveolar plosive /t/ is articulated by placing the tip and the lateral edges of the tongue against the upper gum and then releasing the contact. The velum is raised and the vocal lips are open.

The plosive /t/ has positional allophones analogous to those of /p/. Before a stressed vowel, whether alone or followed by a sonorant, it is aspirated, as in *tin, true, twist, tube*, in BE also, though less strongly, in the cluster /st/, as in *stand, stubborn*. In other positions, /t/ is unaspirated, except between a stressed and an unstressed vowel in BE *butter, motor, little*, etc. In AE the /t/ is often voiced in that position, as in *better, bottle, button, tomato, elevator*, but usually distinct from /d/ by being articulated as a swift and snappy tap against the upper gum. Thus *latter, kitty* are usually not homophonous with *ladder, kiddy*.

In the /tr/ cluster, the tip of the tongue may be somewhat retracted.

Distribution

The plosive /t/ occurs initially, finally, and medially, as in *tale, foot, meter, bitter*. Initially it can be followed by the resonants /r, w, j/, as in *tree, twin, tune, Teuton*, and preceded by /s/, as in *still, stream, student*. At the end of a morpheme, it can be preceded by the resonants /n, l, r/ and the fricatives /s, f/, as in *hunt, belt*, AE *heart* and *fist, gift*; medially only by /n, l, r/, as in *banter, winter, alter, sultan*, and AE *barter, tortoise*.

Foreign final clusters consisting of plosives appear in *apt, adept, act, infect*. Initial and final /ts/ occurs only in foreign words, mostly names, as in *tsetse, Tsingtao, tsar* (beside *czar* /zar/), and *Fitzgerald, Fritz, Schlitz, Spitzbergen*.

Alternation

In many foreign morphemes, /t/ alternates with /č/ or /š/, as in *native ~ nature, cent ~ century, cult ~ culture, digest ~ digestion, Christ ~ Christian* and *act ~ action, native ~ nation, permit ~ permission, relate ~ relation, part ~ partial, predict ~ prediction*, respectively. /t/ also alternates with /s/, as in *convért ~ cónverse, narcotic ~ narcosis, elegant ~ elegance*.

History

MnE /t/ is derived from ME /t/, where it occurs both in native and foreign words. In *against, amongst*, /t/ was added, apparently in such contexts as *agains the law, amongs them*. Some Americans have a /t/ after the /n/ in *fence, advance*, which is probably as old as the /p/ in *glimpse*, though not shown in the spelling at any time.

The /t/ has been lost in the clusters /st, ft/ before /m, n/ and when followed by syllabic /n, l/, as in *Christmas, chestnut, hasten, listen, soften, castle, whistle*. In *often* the /t/ is sometimes retained.

Spelling

The spelling *t* is used for the /t/ phoneme in all positions, regularly so initially and finally, as in *take, trail, twist, tube* and *hit, hint, colt, hart*.

The diagraph *tt* is written for /t/ (a) between a stressed checked vowel and a following unstressed vowel or syllabic /n, l/, as in *fitting, setting, bitter, batter, bitten, button, little, battle, bottle*; (b) in words taken from Latin and Old French, between /ə/ and a following stressed syllable, as in *attend, attract, attune*; (c) finally, in *butt, butte*.

The spelling *th* appears in words taken from Greek and in foreign names, as in *thyme, phthisic* /tízɪk/, *Thames, Anthony, Thomas, Esther, Goethe*. In *bouquet, depot, valet, mortgage* (earlier also spelled *morgage*), adopted from French after the loss of /t/, the *t* has always been silent in English.

8.4 The Plosive /d/

Articulation

The voiced alveolar plosive /d/ is articulated in the same manner as /t/, except that the vocal lips vibrate. In final position, it may be partially unvoiced. In the cluster /dr/, as in *drive, draw*, the tip of the tongue may be somewhat retracted.

Distribution

The voiced alveolar plosive /d/ occurs initially, finally, and medially, as in *din, do, dawn, sad, road, meadow, powder, sudden, needle*.

Initially, /d/ can be followed by the resonants /r, j, w/, as in *draw, dregs, dew, duty, dwell, dwindle*. Finally and medially it can follow /n, l, r/, as in *land, find, weld, bold*, AE *beard, board*, and in *wonder, flounder, elder, moulder*, AE *warden, order*. An exceptional final cluster appears in *adz*, a rare medial cluster in *cauldron*.

Alternation

The phoneme /d/ alternates with /s/ in *defend ~ defense, expend ~ expense, respond ~ response*, etc.; with /š/ in *expand ~ expansion*; and with zero in *spindle ~ spin, sound ~ sonant, hand ~ handsome, handkerchief*.

History

MnE /d/ is largely derived from ME /d/, both in native words, as *deal, dread, dwell, dew, bind, yield, beard, adz* (ME *ad(e)se*), *saddle, ladle, body*; and in words adopted from OF and L, as *dine, drug, due, round, cord, sudden, cauldron*.

In *sound* 'noise', *spindle* (cp. *spin*), *weld* v., /d/ was added in late ME or early MnE; in *handkerchief, handsome* it was lost c1600. The intervocalic /d/ in *paddock* 'enclosure' took the place of earlier /r/ in early MnE. The original /rð/ cluster of *burden, murder* and the /ðr/ cluster of *rudder* changed to /rd/ and /dr/, respectively, in ME; but *burthen, murther, ruther* were also current as late as 1800.

Spelling

The spelling *d* occurs in all positions, regularly so initially and finally. Medially, *d* is used after free vowels, as in *beadle, cradle, dawdle, hurdle, yodel, noodle, sidle, powder, dd* after checked vowels, as in *griddle, peddle, adder, coddle, huddle, pudding*, and *bidding, bedding, madden, plodder, budding*, except in *widow, meadow, shadow, body* and some foreign words like *medal, madame, model, nodule*.

In *handkerchief, handsome, d* is still written, though no longer sounded.

8.5 The Plosive /č/

Articulation

The voiceless prepalatal plosive /č/ is articulated by the grooved blade
of the tongue against the front of the hard palate. The release of the
closure is accompanied by a [š]-like offglide. Since /č/ enters into the
same types of final clusters with resonants as /p, t, k/, it is better to
treat it as a unit phoneme than as a cluster of obstruents, /tš/. In BE,
the /č/ phoneme is generally somewhat rounded, in AE only when a
rounded vowel follows it, as in *chew, chosen*.

Distribution

The plosive /č/ occurs initially and finally, both in the native and the
adopted French vocabulary, as in the English words *chaff, cheek, child,
chin, chose, churl* and *bitch, wretch, much, thatch, watch, beech*; and in
chance, chase, charm, cherry, choice, and *rich vetch, catch, notch, peach,
ache* 'letter h', *poach, pouch, pooch,* adopted from Old French. Medial /č/
appears almost exclusively in words taken from French or Latin, as in
bachelor, butcher, statue, virtue, nature. Righteous, formed on an English
base, has a foreign suffix. After free vowels, the /č/ phoneme is rare,
occurring in native words only after /i/ and /ɜ/, as in *beech, birch*.

Unlike other voiceless stops, initial /č/ is never followed by a resonant
or preceded by /s/; but like /p, t, k/, it enters into final clusters, as in
bench, blanch, belch, mulch, AE *larch, march*.

Alternation

In some morphemes, mostly foreign, /č/ alternates with /k/, as in
*chill ~ cool, chary ~ care, chaplet ~ cap, chant ~ cantor, chandler ~
candle, chart ~ cartulary, chalice ~ calix* and *speech ~ speak, wreck ~
wretch, leach ~ leak, kitchen ~ cook.* For the alternation /č ~ t/ see
under /t/.

History

Initial and final /č/ of MnE are derived from ME /č/.

In OE, the phoneme /č/ occurred (1) initially before front vowels, as
in *čīdan* (> *chide*), *čin* (> *chin*), *čiern* (> *churn*), *čēce* (> *cheek*), *čest*
(> *chest*), *čēosan* (> *choose*), *čeorl* (> *churl*), *čēap* (> *cheap, chap-man*),
čeaf (> *chaff*); and (2) medially after front vowels, as in *čiriče* (> *church*),
bēče (> *beech*), *ræčan* (> *reach*), *wrečča* (> *wretch*). After certain ME
vowel changes and analogic shifts, /č/ appeared also before back vowels,
as in *choke, choose, chosen, chough*.

In words adopted from OF, /č/ occurs in all the positions peculiar to
the native word stock. In addition, it makes its appearance after some

free vowels that are not followed by /č/ in native words, as in *poach*, *couch*, *pouch*, *ache* 'letter h', and (apparently) *mooch*.

Medial /č/ is mostly derived from the earlier cluster /tj/, as in *question*, *invention*, *culture*, *nature*, *furniture*. AE has /č/ also in *century*, *actual*, *eventual*, *textual*, *actuary*, *mortuary*, *Christian*, *fustian*, where BE usually preserves the /tj/ cluster.

The phoneme /č/ occurs also in words adopted in modern times from (or via) Spanish and from other languages, as in *chaparral*, *chigger*, *chocolate*, *Czech*, *Tchaikovsky*.

Spelling

Initially and in final consonant clusters, /č/ is regularly spelled *ch*, as already in ME. When not preceded by a consonant, final /č/ is written *ch* after free vowels, as in *beech*, *birch poach*, *pouch*, *urchin*.

After checked vowels the usual spelling is *tch*, as in *bitch*, *fetch*, *latch*, *notch*, *hutch*, *butcher*, etc.; but *much*, *such*, *rich*, *touch*, *bachelor* have *ch*.

Medial /č/ is represented by the diagraph *ti* in *fustian*, *Christian*, etc.; in *nature*, *actual*, etc., the combination *tu* stands for /č/ plus a vowel.

In names and technical terms adopted from other languages, the foreign spelling is usually retained, as in *cello*, *Cenci*, *Puccini*, *Czech*, *Tchaikovsky*.

8.6 The Plosive /ǧ/

Articulation

The voiced prepalatal plosive /ǧ/ is articulated by the blade of the tongue against the front of the hard palate. The release of the contact has a [ž]-like offglide. Like its voiceless counterpart /č/, it should be taken as a unit phoneme rather than as a cluster of obstruents, /dž/. In BE it is usually rounded, in AE only before rounded vowels. It is fully voiced, except finally.

Distribution

The plosive /ǧ/ occurs initially, as in *gin*, *gem*, *jangle*, *genius*, *joy*; finally, as in *edge*, *lodge*, *age*, *huge*; and medially, as in *badger*, *budget*, *Roger*, *wager*, *major*, *allegiance*.

Finally and medially, /ǧ/ enters into clusters with the resonants /n, l, r/, as in *cringe*, *strange*, *bilge*, *bulge*, AE *large*, and *banjo*, *manger*, *algae*, *soldier*, AE *margin*. Like /č/, the phoneme /ǧ/ does not cluster initially.

Regionalisms

There are some regional and social differences in the incidence of /ǧ/. AE regularly has /ǧ/ in *educate*, *gradual*, *individual*, where BE usually preserves the sequence /dj/. In *garage, massage, prestige*, both /ǧ/ and /ž/ are current in AE. The cluster /nǧ/, as in *strange, stranger*, is often replaced by /nž/ in BE, but not in AE. The historic pronunciation /-ıǧ/ of the final part of *Greenwich, Norwich* is in America usually replaced by the spelling pronunciation /-wıč/.

Alternation

The phoneme /ǧ/ alternates with /g/ in *leg-islate ∼ leg-al*, with /k/ in *larynge-al ∼ larynx*.

History

The phoneme /ǧ/ has a rather complicated history. In OE it occurred only after short front vowels and after /n/, as in the parent forms of MnE *bridge, ridge, edge, wedge, cudgel, hinge, singe, Stonehenge*. After other vowels, both short and long, in the clusters /lǧ, rǧ/, and initially, it became established during the ME period through the large-scale adoption of French and Latin words, such as *gem, jewel, joke, join, allege, badge, lodge, budge, cajole; sage, huge, gouge; avenge, lunge, range, manger, bulge, forge, charge; religion, ledger, budget*.

Scattered sources of MnE /ǧ/ are: (1) medial /dj/, as in *soldier, grandeur, verdure* and AE *educate, individual, residual* (where BE still has /dj/); (2) final /č/ in *hodgepodge* (earlier *hotch-pot*) and in unstressed *-wich*, as in BE *Greenwich, Harwich*; medial /č/ in *ajar*, from earlier *achar, on char*.

The phoneme /ǧ/ also occurs in words adopted from various languages in modern times, such as *jean, jejune, jar* (a container), *jungle, jute, junk* (a sailing vessel), *Japan, banjo*, and *jerked beef* (with /ǧ/ for Spanish /č/).

Spelling

Initial /ǧ/ is often spelled *g* before front vowels, as in *gibbet, gin, gem, gentle*, but also *j*, as in *jig, jilt, jelly, jet*. Before back vowels, *j* is the regular spelling, as in *jaundice, joint, jolly, June*, also before front vowels derived from ME back vowels, as in *jail, jewel*.

Final /ǧ/ is written *ge* after free vowels, as in *gage, dirge, gouge, huge*, and after resonants, as in *singe, strange, bulge, forge*. After checked vowels the usual spelling of /ǧ/ is *dge* (which gradually replaced *-gge* in early MnE), as in *hedge, pledge, bridge, lodge, knowledge*; but note *college, salvage*.

The spelling of medial /ǧ/ varies considerably. After checked vowels, *dg* is common, as in *badger, budget, cudgel, ledger*, but *g* is used in *legend, vegetable, gi* in *religion, ge* in *laryngeal, pigeon, gg* in *exaggerate*. After free vowels we have the spellings shown in *wager, major, allegiance*, after resonants those appearing in *danger, algae, margin, banjo, soldier, cordial*. Before the *u* of *verdure* and AE *educate, gradual, individual*, the /ǧ/ is spelled *d*, as also in *grandeur*.

This variety of spellings of /ǧ/ reflects in part the ME spelling of this sound, where *gg* (later replaced by *dg*) indicated that the preceding vowel was short, in part the Old French and Latin spellings, and beyond that the MnE change of medial /dj/ to /ǧ/.

8.7 The Plosive /k/

Articulation

The voiceless velar plosive /k/ is articulated by the back of the tongue against the roof of the mouth, farther forward before and after front vowels than near back vowels. Before a rounded vowel the lips are more or less rounded.

/k/ is aspirated before a stressed vowel, even when a resonant intervenes, as in *kin, keen, cold, clown, crow, quiet, cube*; in BE also in the cluster /sk/, as in *skin, school, scribe*. In other positions it is unaspirated, as in *shake, milk, bark, fox, act, action*, and in AE *skin*.

In AE, a voiced [k] is sometimes heard between voiced sounds, as in *bucket, knuckle, reckon*, which nevertheless is distinct from /g/, so that *knuckle* and *snuggle* do not rime.

Distribution

The plosive /k/ occurs initially, as in *king, keen, cat, cool*, finally, as in *lick, luck, make, like*, and medially, as in *dicker, tackle, Michael, bouquet*.

Initial /k/ can be followed by the resonants /l, r, j, w/, as in *clean, crop, cure, quick*, and preceded by /s/, as in *skin, sclerosis, scribe, skewer, square*. Final /k/ can follow the resonants /ŋ, l, r/, as in *sink, milk*, AE *dark*. Final and medial clusters of obstruents occur in *ask, fox, fact* and *action, anxious*.

Regionalisms

Regional differences in the incidence of /k/ are rare. AE has /sk/ in *schedule, ski*, where BE has /š/. In Virginia and South Carolina *car, card*, etc., sometimes appear as /kjɑ, kjɑd/, more frequently in popular than in cultivated speech. This /kj/ cluster presumably derives from a palatalized /k/ preceding earlier /æ/, which was later lowered and backed before historical /r/.

Alternation

For the alternation /k ~ č/ see under /č/. In *a-cknowledge ~ knowledge*, /k/ alternates with zero, in *suspec-t ~ suspici-on* with /š/.

Homophones

The reduction of the initial cluster /kn/ to /n/ produced the homophones *knave = nave, knead = need, kneel = Neil, knell = Nell, knew = new, knight = night, knit = nit, knot = not, know = no*.

History

MnE /k/ derives from ME /k/, both in words inherited from OE, as *keen, climb, crow, queen, bake, think, milk, dark*, and in words adopted from Old French or Latin, as *camel, cover, clerk, crew, quaint, quart*.

After the OE cluster /sk/ had become /š/, as in *shine, flesh*, the cluster /sk/ was introduced into English from Old Norse, as in *skate* (a fish), *skin, skill, skirt, sky, bask*; from OF, as in *skein, skim, skirmish, screw, basket*; and from L, as in *scribe*.

The phoneme /k/ occurs also in numerous words introduced from Latin, Greek, French, and other languages in modern times, such as *scholastic, chaos, scheme, kilometer, bouquet, coquette, liqueur, cache, ski, scherzo, kowtow, kremlin, kayak, kumquat, skunk, squash* n.

Initial /k/ before /n/ was lost in the 17. century, as in *knee, knight, know, knowledge*. In *acknowledge* the /k/ survives because the syllabic boundary fell between the /k/ and the /n/. In the former medial clusters /kg/ of *blackguard* and /skl/ of *muscle*, the /k/ is lost.

Spelling

The phoneme /k/ is written in seven different ways: *c, k, ck, q, qu, que, ch*, as in *cat, keen, lick, queen, bouquet, physique, chorus*. Moreover, the letter *x* spells the cluster /ks/, as in *fox*.

The spelling *c* is used (1) for initial /k/ when it is followed by the vowel graphs shown in *cab, cage, cairn, cock, core, cow, count, court, cut, cure*; (2) in the initial cluster /sk/, when followed by the same vowel graphs, as in *scab, Scot, scold, scour, scuffle*, but also in *sceptic*; (3) in the initial clusters /kl, kr, skl, skr/, as in *clear, climb, cream, crow, sclerosis, scream, scribe*; but *klieg, Klondike*; (4) in the clusters /kt, kš/, as in *act, elect, action, election*; (5) in the suffixes *-ic, -ics, -ical, -acle*, as in *logic, physics, comical, spectacle*.

The spelling *k* is used (1) before the vowel graphs shown in *kin, kilometer, kettle, keen, kite* and *skill*, AE *ski, skeptic, skein, sky*; but also in *kulak, kumquat* and *skald, skate, skull, skunk, skew, Kuklux*; (2) finally after free vowels, as in *seek, sake*, BE *bark, lurk, Sauk, talk, soak, spook, pike*; also in *book, took*, which formerly had the free vowel /u/; (3) in the final clusters shown in *thank, link, milk, bulk, ask, brisk*, AE *dark*.

After checked vowels, /k/ is spelled *ck*, as in *sick, neck, back, rock, luck* and *quicken, speckle, cackle, cockle, knuckle*.

In the clusters /kw, skw/, the spelling *q* is regularly used for /k/, as in *quart, question, quit, quota, square, squire* (from Latin and Old French) and *quake, queen, quick, quote* (of English stock).

In words adopted from French in modern times, /k/ is spelled *qu, que*, as in *quay, queue, bouquet, liqueur, critique, physique, barque*.

In words adopted from Latin (most of them ultimately Greek), *ch* is a frequent spelling of /k/, as in *character, chaos, chirograph, chorus, chlorin, chronic, Christ, school, scholar, scheme, stomach, Michael, autochthonous.*

The spelling *ch* occurs also in a few words taken from other languages, as in *scherzo, Czech,* the Dutch names *Schuyler, Schuykill* current in America, and the AE coinage *schooner.* The spelling of the verb *ache* for earlier *ake* is taken over from the noun *ache*, which had /č/ in ME and EMnE. Later the /k/ of the verb replaced the /č/ in the noun. The unique spelling *cc* for earlier *ck* in *hiccup* is taken over from the alternate spelling *hic-cough*, which is based upon the popular analysis of *hick-up* into *hick-cough* (cp. hacking cough). The peculiar spelling *choir* for earlier *quire* is partially modeled on *chorus.*

The cluster /ks/ is regularly spelled *x*, as in *fox, fix, fixture, textile.* In *anxious* and BE *connexion, inflexion,* the spelling *x* stands for the cluster /kš/.

Though lost in the 17. century, /k/ is still written in *knee, know*, etc. *Victuals* is a Latinized spelling of *vittles*, introduced in the 16. century.

8.8 The Plosive /g/

Articulation

The voiced velar plosive /g/ is articulated by the arched tongue against the roof of the mouth, which forms full contact with it, thus blocking the oral channel momentarily. The contact of the tongue with the roof of the mouth shifts with the adjoining vowel, being farther forward near front vowels than near back vowels. The lip rounding of adjoining vowels may be anticipated or retained during the articulation of /g/, as in *good, vogue.* In final position, /g/ can be partially unvoiced and unreleased.

Distribution

The plosive /g/ occurs initially, as in *give, good, guest, ghost, gain,* finally, as in *egg, dog, league, fugue,* and medially, as in *vigor, rugged, juggle, eagle, tiger.*

Initial /g/ can be followed by the resonants /l, r, w, j/, as in *glad, gloom, greet, grand, guano, Guelph, gubernatorial.* A final /g/-cluster seems to occur only in AE *morgue.* Medial clusters consisting of /g/ and either a preceding or/and a following resonant are numerous, as illustrated in such words as *finger, hungry, language, vulgar, pilgrim, ague, figure, saguaro, signal, stigma, vagrant,* and AE *largo, sorghum, argue.*

The unusual medial clusters /gz/ and /gž/, consisting of two obstruents, appear in *exalt, exist, exhibit* and in *luxurious*, respectively.

Regionalisms

In Virginia and South Carolina, the initial /g/ of *garden, guard*, etc.,
is sometimes followed by /j/. Note the parallel phenomenon in *car, card*.

Alternation

Owing to the loss of /g/ in the final /ŋg/ cluster, and its preservation
in medial position, *long, strong, young* have the allomorphs /lɔŋ ~ lɔŋg-ə/,
etc. /g/ varies with zero also in *sign-al ~ sign, dign-ity ~ deign, con-dign,
malign-ant ~ malign, co-gnate ~ nat-ive*. For the alternation /g ~ ǧ/
see under /ǧ/.

History

The voiced velar plosive /g/ descends from ME /g/ in all positions.
In the native vocabulary, initial /g/ is common before old back vowels,
as in *good, gold, ghastly*, and in the initial clusters /gl, gr/, as in *glow, glee,
ground, grim*; before front vowels it is rare, surviving in MnE only in
gild, gilden, gird, girdle, geese. Postvocalic /g/ occurs only in a small
number of native words, as in *twig, rag, stag, dog, frog*, always preceded
by a checked vowel. /ŋg/, as in *finger, longer*, is the only native postvocalic cluster. This restricted distribution of the plosive /g/ is inherited
from OE, where the plosive [g] was a positional allophone of the fricative
[j ~ g], which appear as the phonemes /j/ and /w/ in MnE.
Initial /g/ before front vowels, rare in the native vocabulary, became
rather common in ME and later by the adoption of foreign words, as
gill, gear, guess (from ON), *gimlet, gizzard, guillotine* (from French),
giggle, Ghent, gherkin (from Dutch). In *get, forget, gift, give, guest*, the
native /j/ was replaced by the /g/ of the corresponding Scandinavian
words in the Danelaw and adopted in the London area after Chaucer's
time; but *begin* has the /g/ from *began, begun*.
The great majority of words that have final or medial /g/ in MnE
were taken into English during the Middle Ages or early modern times.
Thus *bag, egg, hug, leg, rig, wag, rugged, swagger, ugly*, from ON; *brag,
dig, drug, fig, haggard, juggler, spigot*, from French; *plug, sag, smuggle,
stagger, wiggle*, from Dutch; *ignious, lingual, stigma, vulgar*, from Latin;
bog, from Irish.
It is worth noting that free vowels occur before /g/ only in words
adopted from foreign languages, as in *league, eagle, legal, plague, vague,
toga, vogue, ogle, bugle, fugue, tiger, migrate*. Moreover, the initial clusters
/gw, gj/ occur only in foreign words, as in *guano, Guelph, gubernatorial*.
At the end of a syllable the /ng/ cluster became /ŋ/ (c1600), as in *sing,
long*, but in the medial cluster the /g/ survives, as in *finger, single, longer,
longest, English*, because here the /g/ began the second syllable. In the
initial cluster /gn/, the /g/ was lost in the seventeenth century, as in

gnaw, gnat, gnash, gnome. Intervocalic /gz/ and /gž/, as in *exalt, exist, exhibit, exhort, anxiety* and in *luxurious*, are derived from /ks/ and /kš/ preceding a stressed vowel. The voicing of these clusters parallels the voicing of /s/ to /z/ in *possess, observe*. In *sugar* (from OF *sucre*), the voiced stop /g/ replaced the /k/ in late ME.

Spelling

Initial /g/, alone or in clusters, is usually written *g*, as in *give, get, gap, good* and *glad, glow, grand, grim, guano*. Before front vowels and /ai/ (from ME /ī/), the French spelling *gu* is fairly common, as in *guerdon, guide, guile* and the native (or ON) words *guess, guest, guild, guilt*; it occurs also in *guard, guaranty*. In a few words, /g/ is written *gh*, as in foreign *gherkin, ghetto, Ghibelline, ghee, Ghurka* and in native *ghost, ghastly, aghast*.

Final /g/ is spelled *g* after checked vowels, as in *big, leg, lag, dog, bug* (but *egg*); *gu* after free vowels, as in *fatigue, league, vague, vogue, fugue*, BE *morgue*, AE *prologue*.

Intervocalic /g/ following a stressed checked vowel is usually written *gg*, as in *rugged, stagger, juggle, wiggle* and *bigger, lagging, shaggy*. This spelling is also used in forms that formerly had two syllables, as *begged, lagged*. A single *g* is written in this position in some words taken from Latin or French, as *vigor, agony, sugar*. *Agglutinate, aggrandize, aggress* also retain the foreign spelling.

After free vowels, intervocalic /g/ is spelled *g*, as in *ego, eagle, toga, ogre, bugle, tiger*.

In medial clusters the spelling *g* is regular, as in *hunger, vulgar, argue, ague, saguara, signal, migrate*; but note *sorghum*.

The clusters /gz/ and /gž/ are represented by *x*, as in *exact, exhibit, anxiety* and *luxurious*.

In *gnaw, gnat, gnash* the *g* is still written, though no longer pronounced; in *diaphragm, paradigm, sign* it has always been silent. The BE spelling *gaol* beside *jail* reflects an Anglo-French variant of the word.

8.9 The Glottal Plosive [ʔ]

The glottal stop [ʔ] is not unknown in English, but it is not a normal phoneme. It appears in the negating interjections [ʔm̓ʔm, ʔń̓ʔn, ʔʌʔə] and the affirming [ʔm̓hm̓]; as a prosodic onset of overstressed initial vowels, as in *ălways, ăbsolútely, ŏh!, ăh!*; and occasionally as an allophone of medial /t/, as in *bottle, button, Saturday*.

9. The Fricative Consonants

9.1 The Fricative /f/

Articulation

The voiceless labio-dental fricative /f/ is articulated by putting the lower lip against the edges of the upper teeth and forcing breath through the narrow passage. The vocal lips are apart.

Distribution

The fricative /f/ occurs initially and finally in native and in foreign words, as in *feel, foot, fool, foil* and *loaf, laugh, beef, chef*. Medially it is common in foreign words, such as *offer, raffle, suffer, prophet, aphid, dauphin, sofa, rifle, gopher*, rare in words of English stock, as *heifer, gaffer, offal*.

Initial /f/ can be followed by the resonants /l, r, j/, as in *flow, flourish, free, frail, few, fume*. Finally, it can follow the resonants /m, l, r/ as in *lymph, nymph, self, wolf, sylph*, and AE *wharf, scarf*. The medial clusters /mf, lf, rf, fn, fl/ occur only in foreign words, e.g. *comfort, camphor, pilfer, sulphur, orphan, daphne, Laughlin*.

The final and medial cluster /ft/ occurs in native *left, soft, draught, rafter, laughter*; the clusters /sf, sθ, fθ/ in foreign words, such as *sphere, sphynx, asphalt, asphodel, sthenic, asthenia, diphthong, diphtheria*.

Regionalisms

In BE, *lieutenant* is pronounced /lɛfténənt/, in AE /luténənt/, both types going back to ME. BE preserves the /v/ of OF *neveu* in *nephew*, while AE has /f/, except for some relics of /v/ along the Atlantic coast.

In the phrase *you have to* the /v/ is sometimes replaced by /f/.

Alternation

In some morphemes, both native and foreign, voiceless /f/ alternates with its voiced counterpart /v/, e.g. *half ~ halv-es, calf ~ calv-es ~ calve, self ~ selv-es, life ~ liv-es ~ live, wolf ~ wolv-es, leaf ~ leav-es, give ~ gif-t, drif-t ~ drive, lef-t ~ leave* and *re-lief ~ re-lieve, grief ~ grieve, proof ~ prove, serf ~ serve*. This alternation results from the phonemicization of the positional allophones [f ~ v] of OE /f/ in ME.

History

MnE /f/ is derived from ME /f/, finally and before /t/ also from the ME velar fricative /x/.

In the native vocabulary of ME, /f/ was common initially and finally, rare medially, since the voiced medial allophone [v] of the OE /f/ phoneme became a separate phoneme /v/ in ME. Among the many native words that had initial and final /f/ in ME are the following: *fish, fly, friend, few, hoof, self, wharf, soft.* Medial /f/ from OE long /ff/ survives in *offer* (ultimately Latin). In *gaffer* (from *god-father*), *heifer* (from *hekfer*), *offal* (from *of-fall*) the /f/ comes from earlier clusters.

In words introduced from OF and L during the Middle Ages or later, /f/ occurs in all positions, as in *fail, flute, frail, fragile, fury, chief, nymph, sylph, scarf, raffle, suffer, dauphin, sofa, camphor, dolphin, orphan, daphne.* It should be noted that all medial /f/ clusters of MnE are of foreign origin.

The foreign clusters /sf, sθ, fθ/, consisting of two fricatives, occur in a number of words taken from Greek, as *sphere, hemisphere, sphynx, sthenic, asphalt, asphyxiate, diphthong, diphtheria.* Since the spellings *spere, hemispere* still appear in the 16. century, it is clear that /sf/ was first Anglicized as /sp/. *Diphthong, diphtheria* now have the cluster /fθ/, but /pθ/ is still heard.

In a number of words, final /f/ and /f/ before /t/ are derived from the ME velar fricative /x/, as in *cough, dwarf, enough, tough, trough, laugh, laughter, draught, draft* and the surnames *Gough, Goff, Auchinleck.* This change of /x/ (presumably articulated with rounded lips) to /f/ occurred before 1600.

In *sheriff* (ME *shir-reve*) earlier /v/ was replaced by /f/, perhaps through the influence of *bailiff.* BE /f/ in *lieutenant* /lɛftɛnənt/ goes back to ME /f/ from /v/ before /t/. AE *nephew* has /f/, which may be a spelling pronunciation; however, /f/ is common in English folk speech of the Midland and the North, and in Scotland. In BE *halfpenny, halfpence* /hepəni, hepəns/ the /f/ was dropped c1600.

Spelling

Initially, in final clusters, and after free vowels, the phoneme /f/ is usually spelled *f*, as in *food, flood, fresh, self, gulf, wharf, soft, reef, safe, loaf, rife, sofa, surface, stifle.* Exceptions are: AE *off, office.*

Double *ff* is written after checked vowels, as in *stiff, bluff, riffle, raffle, suffer, offer.* Exceptions are: *if, chef, heifer.*

In words that formerly had the velar fricative /x/, the old spelling *gh* is usually retained, as in *cough, enough, laugh, laughter*; but *f* has been introduced in *dwarf, draft* (beside *draught*), *Goff* (beside *Gough*), and the Scottish spelling *ch* appears in the surname *Auchinleck.*

In words taken from Latin (ultimately mostly Greek), the foreign spelling *ph* is regularly used, as in *philosophy, physics, sphere, prophet, aphid, nymph, sylph, camphor, orphan, asphodel, diphthong.* As a pseudo-learned spelling, *ph* was introduced in *nephew* (from OF *neveu*) during

the 16. century, and came to be pronounced /f/ in AE. The earlier spelling
ƒ has been replaced by *ph* in *Guelph, Ralph, Randolph* and some other
names. AE *gopher,* attested since c1800, is probably of American Indian
origin.

9.2 The Fricative /v/

Articulation

The labio-dental fricative /v/ has the same articulation as /f/, but it
is voiced.

Distribution

In native words, the voiced labio-dental fricative /v/ occurs medially,
as in *liver, ever, heaven, seven, oven, even, raven, over*; and finally in words
where it was followed by /ə/ in ME, such as *live, love, have, leave, knave,
grove, groove, drive* and *selv-es, wolv-es, carve, starve.* Also the medial
clusters /lv, rv/ occur in native words, as in *anvil, silver,* AE *harvest.*

In foreign words, /v/ is found in all positions characteristic of the
native vocabulary, as in *river, revel, savage, novel, cover, fever, favor, oval,
fluvial, rival; receive, save, serve, move, arrive, valve*; and *salvage, marvel.*

Initial /v/ became established in ME through the adoption of such
French and Latin words as *vigor, vex, valley, vulgar, veal, veil, virtue,
vault, vote, vice, vouch, voice.* The only initial cluster is /vj/ in *view,
purview, review.*

Regionalisms

In BE, *nephew* preserves the historic /v/, which survives in America
only in scattered fashion along the Atlantic coast. The plural form
hooves survives (by the side of *hoofs*) in parts of Pennsylvania.

Alternation

For the alternation /v ~ f/ see under /f/. The phoneme /v/ also alternates with /b/, in *weave ~ web*; with /p/, in *de-ceive ~ de-cep-tion*; with /u/,
in *solve ~ solu-tion, re-volve ~ re-volu-tion*; with zero, in *re-ceive ~
re-ceip-t.*

Homophones

Vane, which replaced earlier *fane,* is homophonous with *vein, vain.*

History

MnE /v/ is derived from ME /v/. In the native vocabulary of ME and
in words adopted from ON, /v/ occurred only between voiced sounds,
having split off from /f/ in this position. In initial position it was introduced from OF with the many words taken from that language or from
Latin.

In modern times the Southern dialect forms *vane, vat, vixen* have replaced the Midland forms *fane, fat, fixen* (akin to *fox*).

The singular past tense forms *gave, drove,* etc., now have the /v/ of the formerly disyllabic plural forms instead of earlier /f/; the imperative forms *give, drive,* the /v/ of the indicative stem.

In the unstressed preposition *of* (historically the same as *off*), the original final /f/ became voiced.

The suffix *-ive,* as in *active, native,* had the variant *-if* in ME (from OF), which was abandoned shortly after 1500.

Spelling

The /v/ phoneme is usually written *v*. Occasional spellings occur in *navvy* (short for *navigator*), AE *savvy* (from Spanish); in *Stephen, Stephenson,* BE *nephew* (in which Latinate *ph* replaced the earlier spelling *v* in the 16. century), AE *gopher*; and in the preposition *of*.

9.3 The Fricative /θ/

Articulation

The voiceless dental fricative /θ/ is articulated by putting the flattened blade of the tongue close to the upper gums and teeth and forcing the breath through the narrow passage. The tip of the tongue may protrude between the teeth. The vocal lips are open.

Distribution

The fricative /θ/ occurs only initially and finally in the native vocabulary, as in *thin, thank, thumb, thaw, thief* and *bath, moth, both, south.* The adjective *earth-en* has the final /θ/ of *earth*.

/θ/ enters into the initial clusters /θr, θj, θw/, as in *three, throw, thwart, thwack* and literary *thew* 'strength, vigor'; and into final /rθ/, as in AE *hearth, north.* In *health, length, fifth, width,* etc., the /θ/ is a separate morpheme.

In words adopted from Greek, usually by way of Latin, /θ/ occurs not only initially and finally, as in *theater, theory, throne, myth,* but also between vowels, as in *catholic, mathematics, method, sympathy, python,* and in medial clusters, as in *anthology, anthropology, esthetic, autochthonous,* and AE *Martha, orthodox*.

Regionalisms

In AE, *smithy* usually has /θ/, in BE /ð/. *Withe, withy* have /ð ~ θ/ in AE; in BE the former has /θ ~ ð/, the latter /θ/. The prepositions *with, without* have /ð/ or /0/ in AE, largely in regional dissemination,

/ð/ in BE. The adverbs *thence, thither* begin with /θ/ or /ð/ in AE, with /ð/ in BE. In *northwest, southwest* seafaring people drop the /θ/.

Alternation

In some morphemes, /θ/ alternates with its voiced counterpart /ð/. Thus, *bath ~ bathe, breath ~ breathe, cloth ~ clothe, loath ~ loathe, wreath ~ wreathe; path ~ path-s* /-ðz/, *lath ~ lath-s* /-ðz ~ -θs/, *moth ~ moth-s* /-ðz ~ -θs/, *wreath ~ wreath-s* /-ðz ~ -θs/; *worth ~ worth-y, smith ~ smith-y* /θ ~ ð/, *north ~ north-ern, south ~ south-ern, heath ~ heath-er*. This alternation arose in ME through the phonemicization of the positional allophones [θ ~ ð] of OE /þ/.

History

In the native vocabulary, /θ/ descends from ME /θ/ in initial and final position, as in *thin, thunder, thread, thwart* and *path, death, cloth, loath, north*. Final /θ/ in *moth, wrath* is derived from the long medial /θθ/ of ME *moþþe, wraþþe*. *Booth* was adopted from ON in early ME, *faith* from OF.

It is worth noting that, contrary to the general rule, the archaic forms *giveth, loveth*, etc., have voiceless /θ/ in an unstressed syllable.

Most of the Greek words containing /θ/ in MnE came into the language in the last decades of the 16. century or later. Contrary to the English distribution pattern, /θ/ occurs in these words not only initially and finally, but also between vowels and in medial consonant clusters. Examples are given above.

There are several spelling pronunciations. In *panther*, for earlier *panter*, the spelling *th* was introduced c1500 from L *panthera* (ultimately Greek) and came to be sounded /θ/. *Anthem* for earlier *antem* (OE *antefn*) has a pseudo-Latin *th*. *Thug*, adopted from Hindi c1800, has the fricative as a substitute for the aspirated stop of Hindi.

Spelling

The phoneme /θ/ is regularly spelled *th*. The spelling *th* gradually replaced earlier *þ* and *ð* during the latter part of the ME period.

The *th* of *asthma* is not sounded. In *Thomas, Anthony, Thames* the spelling *th* stands for /t/.

9.4 The Fricative /ð/

Articulation

The dental fricative /ð/ is articulated like /θ/, but it is voiced.

Distribution

The phoneme /ð/ occurs in all major positions, but does not enter into clusters. Initial: *the, that, they, thou, then, there, thus, though*; final: *bathe, breathe, clothe, blithe, path-s, clothe-s, with, with-out*; medial: *whither, weather, lather, bother, mother, heathen, father, worthy*.

Regionalisms

The plural forms *baths, clothes, paths* regularly have the /ð/ of the old disyllabic forms, but *laths, moths, wreaths* waver between /ð/ and /θ/. In *smithy*, /ð/ is more common than /θ/ in England, whereas the /θ/ of *smith* is usual in America, where the word is little used. *Thence* and *thither* have initial /ð/ in BE, /θ ~ ð/ in AE. In *clothes, baths* the /ð/ is sometimes omitted in rapid speech.

Alternation

/ð/ alternated with /θ/ in some morphemes. See the list under /θ/.

History

MnE /ð/ is largely derived from late ME /ð/. It occurs only in native words.

In early ME, the /ð/ sound was a positional allophone of the phoneme /þ/, occurring only between voiced sounds, as in OE. Three phonetic changes in late ME raised [ð] to phonemic status: medial long /θθ/ became short /θ/, as in *moþþe, wraþþe* (MnE *moth, wrath*); initial /θ/ became [ð] in frequently unstressed words, as in pronouns and prepositions; after the loss of final /ə/, as in *bathe*, [ð] became established in final position. These three successive changes created the voiced phoneme /ð/ to contrast with voiceless /θ/ in medial, initial, and final position.

As in late ME, initial /ð/ occurs in MnE only in words that are frequently unstressed, as *the, this, them, they, there, thus, though*, /ð/ being retained if such words received the sentence accent, as in *I mean thém, he wasn't thére*. Final /ð/ appears in formerly disyllabic *bathe, breathe, clothe-s, path-s, lath-s* and in normally unstressed *with, without, within*; medial /ð/ in *brother, heathen, wether, worthy*.

Medial /ð/ is in part derived from earlier /d/ in the cluster /dr/, as in *father, gather, hither, mother, weather, whither*. This change took place in late ME. As a result, *weather* became homophonous with *wether*.

Spelling

The phoneme /ð/ is always spelled *th*, a diagraph used also for /θ/.

9.5 The Fricative /s/

Articulation

The voiceless prepalatal fricative /s/ is articulated by the grooved blade of the tongue against the front part of the hard palate in such a manner that the concentrated stream of breath is hurled against the edges of the lower teeth, producing a 'hissing' sound. The narrowing of the breath channel is farther forward than in the /š/ of *she, shoe*.

Distribution

The fricative /s/ occurs in all positions, both in native and foreign words, and enters into more clusters than any other consonant.

It occurs initially, as in *sing, sun, soon, side* and *city, cent, seal, soup, science*; finally, as in *glass, less, goose, mice* and *press, plus, face, nice*; medially, as in *listen, whistle* and *tassel, faucet, basin*.

/s/ enters into clusters with resonants: initially with /m, n, l, j, w/, as in *smoke, snow, slide, sweet*, BE *suit*; finally with /n, l, r/, as in *chance, else, false*, AE *horse*; medially with /m/, as in *isthmus*.

Unlike other fricatives, /s/ freely forms clusters with the plosives /p, t, k/: initially, as in *spin, split, spring, star, stream*, BE *stew, skill, scrub, skew, square*; finally, as in *grasp, fist, ask* and *lapse, fox, Fitz*; medially, as in *aspen, master, biscuit* and *dropsy, buxom, toxin*. In a few words adopted from Greek, /s/ is followed by a fricative, as in *sphere, Sphynx, sthenic, asthenia*.

Regionalisms

There are some differences and fluctuations in the incidence of /s/. The prefix *trans-* has /s ~ z/ when followed by a stressed syllable beginning with a vowel or a voiced consonant, as in *transact, translate*. Both AE and BE have /s ~ z/ in *discern*. In AE the same variation occurs also in *blouse, spouse, suffice, sacrifice*, but BE has /s/. BE appears to have predominantly /z/ in *greasy*; AE usage varies regionally, /s/ predominating in the New England settlements and in eastern Pennsylvania, /z/ farther south. *Louisville* (Ky.) and *St. Louis* (Mo.) are often pronounced without /s/ locally and in adjoining areas. The cluster /sj/ is usually preserved in BE, as in *sue, super* and *issue, sexual*; AE has *sue* /su/, *sexual* /sɛkšuəl/, *issue* /ɪš(j)u/.

Alternation

The phoneme /s/ alternates with /z, š, ž, d, t/.

The nouns *glass, grass, grease, house, close, use* have /s/, the corresponding verbs *glaze, graze, grease, house, close, use* have /z/. *Brass, goose, house, grease* end in /s/, the derivatives *brazen, gosling, lousy, greasy* have /z/

(the last only regionally). Note also *house ~ hous-es, los-t ~ lose*. Morpheme-initial /s/ varies with /z/ in *sign ~ de-sign, solve ~ dis-solve ~ ab-solve, sound ~ re-sound*, etc.

The inflectional morphemes of the plural of nouns and of the third person singular of verbs have the variants /s ~ z ~ əz/, as in *book-s ~ leg-s ~ hous-es* and *write-s ~ sing-s ~ catch-es*.

The alternation /s ~ š/ occurs in the base morphemes of *con-fess ~ con-fession, possess ~ possession, emerse ~ emersion, inverse ~ inversion, race ~ racial, grace ~ gracious*, etc. Instead of /š/, *emersion, conversion* may have /ž/.

/s/ varies with /ž/ in *case ~ casual, use* n. *~ usual, glass ~ glazier*. For the alternations /s ~ t/ and /s ~ d/ see under /t/ and /d/.

History

The /s/ of MnE continues ME /s/ in all major positions, both in native and in foreign words. Most of the /s/ clusters occur both in the native and in the foreign vocabulary, but /sk, skr, skj, skw, sf, sθ, sj, ps, ts/ are peculiar to such foreign words as *skim, skirmish, biscuit, scribe, skew, square, sphere, sthenic, Fritz, Fitzhugh, waltz, lapse, dropsy*, and BE *suit*.

The incidence of /s/ was somewhat reduced in early MnE by the voicing of intervocalic /s/ before stressed vowels, as in *possess, deserve* (see under /z/), and the reduction of the cluster /sj/ to /š/, as in *nation, vicious* (see under /š/).

Spelling

The phoneme /s/ is most commonly spelled *s*, especially in clusters; but a rather bewildering variety of other spellings also occur.

Initial /s/ is usually written *s*. But in foreign words *c* is common before old front vowels, as in *city, cent, certain, circle, cite, receive*, and *sc* is used in *science, scion, scissors*, and even in native *scythe*.

After checked vowels, *ss* is the usual spelling of /s/, as in *miss, less, glass, fuss, puss*, and *missing, missile, lessen, essence, tassel, massive, fossil, fussy, pussy*. After free vowels, /s/ is written *ce* or *se*, as in *fleece, caprice, face, sauce, juice, nice, mice, choice* and *geese, base, close, noose, goose, souse, mouse*. It should, however, be noted that the *e* in the digraphs *ce, se* is at the same time an indicator of free vowels.

The diagraphs *ce* and *se* also spell final /s/ following a consonant, as in *quince, since, fence, pence, chance, once*, AE *farce, force* and *sense, else, false, pulse*, AE *horse, hoarse, course, bourse*. Final *ce*, moreover, appears after unstressed vowels in such words as *lettuce, palace, service, necklace*.

Inflectional /s/, as in *books, cups* and *keeps, sits* is written *s*. A single *s* also spells final /s/ in *us, plus, octopus, (omni)bus, fungus, alumnus*, etc.

Rare spellings of medial /s/ appear in *basin, facet, faucet, lascivious*.

After initial /ə/, the foreign spelling is retained in *ascend, ascetic, assault, assimilate,* etc.

The cluster /ks/ is written *x* or *xc*, as in *fox, fix, buxom, exit* and *excel, excite*; the cluster /ts/ is spelled *tz*, as in *Fitz, Fritz, waltz.*

The *s* in *isle, island, aisle* has always been purely graphic.

9.6 The Fricative /z/

Articulation

The prepalatal fricative /z/ has the same oral articulation as /s/, but it is voiced.

Distribution

In the native vocabulary, the phoneme /z/ occurs only finally, as in *graze, ooze, rise, fizz, buzz, was, as,* and medially, as in *dizzy, dazzle, thousand, weasel.* In foreign words it is common in these positions, as in *ease, rose, use, noise* and *dozen, prison, reason, possess, resign, citizen, spasm,* respectively.

Initially, /z/ is found only in words adopted from foreign languages, as *zeal zest, zigzag* (from French), *zoology, zone, Xerxes, xenophobia* (ultimately Greek); and from various languages, *zero, zebra, Zulu, Zion, Zuider Zee, zeitgeist, czar.*

The phoneme /z/ appears as a separate morpheme in *bring-s, hang-s* and *son-s, head-s* (fuller form in *blush-es, bench-es*), and in *her-s, hi-s.* Initial /z/ in the archaic exclamation *zounds!* is reduced from *His wounds.*

Finally and medially, /z/ can follow a resonant, as in *cleanse, brouse,* AE *Mars,* and in *clumsy, crimson, pansy, palsy,* BE *visual,* respectively. Initially, /z/ occurs only in the rare clusters shown in *zloty, Zwingli,* BE *Zeus, zeugma.*

Medially, /z/ can follow a voiced plosive, as in *absolve, observe, exist, exhibit, Alexander, anxiety.*

Regionalisms

BE usually preserves the cluster /zj/ in *glazier, transient, casual, visual, Jesuit, Parisian,* where AE has /ž/. *Illinois* (in French spelling) regularly ends in /oi/ in the Midwest, but elsewhere /z/ is sometimes added. For the variation /z ~ s/ see under /s/.

Alternation

For the alternation /z ~ s/, see under /s/. In *seize ~ seizure, please ~ pleasure, use* v. *~ usual,* AE *Jesus ~ Jesuit,* /z/ alternates with /ž/; in *anxiety ~ anxious,* the cluster /gz/ varies with /kš/.

History

In the native vocabulary, the phoneme /z/ came into being in ME through the phonemicization of the voiced allophone [z] of the /s/ phoneme, which occurred only between voiced sounds. In MnE, the /z/ from this source occurs medially, as in *hazel, weasel, thousand, houses, risen, rising, rises, dizzy*; and, owing to the loss of final /ə/ in late ME, finally, as in *nose, ooze, wise, graze, rise*.

In words adopted from OF and L, /z/ is common in these positions, as in *prison, embezzle, hazard, reason, horizon, venison, citizen*, and in *please, rose, amuse, noise*.

Initial /z/ was introduced into late ME and early MnE in Greek and Arabic words current in Latin and French, as *zeal, zone, zodiac, zoology, zenith, zero*. The stock of words beginning with /z/ has been considerably increased in more recent times through the adoption of such foreign words as *zest, zigzag, zany, zink, Zeeland, zebra, Zulu, xenophobia, xylophone, czar*.

The incidence of the voiced fricative /z/ in final and in medial position was increased by the voicing of final /s/ in unstressed position and of medial /s/ before a stressed vowel.

The final /s/ of the unstressed ME inflectional suffix /-əs/ of the genitive singular and the plural of nouns, and of the 3. person singular indicative of the verb, became voiced in the 15. or 16. century. In *riches*, from earlier *richesse*, the final /s/, taken as the plural inflection, also became /z/.

Voicing of final /s/ to /z/ occurred also in the normally unstressed monosyllables *has, is, was, hers, his, as*, and in the title *Mrs.* (from *mistress*). On the other hand, final /s/ survived in the normally stressed monosyllabic adverbs *once, twice, thrice, hence, since, else* and the plurals *pence, truce*, in which the inflectional /-əs/ of ME was reduced to /-s/ at an early date.

Voicing of ME /s/ to /z/ before a stressed vowel took place in the 16. century, as in *possess, dessert, deserve, design, disaster, disease, dishonor, disown, dissolve, discern; resemble, resent, preserve, presume, transact, absolve, observe, exalt, exist, exhort, anxiety*. This phonemic change was not carried out consistently because many morphemes had variants in which /s/ was preceded by the stress, was followed by a consonant, or stood in initial position, and therefore remained unchanged.

Spelling

The complicated history of the fricative /z/ is reflected in an almost bewildering variety of spellings.

Initial /z/ is usually written z, as in *zone, zodiac, zero, zoology, zink, zebra, zigzag*, and the recent *zip, zipper*. But x is used in *Xerxes, xylophone, xenophobia* and cz in *czar, czarina* (Russian).

Final /z/ is written *s* in the normally unstressed words *as, was*; in the inflectional suffixes of *blush-es, run-s, ha-s, i-s, bench-es, log-s*; and in *Mrs.,* AE *Mars.* After a stressed or half-stressed free vowel, final /z/ is spelled *se* or *ze*, as in *ease, nose, choose, fuse, rise, browse, noise, chastise* and *seize, graze, haze, ooze, baptize.* In the few words in which /z/ occurs after checked vowels, it is written zz, as in *fizz, fuzz, buzz, razz.* The diagraph *se* is used in the final cluster of *cleanse, bronse.*

The spelling of medial /z/ is rather chaotic, but there are some general rules.

After a stressed free vowel either *s* or *z* is written, as in *season, daisy, miser, thousand* and *sleazy, lazy, hazel, cozy, woozy, horizon.* After a stressed checked vowel, the distinctive zz appears in *dizzy, fizzle, dazzle, mizzin* (beside *mizen*); but *s* is used in *risen, prison, misery, desert, z* in *dozen, mizen* (beside *mizzin*), and *ss* in *scissors.*

Before a stressed vowel, we have *s* in *design, disaster, preserve, resent, ss* in *dessert, dissolve, possess,* and *sc* in *discern.*

Between unstressed vowels, /z/ is spelled *s* in *artisan, venison, z* in *citizen.*

In medial clusters, the usual spelling of /z/ is *s*, as in *crimson, pansy, palsy, transact, observe*; but *frenzy* has *z.* In *exact, exhibit, Alexander,* etc., the graph *x* spells the cluster /gz/.

Silent *z* appears in *rendezvous.*

9.7 The Fricative /š/

Articulation

The voiceless palatal fricative /š/ is articulated by the grooved blade of the tongue against the front of the hard palate, decidedly farther back than /s/. The breath, escaping through a narrow channel, strikes the edges of the lower teeth to produce a 'hushing' sound. In BE the lips are often rounded, but not in AE.

Distribution

In the native vocabulary, the phoneme /š/ occurs initially, as in *ship, shed, shot, sheep, shoe, shine,* and finally, as in *fish, flesh, ash, wash, gush, bush.* In foreign words it is found in the same positions, as in *shock* v., *shay, chagrin, chivalry* and *bashful, squash* v., *crush, push, finish.*

In ME and in early MnE, /š/ occurred only after short (checked) vowels. The change of /ar/to /ɑ/ in BE, as in *harsh, marsh,* and of /v/ to /ɔ/ in regional AE, as in *wash, Washington,* introduced free vowels before /š/ in native words. Free vowels appear before /š/ also in a few words taken from French in modern times, namely *douche, gauche, creche,* BE *moustache.* It seems that *leash,* from OF, was the only word with a long vowel before /š/ in ME.

Initially and finally, /š/ clusters only with /r/ in native words, as in *shred, shrink, shrub, shrew, shrine, shroud* and AE *harsh, marsh*. Initial clusters of /š/ plus /m, n, l, w/ occur only in recently adopted German words, such as *schmalz, schnapps,* AE *Schlitz, Schwartz,* and are frequently replaced by the native clusters /sm, -sn-, sl-, sw-/. Note that final /š/ in *Welsh* is a separate morpheme.

Medial /š/ and medial /š/-clusters occur only in words from foreign languages, chiefly French and Latin. Thus, *bishop, fissure, session, fashion, Russia, bushel, specious, nation, caution, ocean, crucial, cliché, machine* and *ashlar, compulsion, extortion, mention, luxury,* AE *sexual*.

Regionalism

Regional differences in the incidence of /š/ are rather rare.

In *aspersion, emersion, conversion, version,* AE has /ž/ beside /š/, BE only /š/. BE usually preserves the sequence /sj/ in *issue, sensual, sexual, sumac,* while AE has predominantly /š/. BE has a peculiar /š/ for earlier /s/ in *schedule,* AE the spelling pronunciation /sk/. In *nausea* the phoneme /š/ is less common than /ž ~ z/ in America, in England less common than /s/. Some Americans have /š/ in the phrase *this year*.

Alternation

For the alternation /š ~ s/, see under /s/. /š/ alternates with /ž/ in *lúxury ~ luxúr-ious;* with /z/ in *ánxious ~ anxíety;* with /t/ in *exertion ~ exert, extortion ~ extort, conversion ~ convert, commission ~ commit, ignition ~ ignite;* with /k/ in *suspicious ~ suspect*.

Homophone

The assimilation of /sj/ to /š/ in *fissure* made it homophonous with *fisher*.

History

In the native vocabulary, MnE /š/ descends from ME /š/, as in *shall, shot, shame, shoot, shrink, shrug* and *wish, fresh, rash, hush, wash, marsh*. Since in the native words of ME all vowels before /š/ were short, final /š/ occurs in MnE chiefly after checked vowels, following only the newly developed free vowels /ɑ/ of BE, as in *harsh, marsh,* and /ɔ/ of AE, as in *wash, Washington*.

In words adopted from French and Latin, MnE /š/ has four different sources.

(1) During the Middle Ages the English phoneme /š/ took the place of a palatalized long sibilant written *ss* in OF, as in *cherish, finish, crush, leash, cushion, bushel* (OF *cheriss-, finiss-, croiss-, laisse, coissin, boissiel*).

(2) Many words taken from OF or L had the medial sequence /si/ in ME, which, passing through /sj/, became /š/ in early MnE (c1600), as in *caution, nation, ocean, mansion, patience, vicious, special*.

(3) In *sugar, sure, assure, fissure, pressure* and AE *sumac, issue, tissue, sensual, sexual*, /š/ is derived from /sj/ in the sequence /sju/ (from earlier /siu/). The shift of /sju/ to /šu/ did not become established in *suit, assume, super-* and in BE *sumac, issue, sexual*, etc.

(4) In words adopted from French in modern times, /š/ appears in all positions, as in *chamois, shammy, shock* v., *chagrin, chic, chauvinism, cliché, mustache, gauche, douche*.

These four separate events established the phoneme /š/ in all major positions in foreign words, even after free vowels, as in *leash, relation, motion*.

Spelling

The most common spelling of /š/ is *sh*. It is used in all native words, as in *ship, shade, shrug, fish, fishing, marsh*; in words adopted from OF, as in *flourish, crush, lash, bushel*; in some words taken from French into early MnE, as in *shock* v., *shallot, shammy*; and in words adopted in modern times from various other languages, as in *shampoo, shawl, shamrock, sherry, kosher*.

In words taken from French in modern times, the foreign spelling *ch* is usually retained, as in *chaperon, chicanery, chic, cache, douche, moustache, machine, cliché* and in *Chicago, Michigan*.

Words adopted from German retain the foreign spelling of /š/, as in *schist, schnapps, schnauzer* and the names *Schiller, Schmidt, Schleswig, Schlitz, Schweizer*. The spelling *sch* appears also in *schedule* (for earlier *sedule, cedule*, since c1600), which has lead to the spelling pronunciation /skɛǧul/ of AE and to aberrant BE /šɛdjul/.

Medial /š/, derived from the cluster /sj/, has a variety of spellings: *ss* in *issue, fissure*; *ssi* in *session, profession, Russian*; *si* in *compulsion, conversion*; *se* in a variant of *nausea*; *sci* in *luscious, conscience*; *shi* in *cushion, fashion*; *ci* in *precious, vicious, crucial, special*; *ce* in *ocean*; *ti* in *nation, damnation, mention*. In *luxury, anxious*, the *x* spells the cluster /kš/.

9.8 The Fricative /ž/

Articulation

The palatal fricative /ž/ has the same oral articulation as /š/, but it is voiced.

Distribution

In words more or less widely used, the phoneme /ž/ occurs only medially and finally, and only in a small number of words. It appears medially in *decision, vision, lesion, collusion,* AE *version, glazier, osier,* AE *Hoosier, Parisian, Vespasian,* AE *Asia, measure, pleasure, leisure, casual, usual, visual,* AE *Jesuit, bijou;* finally, in *massage, mirage, prestige, loge, rouge;* initially, in *jabot, jeu d'esprit, jour maigre.*

A /ž/ cluster occurs only in *luxúrious.*

Regionalisms

BE has preserved the cluster /zj/ in *Jesuit, visual, casual,* and /zɪ/ or /zj/ in *glazier, Parisian,* at least to some extent. In AE these words usually have /ž/. In *Asia, Asian, emersion, aspersion, dispersion, version, conversion, diversion,* where BE has only /š/, AE has /ž/ beside /š/. Phrases like *as yet, all these years* sometimes have /ž/ for /z/ in AE, /z/ being fully or partially assimilated to the following /j/.

Alternation

For the alternation of /ž/ with /z/ and /š/, see under /z/ and /š/. In some morphemes, /ž/ alternates with /d/, as in *decision ~ decide, derision ~ deride, division ~ divide, provision ~ provide, provident.*

History

The phoneme /ž/ did not exist in ME. It arose (c1600) through the assimilation of the medial sequence /zj/ to /ž/, a development parallel to the change of /sj/ to /š/. In *lesion, vision, glazier, Parisian,* etc., early MnE /zj/ is derived from earlier /zi/; in *measure, treasure, usual, visual, luxurious,* it developed in the sequence /ziu/. Thus, for instance, tri-syllabic *vision* /vɪzɪən/ became disyllabic /vɪzjən > vɪžən/, and *visual* /vɪzɪuəl/ became /vɪzjuəl > vɪžuəl/.

In words adopted in recent times, /ž/ has been accepted directly from French, as in *bijou, mirage, prestige, loge, rouge, jeu d'esprit.*

It should be pointed out that /ž/ is the only consonant phoneme not native to English. The sequenze /zj/ of early MnE, from which /ž/ is derived, occurred only in words taken into ME from French or from Gallicized Latin.

Spelling

The spelling reflects the sources of the /ž/ phoneme.

Medial /ž/ from /zj/ is written *si,* as in *lesion, vision, collusion, Asia, Parisian, osier;* in *glazier,* formed on *glaze* with an OF suffix, it is spelled *zi.* In *casual, visual,* where *u* spelled /ju/ in early MnE, /ž/ is written *s.*

The French spellings of /ž/ are used in words adopted in modern times, as in *rouge, mirage, prestige* and *bijou, jeu, jour.* In *luxúrious* the cluster /gž/ is written *x.*

9.9 The Fricative /h/

Articulation

The fricative /h/ differs from all other consonants of this class in that
it lacks any fixed articulation in the oral-pharyngeal cavity, except that
the velum is raised to close the entrance to the nasal cavity. The friction,
however slight, is produced at the half open vocal lips, its timbre modified
by the resonance of the oral cavity as determined by the position of the
tongue and the lips assumed for the following vowel or semivowel.
Hence /h/ has as many positional allophones as the number of vowels
and semivowels that can follow it.

Though normally voiceless, /h/ is sometimes voiced between voiced
sounds, as in *perhaps, Sahara, inhibition, to his liking*. A nasal /h/ occurs
in the interjection /hm, hn/, conventionally spelled *hem!, hum!*

Distribution

The fricative /h/ occurs only before vowels and in the initial clusters
/hj/ and AE /hw/. It does not appear finally.

Initial /h/ is found both in native and in foreign words, as in *head,
heart, high, house, whole, who, behold, perhaps* and in *haste, haunt, host,
hero, habitation, heroic, hilarity, Jalisco, habitual, horizon*.

Medially, /h/ occurs only in foreign words, as in *vehicular, Jehova,
Sahara, mahogany, Manhattan, Oaxaca, mahatma, Mohawk, maharaja*.

Initially, /h/ clusters with /j/, as in *hew, hue, huge, human, humor*; in
AE also with /w/, as in *whet, whale, wheel, whirl, wharf, white* and *San
Juan, Juarez, Joaquin* /hwákɪn/.

Regionalisms

The initial cluster /hw/, as in *whet, white*, etc., survives in America,
except for an area extending from the Hudson Valley to Chesapeake Bay
(including New York, Philadelphia, and Baltimore), and in a narrow
coastal belt in New England and South Carolina.

In sections of America in which /hw/ is regularly used before a stressed
vowel, as in *wheel, white*, the /h/ is rather frequently dropped in *what,
when, where, which, why!*, when they are unstressed. Some Americans omit
the /h/ in *huge, humor, human*, and *herb* usually lacks the /h/ in America.

Alternation

Before an unstressed vowel, /h/ is usually omitted, as in *mayhem,
annihilate, vehemence, prohibition*. Since /h/ is regularly retained before
a stressed vowel, we have allomorphs with and without /h/ in *vehicular ~
véhicle, prohíbit ~ prohibítion, inhíbit ~ inhibítion*.

The frequently unstressed words *have, has, had, he, him, his, her* have allomorphs without /h/, as in *we've seen it, don't tell her*.

Homophones

The reduction of /hw/ to /w/ in BE and in some coastal American dialects produced the homonyms *whit = wit, whither = wither, Whig = wig, which = witch, whet = wet, whether = weather, wether, wheel = weal, whey = way, weigh, whine = wine*.

History

Initial /h/ and AE /hw/, as in *heart* and *white*, descend from ME /h/ and /hw/, respectively; the sequence /hju/, as in *hew, huge*, from ME /hiu/. (For the shift of /iu/ to /ju/ see under /u/.)

In BE, the initial cluster /hw/ was reduced to /w/, apparently in the latter part of the 18. century. In America, the loss of /h/ in this position is confined to certain areas on the Atlantic coast (see above under regionalisms) that had intimate contacts with England before the Revolution.

Initial /h/ of unstressed final members of compounds is frequently lost, as in *shepherd, Birmingham, Haverhill*; but in American place names /h/ is usually restored.

Medial /h/ occurs in MnE only in words taken from other languages in modern times, as in *vehicular, mahatma, mahogany, Manhattan, Navaho, Sahara*.

Spelling

Except for *who, whole, whoop, whore* and some recently adopted Spanish place names, such as *San Juan, Joaquin, Guadalajara, Oaxaca*, the phoneme /h/ is spelled *h*.

The AE cluster /hw/, as in *wheel, whelp*, is spelled *wh*, as if the /h/ followed the /w/. This awkward reversal of the older spelling *hw* was introduced in the 13. century.

The letter *h* has various other functions. It enters into digraphs spelling other phonemes, as those in *thin, that, phoneme, shine, school, ghetto, change, rhetoric*. It is intended to suggest stressed free vowels, as in the exclamations *ah!, oh!, hurrah!, bah!* and in *shah, Yahweh*.

In some traditional or foreign spellings *h* has no phonemic value at all, as in BE *wheat, whet*, etc., and in such words as *vehicle, mayhem, Powhatan, Kanawha, Chihuahua*.

9.10 The Phoneme /x/

The voiceless fricative *gh* /x/ of ME, varying from palatal to velar in articulation with the preceding vowel, was either lost (in the East

Midland by c1500), as in *high, dough, night, bought, eight*, or it changed to /f/, as in *tough, trough, laugh, laughter*; but the old spelling *gh* has been retained.

Since /x/ survives in Scotland and in Ulster, Englishmen and Americans are familiar with it and may use it in *loch, lough*, especially in names like *Lochinvar, Lough Neagh,* instead of replacing it by /k/.

After the loss of /x/, the digraph *gh* was introduced in some words that never had /x/, as *inveigh* (from OF *enve-ir*) and AE *sleigh* (from Dutch *slee*).

The loss of /x/ produced the homonyms *high = hie, dough = doe, bight = bite, right = wright = write = rite, sight = site = cite, eight = *AE *ate, weight = wait, threw = through.*

10. The Nasal Consonants

10.1 The Nasal /m/

Articulation

In articulating the nasal bilabial resonant /m/, the lips are closed, the velum is lowered to permit the breath to escape through the nose, and the vocal lips are set in vibration. Before the labiodental /f/, as in *comfort, Sanford, Stamford, Humphrey, Banff,* the /m/ can be labiodental rather than bilabial; if labiodental, it can equally well be regarded as an allophone of /n/.

Distribution

The /m/ phoneme occurs singly in all positions, as in *man, meet, moist* and *dim, hɛm, thumb, home, time, bottom, solemn* and *hammer, summer, chamois, humor.*

In the native vocabulary, /m/ enters only into a small number of clusters. Initially it can follow /s/, as in *smell, small, smoke,* and be followed by /j/, as in *mew* gull); finally it can precede /p/, as in *limp, hemp,* and follow /l, r/, as in *elm, helm* and AE *arm, storm*; medially it can be followed by /p, b/, as in *wimple, timber, thimble.*

In words taken from other languages, /m/ occurs in all of these clusters, as in *smilax, music, camp, alarm, temper, member.* In addition, it can precede final /f, z/, as in *nymph, Thames,* and medial /f, ð, z, n/, as in *camphor, rhythm, clumsy, solemnity.* Medially it can follow also an obstruent as in *acme, atmosphere, zeugma, arithmetic, asthma, spasmodic.*

After the fricatives /ð, z/, as in *rhythm, spasm, purism,* the /m/ is syllabic unless preceded by /ə/.

Alternation

/m/ alternates with /n/ and with zero in the prefixes *com-* ∼ *con-* ∼ *co-* and *sym-* ∼ *syn-* ∼ *sy-*.

History

The sonorant /m/ of MnE largely continues ME /m/ both in native and in foreign words.

In *jetsam* (< *jettison*), *flotsam*, *ransom*, taken from French, an earlier /n/ was replaced by /m/ in ME or early MnE; also in the native *seldom*. In *Pomfret*, *Stamford*, *Sanford*, an earlier /n/ has been assimilated to the following labiodental.

Spelling

The /m/ phoneme is usually spelled *m*.

The digraph *mm* is written: (1) for medial /m/ following a stressed checked vowel, as in *shimmer*, *swimmer*, *hammer*, *ramming*, *summer*, *summit*, etc., but not in *woman*, *limit*, *lemon*, *chamois*, *comet*, etc.; (2) for medial /m/ in all words containing the Latin prefix *com-*, as in *commerce*, *command*, *communist*, *communion*; (3) for /m/ following a checked vowel in formerly disyllabic forms, such as *skimmed*, *hummed*.

Final /m/ to which a following /b/ has been assimilated is spelled *mb* in *lamb*, *dumb*, *dumber*, *comb*, *combing*, *combed*, etc.; also in *crumb*, *limb*, *thumb*, *numb*, *benumbed*, which never had /b/. In *Sanford* the labiodental allophone of /m/ is spelled *n*, in *Stamford*, *Pomfret*, /m/. Silent *m* appears in *mnemonic*, *Mnemosyne*.

10.2 The Nasal /n/

Articulation

The nasal alveolar resonant /n/ is articulated by placing the tip and the sides of the tongue against the upper gums and lowering the velum, so that breath escapes through the nasal cavity. The vocal lips are in vibration.

Distribution

The phoneme /n/ is by far the most common nasal in English. It occurs singly in all positions and enters into many final and medial clusters.

In native words, /n/ occurs in the initial clusters /sn/, as in *snake*, *sneeze*, *snow*, and /nj/, as in *new*, *newt*. Finally it can be followed by the plosives /t, d, č, ǧ/, as in *hint*, *hunt*, *bend*, *find*, *drench*, *stench*, *cringe*, *singe*, or follow the resonants /l, r/, as in *kiln*, AE *barn*, *horn*. Medially it can be followed by /t, d/, as in *winter*, *canter*, *gander*, *under*, and (rarely) by /v, z/, as in *anvil*, *answer*.

The same clusters appear in words adopted from other languages, as in *snare*, *snub* (from ON), *nude*, *neutral* and *aunt*, *point*, *fund*, *round*, *paunch*, *pinch*, *strange*, *lounge* and *center*, *counter*, *fender*, *jaundice*, *pansy*, *frenzy* and *Inverness*.

Other final and medial /n/-clusters appear only in foreign words. Some of these consist of /n/ plus an obstruent, as in *dance*, *sense*, *cleanse*, *bronze* and *fancy*, *counsel*, *mention*, *censure*, *panther*, *menthol*, *century*, *puncheon*, *manger*, *banjo*; others of /n/ plus /j, r/, as in *onion*, *menu*, AE *corner*, *harness*; yet others of a plosive plus /n/, as in *dignity*, *recognize*. Even more complex clusters appear medially, as in *country*, *laundry*, *monster*, *anthropology*, *antler*.

After the obstruents /t, d, s, z, š, ž/, as in *bitten*, *hidden*, *mason*, *reason*, *rational*, *visionary*, the /n/ is syllabic unless preceded by /ə/.

Variants

Some speakers have /n/ for /ŋ/ in *length*, *strength*. In rapid speech, the /n/ is sometimes assimilated to a preceding /p/, as in *happen*, *open* /opm/, less commonly to /f, v/, as in *often*, *seven*. In *nightingale* some speakers have /ŋ/ before /g/.

Alternation

The prefixes *con-*, *in-*, *syn-* have the variants *com-*, *im-*, *sym-*, if the base begins with a labial, as in *compel*, *combat*, *impel*, *imbibe*, *sympathy*, *symbol*.

Owing to the reduction of the final clusters /-ln, -mn/ to /l, m/, the phoneme /n/ alternates with zero in *Miln-er* ~ *mill*, *solemn-ity* ~ *solemn*, *hymn-al* ~ *hymn*.

History

The phoneme /n/ of MnE continues the ME /n/.

In ME, the palatal nasal /ɲ/ of OF was either replaced by /n/, as in *deign*, *reign*, *sign*, or by the sequence /nj/, as in *companion*, *onion*. In modern times, foreign /ɲ/ is regularly rendered by /nj/, as in *minion*, *cognac*, *cañon* (*canyon*), *piñon*, *Bologna*.

In *nightingale*, *messenger*, *passenger* (earlier *nightegale*, *messager*, *passager*), medial /ə/ was replaced in ME by /ən/ at a time when in *Monday Sunday*, *fortnight* (earlier *Monenday*, *Sonenday*, *forten-night*) medial /ən/ was being reduced to /ə/.

The French nasal vowel /ã/ is now rendered by /an/, as in *entourage*, *entrée*, *debutante*.

In the final cluster /ln/, the /n/ has been lost in *ell*, *mill* (ME *ellen*, *eln*; *milne*, *miln*), but in *kiln* many speakers still pronounce it.

Spelling

The phoneme /n/ is usually spelled *n*. Medial /n/ after checked vowels is often written *nn*, as in *minnow, sinning, sinner, penny, manner, funnel, runner*; but a single *n* is common in foreign words, as in *minute, menace, canon, honor, money*, and appears also in native *any, many, honey*. Double *nn* is regularly written after checked vowels in formerly disyllabic verb forms, such as *sinned, canned, punned*.

The spellings *kn, gn* are preserved in *knife, knot, gnat, gnaw*, etc., although these initial clusters were reduced to /n/ in early MnE. In *gneiss, gnomic, gnostic, mnemonic, pneumatic* the spelling of the foreign clusters is kept, although they are replaced by /n/ in English.

In *deign, reign, champaign, sign, design*, the digraph *gn* for the French palatal nasal survives, although alveolar /n/ replaced it in ME times.

The medial /nj/ cluster is spelled *gn* in *cognac, Bologna, ñ* in *piñon, cañon* (also written *canyon*).

10.3 The Nasal /ŋ/

Articulation

The nasal velar resonant /ŋ/ is articulated by placing the back of the tongue against the roof of the mouth and lowering the velum, so that the breath escapes through the nose. The point of contact of the tongue varies with the preceding vowel, being farther forward after front vowels, as in *sing, hang*, than after back vowels, as in *sung, long*. The vocal lips vibrate.

Distribution

The phoneme /ŋ/ occurs only at the end of morphemes, as in *sing, king, hang, tongue* and *sing-er, long-ing, long-ish*; and before /g, k/, as in *finger, hunger, dangle, longer, English, language, angry, angular* and *thank, monk, lynx, tinker, ankle, uncle, anxious, punctual*.

Variants

The prefixes *con-, in-, syn-*, when stressed, have /ŋ/ beside /n/ before a following /k/, as in *conquest, concubine, concord, concourse, concord, conclave, income, incubate, inquest, synchronize, syncope*. Before /g/, the velar /ŋ/ is fully established in *congress, congregate, ingot*, and fairly so in *congruence, congruous*. Occasionally /ŋ/ appears also in unstressed *con-, in-, syn-*, as in *conclude, concrete, include, increase, synchronic*.

In popular speech, the suffix of *laughing, meeting* is frequently pronounced /-ən/. In *length, strength*, some speakers substitute /n/ for /ŋ/, others have the cluster /ŋk/.

History

The velar nasal /ŋ/ came into existence through the reduction of the final cluster /ŋg/ to /ŋ/, as in *thing, sing, rung*, which contrast with *thin, sin, run*. In ME, [ŋ] had been a positional allophone of the phoneme /n/ before the velar plosives /g, k/, as in *thing, singen, thank, sinken*.

The assimilation of [ŋg] to /ŋ/ did not take place medially, as in *finger, longer, longest, angle*, where the /g/ began the second syllable. Medial /ŋ/ of MnE, as in *singing, wringer, longish*, was introduced into the derivatives from the base forms *sing, wring, long*, etc.

In *handkerchief* the earlier /n/ was assimilated to the following velar after the loss of /d/.

Spelling

The phoneme /ŋ/ is written *ng*, unless followed by /g, k/, when it is spelled *n*, as in *hunger, anxiety, think, anxious*. In *tongue, harangue* final /ŋ/ is written *ngue*.

11. The Lateral Consonants

11.1 The Lateral /l/

Articulation

The lateral resonant /l/ is articulated by placing the tip of the tongue against the upper gums and drawing the sides of the tongue away from the gums, so that the breath escapes laterally. The vocal lips vibrate.

Following a vowel, especially a back vowel, the back of the tongue is more or less raised, as in *hill, hull, hall, hole* and in *pillow, fellow, follow*. The degree of this 'velarization' of /l/ varies regionally. In parts of the American South, intervocalic /l/ after a front vowel, as in *Billie, jelly*, is not velarized.

After the aspirated voiceless plosives /p, k/, the /l/ may be partially unvoiced, as in *please, clean*.

In *always, walnut, fall dówn*, the /l/ is sometimes omitted in rapid speech, especially in parts of the American South.

Distribution

The phoneme /l/ occurs singly in all positions and freely enters into clusters with obstruents and resonants.

It occurs initially in *let, luck, lead, lawn, loin*, etc., finally in *fill, feel, fool, foil*, etc., medially in *yellow, sully, tulip, pilot*, etc.

Initially it can follow obstruents, as in *plow, blue, claw, glad, flow, slow, Vladimir*.

Finally it precedes obstruents, as in *help, bulb, melt, wild, belch, bulge, milk, self, valve, false*; and nasals, as in *elm, kiln*. It can follow /r/ in AE *marl, snarl*.

Medially, /l/ can precede obstruents, as in *pulpit, Melba, sultan, moulder, vulture, soldier, Vulcan, vulgate, sulphur, silver, Malthus, ulcer, palsy*; and it can precede resonants, as in *fulmar, ulna, value, Milwaukee*. /l/ also occurs in triple medial clusters, as in *poultry, cauldron, bolster, English*.

After obstruents, as in *ripple, Bible, spittle, riddle, rankle, wiggle, muscle, puzzle, bushel*, the /l/ is syllabic, unless preceded by /ə/.

Homophones

The loss of /l/ before certain consonants has produced the homophones *yolk = yoke, holm = home, would = wood*.

History

MnE /l/ continues ME /l/, which in turn was derived from OE /l/; medially after a short stressed vowel also from long /ll/, as in ME *sellen, fillen* (MnE *sell, fill*). Before /k/ and the lip consonants /m, f, v/, the sonorant /l/ was lost by 1600, if preceded by certain back vowels, as in *balk, chalk, stalk, talk, walk, folk, Norfolk, yolk*, in *calm, palm, psalm, almond, salmon, Holmes*, and in *calf, calve, half, halve, salve*. However, the /l/ sometimes survives in these positions, or is reintroduced, as in *talc, talcum, falcon, Malcolm, polka, psalmody, Stockholm, Ralph, palfrey, Rolf*.

The early MnE fluctuations in the use of /l/ before alveolar stops, as in *solder, soldier, cauldron, fault, vault*, goes back to ME. In such words the /l/ is now fully established, but AE *solder* /sɔdə/ lacks the /l/. Notice also *Wat*, short for *Walter*. The London pronunciation of *Holburn* without /l/ is quite unique.

In the usually unstressed verb forms *shan't, should, won't, would*, the /l/ was lost by 1600.

The Welsh voiceless lateral of *Lloyd, Llewellyn*, and the Spanish palatal lateral of *llama, llano* have been adapted as /l/.

Spelling

The phoneme /l/ is usually spelled *l* or *ll*. With some exceptions, a single *l* is written (1) initially; (2) in all clusters; (3) finally after stressed free vowels, as in *feel, fail, furl, caul, coal, cool, mile, howl, boil*, and after the unstressed vowel, as in *fatal, duel, angel*; (4) medially after stressed free vowels, as in *velar, bailiff, folio, tulip, silent, Rowley*, and after unstressed vowels, as in *políte, malévolent*.

The digraph *ll* is used (1) with some regularity after stressed checked vowels, both finally, as in *still, bell, cull, pull*, and medially, as in *pillow, belly, fallow, hollow, gully, pully*, especially in native words; (2) in some words after the stressed free vowels /ɔ, o/, as in *fall, roll* and *falling, rolling*; (3) in formerly disyllabic verb forms like *spilled, spelled, called, rolled*; (4) before a stressed vowel, in words taken from Latin or French, as in *allege, alleviate, alliance, allow, allude, ellipse*, where the foreign spelling is retained.

Exceptions to these rules are: (1) Single *l* after stressed checked vowels in foreign words, as in *hotél, locále, expél, rebél* (but *expelling, expelled, rebellion, rebelled*), and in *telephone, palace, tolerant*. (2) Double *ll* after unstressed /ə/ in *párallel* and BE *lévelled, trávelled*, etc., and initially in foreign *llama, llano, Lloyd*.

In *able, apple, riddle, puzzle*, etc., the digraph *le* represents syllabic [ḷ], a positional allophone of /l/.

The letter *l* is retained in such words as *talk, folk, half, salve, calm, should*, though /l/ was lost in such words in early MnE.

11.2 The Lateral /r/

Articulation

The lateral resonant /r/ has rather striking allophones and regional diaphones.

Prevocalic /r/ is articulated by putting the tip of the tongue near the upper gum and drawing the sides of the tongue away from the gum, so that the breath escapes both over the tip and the sides of the tongue. The rear part of the tongue is more or less raised.

In the postvocalic /r/ of AE, the body of the tongue is laterally constricted and humped up in the back of the mouth, the degree of constriction varying markedly from area to area. In this 'constricted' /r/ the tip of the tongue is inactive.

Intervocalic /r/, as in *merry, married, vary, glory* and *far out, store it*, is 'constricted' in those dialects of AE in which postvocalic /r/ survives, but 'apical' like the prevocalic /r/ of BE in those dialects of AE that lack postvocalic /r/. In this position, BE usually has a 'tap' /r/, the tip of the tongue forming momentary contact with the gum. This articulation is unknown in America, except as an intervocalic allophone of /t/, as in *better, cutting*.

After aspirated voiceless stops, as in *proud, try, cream*, the /r/ is partially unvoiced.

Distribution

In large sections of North America, /r/ occurs in all positions, in some coastal areas and in BE only before vowels.

I. In all varieties of English, /r/ occurs singly in initial position, as in *rid, rod, read, road, royal*; between vowels, as in *mirror, merry, marry, borrow, burro* and *Mary, story, Moira*; and morpheme-finally, when followed in the same word or utterance phrase by a vowel, as in *hear-ing, car-ing, starr-y, roar-ing, lur-id, fier-y, lower-y* and in *far out, tear up, fair offer, spear it*, etc. BE and some varieties of AE have /r/ also in *hurry, furry*.

/r/ follows obstruents initially, as in *pray, broad, tree, drink, cry, great, free, three, shrewd*; and medially, as in *April, rubric, pantry, quadrant, secret, mongrel, Africa, anthracite* (only foreign words). Medial /rj/ occurs as a variant of /ri/ in *serious, curious, burial*.

II. Aside from some areas along the Atlantic coast and the Gulf of Mexico, the phoneme /r/ occurs in America (as in Scotland, Ireland, and the west of England) also after vowels, both singly, as in *hear, care, far, for, four, poor*, and in clusters.

Finally and medially, /r/ precedes most of the obstruents, as in *harp, barb, heart, hard, larch, large, lark, morgue, scarf, carve, hearth, farce, Mars, harsh* and *harpoon, harbor, mortar, pardon, orchard, sergeant, orchid, organ, orphan, marvel, orthodox, northern, morsel, borzoi, marshal*. Postvocalic /r/ can also be followed by a resonant, as in *charm, barn, snarl* and *harmony, ornament, garlic*.

Medially, /r/ can be followed by two consonants, as in *partridge, arctic, argue, lorgnette, parsnip, parsley*.

Regionalisms and Variants

In BE, the phoneme /r/ occurs only before vowels, as in *read, spirit, dearest, pouring, far away, rather old*. This usage appears in America in the coastal plain along the Atlantic and the Gulf of Mexico: in New England, Metropolitan New York, and the South.

In the greater part of North America the /r/ is preserved in all positions.

In the unstressed medial syllables, the sequence /ər/ is frequently reduced to /r/, as in *different(ly), dangerous(ly), miserably*.

In BE, *curry, furrow, hurry, worry* have the vowel /ʌ/, *furry, preferring*, etc., the vowel /ə/ of the bases *fur, prefer*, etc. In America this practice is followed only in dialects that lack postvocalic /r/. Other AE dialects have the constricted vowel /ɜ/ both in *furry, preferring* and in *furrow, hurry*, etc.

In BE and AE coastal dialects lacking /r/ after vowels, a 'linking' /r/ appears sporadically after the vowels /ə, ɔ, ɑ/ in such phrases as *the idea-r of it, we saw-r it, Mah-r and I*.

In *wash, Washington* a 'transitional' /r/ sometimes appears before /š/ in western Pennsylvania and the southern mountains. In *quarter* the postvocalic /r/ is frequently omitted in American dialects that normally preserve it.

Alternation

In BE and in AE dialects lacking postvocalic /r/, such morphemes as *fear, dare, fur, star, pour, assure, fire, flower, father,* have alternate forms with /r/ when a vowel follows, as in *fearing, daring, furry, starry, assurance, fiery, flowering* and in phrases like *fear it, flare up, pour out, father and I, for all that, your aunt.* However, in the phrases illustrated above, the /r/ is often omitted in the southern United States.

Homophones

In BE, the change of postvocalic /r/ to consonantal /ǝ/ and the later absorption of this /ǝ/ in the free vowel /ɔ/ produced such homophones as *court = caught, lord = laud, source = sauce, floor = flaw, lore = law, more = maw, whore = haw,* and even *poor = paw, sure = shore = shaw.* In similar fashion, the change of /ɑr > ɑǝ/ to the free vowel /ɒ/ created the homophones *farther = father, arms = alms* both in BE and in coastal AE.

History

The /r/ phoneme of MnE descends from the /r/ of ME, which presumably had various allophones and regional diaphones.

During the latter part of the 18. century the /r/ following a vowel became an unsyllabic sonorant /ǝ/ in BE, which survives as such after high and mid-vowels, as in *hear, fare, four, poor,* but merged with the preceding vowel to produce two new vowel phonemes, the /ɜ/ of *fir, learn, hurt* and the /ɒ/ of *far, heart.* In *father, Saturday* the earlier sequence /ǝr/ became /ǝ/. All of these changes appear also in some coastal dialects of AE. The later shift from /oǝ/ to /ɔǝ ~ ɔ/, as in *four, poor,* in BE has not been adopted anywhere in America.

Since /r/ was preserved before a vowel within a word or utterance phrase, all morphemes formerly ending in /r/ now have positional variants in BE and coastal AE. Thus, for instance, phrase final *fear, care, star, four, poor, father* lack /r/, but *fearing, caring, starry, poorest, four and five, father is out,* have it. On the analogy of such 'doublets', a 'linking' /r/ is sometimes introduced in such phrases as *this sofa-r is new, we saw-r it.* In America one can even hear an occasional *saw-r-ing wood, draw-r-ing out* from New Englanders and New Yorkers.

In early MnE, postvocalic /r/ was sometimes lost before /t, s, š/, as in *cartridge, nurse, marsh,* from which the modern folk pronunciations /kætrɪǧ, nʌs, mæš/ of England and America are derived. At the same time, an /r/ was introduced in *parsnip, harslet* as an overcorrection.

Intervocalic /t/ was replaced by /r/ (c1600) in *porridge* (earlier *pottage*).

Spelling

The phoneme /r/ is spelled r in most positions.

The digraph rr is used chiefly for intervocalic /r/ following a stressed checked vowel, as in *merry, carriage, borrow, torrid, hurry*, AE *starry, tarring*; but foreign words often have the single r, as in *spirit, merit, carat, sorority*. The Latin spelling is retained in *corréct, corróde, corrúpt*, etc.

In dialects of English that have lost the phoneme /r/ after vowels, r spells the semivocal /ə/ in *here, fair, four*, etc.; the digraph *ar* represents the phoneme /ɐ/ in *hard, star*, etc., the digraph *or* the phoneme /ɔ/ in *corn, for*, etc. In all dialects of English, the digraphs *ir, er, ur*, as in *bird, confer, burn*, stand for the phoneme /ɜ/.

12. The Semivowels

12.1 The Semivowel /j/

Articulation

The palatal semivowel /j/ is articulated by raising the arched front of the tongue toward the hard palate. The elevation of the tongue varies with the position required for the following vowel. The vocal lips vibrate. After the voiceless plosives /p, t, k/, the /j/ is partly or fully unvoiced, as in *pure, tube, cube*.

Distribution

The phoneme /j/ occurs freely in initial position and in initial and medial clusters, rarely between vowels, never finally.

Single initial /j/ is found before most syllabics, as in *Yiddish, yet, yellow, yarrow, Yankee, yacht, yonder, young* and *year, Yale, yearn, yard, yawn, yoke, youth, ewe, use, yowl*; medial /j/ only in some foreign words, such as *halleluja, Fayum, Goya, Mayan, de Falla*.

In clusters, /j/ is followed only by stressed /u/ and unstressed /ə/, mostly in foreign words. It can follow most obstruents and resonants, both initially and medially: initially, as in *pew, spew, beauty, tune, steward, dew, cube, skew, gubernatorial, few, view, enthuse, sue, pre-sume, hew, huge, mute, new, nude, lewd, lute*; medially, as in *opulent, nebulous, nodule, occupy, argue, curfew, ovule, Mathew, mensuration*, BE *casuist, emulate, annual, onion, canyon, value, stallion, erudite, querulous*.

Regionalisms and Variants

In BE the initial clusters /tj, dj, nj/ as in *Tuesday, due, new*, are fully preserved. In America usage varies. The clusters are regularly current

in the South and to some extent in New England and Metropolitan
New York; elsewhere the /j/ is largely lost, so that *Tuesday, due, new*
begin like *tool, doom, noon*. After the fricatives /θ, s, z/ and after /l/, as
in *enthusiasm, suit, presume, lure*, /j/ usually survives in BE, but is lost
in AE.

Medial /tj, dj, sj, zj/ survive in BE in such words as *virtue, educate,
issue, visual*, where AE has /č, ǧ, š, ž/, respectively.

In the South Atlantic States and in Pennsylvania, *yeast* begins like
east; but in the New England settlements /j/ is retained, as in BE.

As pointed out below, some New Englanders and Midwesterners have
the old diphthong /iu/ in *beauty, few, tube, due, new, human*, etc., instead
of /ju/ or /u/.

In *erudite, garrulous, querulous*, some speakers preserve the /j/, others
not.

The vowel of the medial syllable of such words as *Indian, genius, filial,
curious* may be replaced by /j/, especially in rapid speech. This seems
to be more common in England than in America.

Homophones

The loss of /j/ after /d, n, s, l/ in large sections of America produced
the homophones *dew = due = do; new = gnu; suit = soot* (rare); *sue =
Sioux = Sault* (in *Sault Sainte Marie*, Michigan); *lute = loot*.

History

The MnE semivowel /j/ descends in part from ME /j/; but a more
common source of it is the ME diphthong /iu/, which shifted to /ju/ in
MnE.

Initial /j/ occurred in ME only in native words. It survives in MnE
*yip, yes, yarrow, yarn, yonder, young, yield, Yates, yearn, yawn, yolk,
youth, yowl*, etc. In modern times, a fair number of words beginning
with /j/ were adopted from various languages, as *yen, yam, Yankee,
yacht, younker, yucca, yawl, yodel, yogi, Yukon, Jugoslav*.

Early ME had /j/ also in final and in medial position, but it fused
with the preceding front vowels to form the later ME diphthongs /ai, ei/,
from which the free vowel /e/ of MnE *day, nail, rain* is derived.

The ME diphthong /iu/ (also /eu/) from which the MnE sequence /ju/
is derived occurred in some native words, as *ewe, yew, dew, few, hew,
mew, new, newt, lewd, spew, steward*, and in many words adopted from
Old French or Latin, as *use, usury, pure, tune, student, cube, fume, sue,
huge, view, music, nuisance, lute* and *virtue, occupy, argue, curfew, annual,
value, erudition*. It is of interest to observe that in some folk dialects of
eastern England the change of /iu/ to /ju/ did not take place, and that
/iu/ survives to some extent in the New England settlements, as in *few,
music, Tuesday, due, new*.

The incidence of /j/ has been considerably reduced in modern times.

The medial clusters /tj, dj, sj, zj/ often became /č, ǧ, š, ž/, respectively, as in *question, nature*, AE *virtue*; *soldier, verdure*, AE *educate*; *nation, version*, AE *issue*; *vision, pleasure*, AE *visual*. Initial /sj/ yielded /š/ in *sure, sugar*, AE *sumac*.

In some clusters /j/ has been lost: regularly after /r/, as in *rew, rule*; regionally after alveolar and blade consonants, as in *tune, dew, new, lute, enthusiasm, suit, presume*. The reduction of initial /tj, dj, nj/ to /t, d, n/ is attested in England from 1750 onward—and condemned by lexicographers; it is not an American innovation.

Onion, million, scallion, carrion, taken from OF, have had /j/ since ME times. Intervocalic /j/, lost in ME times except in *halleluja*, now occurs in such names as *Fayum, Goya, Maya, de Falla*.

Spelling

The spelling reflects the history of the /j/ phoneme.

Initial /j/ is usually spelled *y*, as in *yet, yam, young, year, you*, etc.; also the rare intervocalic /j/ of *Mayan, Goya*, etc. But *j* is written in foreign *jaeger* (a bird) and *hallelujah*, *ll* in *de Falla*.

The cluster /ju/ is usually spelled *u* or *ew*, but also *eu, ieu, iew, eau, iu*, as in *use, mute, value, ewe, new* and *neutral, lieu, view, beauty, suit*.

In the medial clusters of *onion, million, carrion*, etc., /j/ is written *i*; but *y* appears in *Bunyan, Kenyon, banyan, canyon* (beside *cañon, Canon City*). Rare spellings of the /nj/ cluster occur in *vignette, cañon*.

The graph *y* has also other uses, as in *fly, happy, day, coy*.

12.2 The Semivowel /w/

Articulation

The labiovelar semivowel /w/ has a double articulation: the lips are pursed and the back of the tongue approaches the roof of the mouth, the position of the tongue varying with the following vowel. The vocal lips vibrate. After aspirated /t, k/, as in *twice, quit*, the /w/ is partially unvoiced.

The AE sequence /hw/, as in *white*, is sometimes pronounced as a voiceless [w̥], but voicing usually starts before the following vowel is articulated.

Distribution

The semivowel /w/ occurs only before vowels.

Initially it appears singly before most of the vowels, as in *wit, wet, wag, want, won, wood, weed, way, a-wake, word, war, re-ward, woe, woo, wife, wound* v.

It can follow certain initial obstruents, as in *twin, dwell, queen, square, Gwin, thwart, swan, suite, schwa*, and in AE *wheat, San Juan*.

Medially, /w/ occurs only in foreign words: singly, in *Hawaii, Iowa, Chihuahua* /čiwáwɑ/; following an obstruent or resonant, as in *equal, kumquat, Susquehanna, language, reservoir, memoir, Milwaukee*.

Regionalisms and Variants

The initial cluster /hw/ has been reduced to /w/ in BE and some coastal dialects of AE (see under /h/).

In America, place names in *-wich, -wick*, as *Greenwich, Berwick*, usually retain the /w/. Both in England and in America, *toward* is usually stressed on the first syllable and pronounced without /w/; if end-stressed, the /w/ is sounded. In AE, disyllabic prosodic variants of *usual, casual*, i.e. /južwəl, kæžwəl/, are not uncommon.

Homophones

The reduction of initial /wr/ to /r/ produced the homophones *wrap = rap, wreak = reak, wrest = rest, wretch = retch, wring = ring, write = right = rite, wrung = rung*. Loss of initial /h/ in BE and some varieties of AE, resulted in the homophones *whale = wail, wheel = weal, when = wen, where = wear, whey = way, which = witch, Whig = wig, while = wile, whine = wine, whir = were, whit = wit, white = wight, whither = wither*. Other homophones are: *two = too = to, one = won, sweet = suite*.

History

MnE /w/ continues ME /w/, which is largely derived from OE /w/. Some words adopted from Norman French have initial /w/, as *wait, war, warden, re-ward*. A considerable number of words taken from Old French or Latin have medial w/-clusters, as in *conquest, equal, language, anguish*.

ME inherited also final and medial /w/ from OE, as in *spiwen, newe, fewe, clawe, snow, knowen, flowen*. But in late ME the /w/ fused with the preceding vowel to form the diphthongs from which the MnE free vowels of *spew, new, few, claw, know, flow* are derived.

In the weakly stressed or unstressed final member of such compounds as *backward, homeward, awkward, Greenwich*, the /w/ is sometimes preserved (or restored), sometimes lost, as in *toward, to the windward, Greenwich*. In *answer* (akin to *swear*) and *conquer* (cp. *conquest*) the /w/ was dropped by 1600. Unstressed *will* and *would* are reduced to /l/ and /d/ respectively in such expressions as *we'll do it* and *I'd rather not*.

In *ooze, sword, zounds*, the /w/ preceding a rounded back vowel was lost in early MnE, in *quoth, thong, two, who* already in ME.

The initial cluster /wr/, as in *wrong, write, wretch*, was reduced to /r/ by 1650. Initial /wl/ became /l/ already in ME, as in *lisp*.

One, once (from ME /ǭn, ǭnǝs/) show West Country development of initial /ǭ/, while *only, alone, lonely* have the normal /o/. The present pronunciation of *one, once* with initial /w/ was adopted in the 16. century.

Intervocalic /w/ has been introduced into MnE in words, chiefly names, taken from various languages, as *powwow, Ottawa, Kanawha, Chihuahwa, Hawaii*.

Spelling

The consonant /w/ is usually spelled *w*. But there are also other spellings.

The clusters /kw/ and /gw/ are written *qu* and *gu*, respectively, in accordance with Latin and French usage, as in *quiet, quarter, square, sequel, esquire* and *language, languid*. Native *queen, quick*, etc., have *qu* for earlier *cw*. The cluster /sw/ is spelled *su* in words taken from French and Latin, as in *suave, suite, persuade*.

In BE and some coastal dialects of AE, where initial /hw/ became /w/, the spelling *wh* (replacing earlier *hw* in ME) is retained, as in *wheat, while, wharf*.

The digraph *wh* replaced older *h* in *whole* (cp. *holesome*), *whoop, whore* in the 16. century, probably on the analogy of *who* (but see below).

The graph /w/ was usually retained after the loss of the phoneme, as in *two, who, sword, wring, wreck, answer, toward*, BE *Greenwich*. When /w/ was fused with a preceding vowel, as in *saw, flow, few*, the *w* became part of digraphs spelling diphthongs in late ME, which yielded free vowels in MnE.

Unique spellings of /w/ occur in *one, once, memoir, reservoir, Kanawha, Chihuahua*.

12.3 The Semivowel /ǝ̦/

Articulation

The mid-central semivowel /ǝ̦/ has the same articulation as the vowel /ǝ/ of *sofa*. It differs from the vowel /ǝ/ in that it is consonantal, i.e. does not occupy the peak of a syllable.

Distribution

The semivowel /ǝ̦/ appears only in those dialects of English in which postvocalic /r/ is not preserved as such. It does not occur initially.

In BE and in the dialect of Metropolitan New York, it is found in two positions: (1) finally and before a consonant, as in *dear, beard, fair*, la·rd, *pour*, *board*, *poor*, and (2) before intervocalic /r/, as in *dearest*, *dreary*, *fairest*, *dairy*, *pouring*, *story*, *poorest*, *boorish*. In other coastal dialects of America it is confined to the first of these positions.

In BE, the final sequence /ɔə̣/ appearing in such words as *more*, *pour*, *poor* is frequently reduced to /ɔ/, so that *more*, *pour* become homophonous with *maw*, *paw*.

The incidence of vowels before /ə̣/ varies greatly both in American and in British English.

Regionalisms

In America, /ə̣/ is current only in some sections of the coastal plain along the Atlantic and the Gulf of Mexico: Eastern New England, Metropolitan New York, and most of the South (from Chesapeake Bay to eastern Texas).

Alternations

Owing to the fact that /r/ is preserved before vowels, as in *dear-est*, *dar-ing*, *stor-y*, *boor-ish* and in phrases like *steer it*, *flare up*, *fair and foul*, *poor as can be*, but lost in other positions, morphemes like *dear*, *dare*, *store*, *boor* have doublets in all dialects in which only prevocalic /r/ survives as such.

History

The semivowel /ə̣/ is derived from postvocalic /r/. It became current in cultivated BE during the latter part of the 18. century, but was in use in the folk speech of eastern England much earlier. Its currency along the Atlantic seaboard of America may be due in part to English folk speech (since it is regular in rural Maine and New Hampshire); but its predominance in the old Atlantic seaports (Boston, New York, Charleston) and their hinterland points to a strong later influence of BE, despite the War for Independence.

The phoneme /ə̣/ appears now chiefly after high and mid-vowels, as in *here*, *care*, *more*, *poor*. After low vowels it merged with the vowel, as in *hard* /hɑd/ and BE *ford* /fɔd/, *more* /mɔə̣ ~ mɔ/.

The sequence /ɪə̣ ~ iə̣/, as in *here*, *beard*, sometimes shifts to /jə̣/ in England and in Virginia.

Spelling

The phoneme /ə̣/ is written *r*, as in *hear*, *beard*, *more*, *lord*, etc. In BE *hearing*, *Mary*, *glory*, *mooring*, etc., the letter *r* spells the sequence /ə̣r/.

13. The Checked Vowels

13.1 The Checked Vowel /ɪ/

Articulation

MnE checked /ɪ/ is an open high-front monophthong [ɪ] in BE. In America, this phonic type is usual in the North and parts of the North Midland. In the South and the South Midland it is more commonly an ingliding diphthong [ɪə ~ ɪ·ə], especially before voiced consonants, as in *bid, rib, give, fizz, sin, bill*. Near consonants in which the back of the tongue is raised, /ɪ/ is sometimes retracted to mid-central [ɨ ~ ɨə], as in *whip, crib, hill*.

In unstressed syllables, as in *careless, bucket, houses*, /ɪ/ is centered to [ɨ]. Some varieties of AE have /ə/ instead.

Distribution

The phoneme /ɪ/ does not occur finally or before vowels.

Stressed /ɪ/ occurs before all consonants, as in *lip, bit, ditch, lick; rib, bid, bridge, big; stiff, pith, hiss, fish; give, wither, dizzy, vision; swim, win, sing; hill, hear*. It can be followed by clusters consisting of a resonant and an obstruent, as in *limp, hint, finch, think, wind* n., *hinge, nymph, mince, hilt, build* and *simple, limber, hinder, finger*; also by some clusters of obstruents, as in *lift, lisp, fist, risk*.

/ɪ/ is frequent in unstressed syllables, especially in BE and some types of AE. It occurs in the final member of old compounds and complex words, in prefixes and suffixes, and medially. Examples are: *kerchief, mischief, biscuit, forfeit, benefit, midriff, sheriff* and *abdicate, diffident, infinite, intelligent*.

The unstressed prefixes illustrated in the following examples regularly have /ɪ/: *discover, illegible, impossible, impose, invalid, inspect, interpret, irregular, mistake, withdraw*. In BE and some dialects of AE, unstressed /ɪ/ is used beside half-stressed /ɛ/ in the prefixes found in *engage, enjoy, embrace, employ, exact, example, excuse*.

In the unstressed suffixes illustrated below, /ɪ/ is regularly used: *article, music, musical, physics, justice, officer, rapid*, AE *hostile, imagine, laughing, basis, English, finish, monism, linguist, credit, opposite, composite, active, dative, lambkin, Wilkins, friendship*.

BE and some varieties of AE have /ɪ/ also in the suffixes illustrated in the following examples: *peaches, pushes, hated, wicked, private, senate, actress, tallest, pocket, ruthless, darkness, sausage, ravage*.

In the medial unstressed syllable of such words as *armistice, hemisphere, homicide, magistrate, privilege, satisfy, artifice, benefit*, and *cardinal, nominal, geminate, juniper, appetite, capital, gratitude, genitive, hesitate*, *hospital*, BE has /ɪ/, AE /ɪ/ or /ə/. In the final syllable of *Joseph, bargain, fuel, poem, poet, college, knowledge, nostril*, etc., BE also has /ɪ/, AE /ə/ or /ɪ/.

Regionalisms

Before unsyllabic /ə/, as in *hear, beard*, and before intersyllabic /ər/, as in *hearing, herein, hero*, BE has the checked vowel /ɪ/, thus /hɪə, hɪəro/, etc. Instead of the sequence /ɪə/, some English speakers have the sequence /jə/ in some words, as in *hear, deer*.

In America, the vowel in such words varies regionally. Generally speaking, areas in which postvocalic /r/ has become /ə/ have the free vowel /i/, articulated as a lowered long [i·]; areas in which /r/ is preserved have a short checked /ɪ/. The Lower South, however, has preserved the mid-vowel /e/ in some words of this group.

Squirrel, stirrup, syrup have the vowel /ɪ/ in BE. This pronunciation of *syrup, stirrup*, but not of *squirrel*, is fairly common in New England, New York State, eastern Pennsylvania, and South Carolina. Elsewhere in America these three words have the same vowel as *furrow*.

The suffix *-ile*, as in *agile, futile, hostile, servile*, has /ɪ/ in America, /ai/ in England. In the suffix *-ine* the vowel varies, but *genuine, jessamine* regularly have /ɪ/.

In *creek* the vowel /ɪ/ predominates in the American North and North Midland, /i/ in the South.

In the unstressed suffixes of such words as *careless, ringlet, bucket, village, houses, hated*, BE has a centered allophone of /ɪ/. In America, this pronunciation is common in the North and in the coastal South, but not in the Midland, which has /ə/.

Alternation

In some morphemes, /ɪ/ alternates with /ai/, as in *bit ~ bite, writ ~ write, fifth ~ five, drift ~ drive, filth ~ defile, wisdom ~ wise, Christmas ~ Christ, signal ~ sign, biblical ~ Bible, tyrannical ~ tyrant*. Other alternations are rare: /ɪ ~ ɛ/ in *bier ~ bear*, /ɪ ~ i/ in *obliquity ~ oblique*, /ɪ ~ ə/ in AE *vehicular ~ vehicle*.

Homophones

The merging of several ME vowels in MnE /ɪ/ has produced such homophones as *bin* = AE *been, crick* = AE *creek* (in some areas), *hip* (part of body) = *hip* (seed pod). Other homophones, old or recent, are: *kill* = *kiln, guild* = *gild, guilt* = *gilt, miss* = *Miss, mist* = *missed*.

History

The chief source of the MnE checked vowel /ɪ/ is ME short /i/, which in turn is derived from various sources, as indicated below: *rib, sing, driven* (OE *i*); *hill, bridge, listen* (OE *y*); *link, hinge, English* (OE *e*); *grist, fifty, Christmas* (OE *ĭ*); *fist, filth, thimble* (OE *ȳ*); *issue, mirror, liberty* (OF *i*); *infant, history, mystery* (L).

In a number of words, MnE /ɪ/ is derived from ME long close /ē/, which was raised to /ī/ before 1500 and then shortened to /i/, as in *breeches, hip* (rose pod), *nickname, rick* (stack), *wick*, in the unstressed syllable of *garlic, sheriff*, and in the first element of *Greenwich, three-pence*. In the weakly stressed second element of such place names as *Woolwich, Berwick*, /ɪ/ is derived from ME long /ī/.

It should be noted that, contrary to the general rule, /ɪ/ appears before /ld/ in *build, gild, guild* and before /nd/ in *wind* n.

The phoneme /ɪ/ occurs also in many words adopted from various languages in modern times, as in *billion, Hindu, hinterland, irritate, myth, shindig, tyrannize*.

In addition to ME /i/, unstressed /ɪ/ has several other sources: ME /e/ in the affixes *em-, en-, ex-, -ness*; ME /i ~ ə/ in inflexional *-es, -ed, -est*, as in *houses, pushes, longest*; ME /ĕ/ in the suffixes *-el, -less*, as in *cruel, careless*; ME /ắ/ in the suffixes *-age, -ate*, as in *desolate, senate, savage*; ME /ai/, as in *bargain, certain*. The present pronunciation of the vowel in these affixes became established in early Modern English.

Spelling

The usual spelling of /ɪ/ is *i*, as in *bridge, hill, link, little, liver, issue, liberty, spirit*. The split digraph *i-e* is written in *give, live, hinge, fringe* and in the suffixes *-ice, -ile, -ine, -ive*, as in *justice, genuine, native*, AE *hostile*.

Before /r ~ ə/ various spellings are current, as in *here, experience, hear, weary, weir, weird*.

Uncommon spellings, largely reflecting sources other than ME /i/, are: *e*, in *England, English, pretty*; BE *embrace, enjoy, exact, excuse, houses, hated, kindness, poet*; *ee*, in *been, breeches, creek, Greenwich, threepence*; *ei*, in *forfeit, surfeit*; *ui*, in *build, guilder, guilt*; *y*, in words taken from Greek, as *lyric, myth, syllable, tyranny*, and in English names, as *Plymouth, Smyth*; *ie*, in *sieve, kerchief, mischief*; *u*, in *busy*; *o*, in *women*; *a*, in BE *private, senate, cabbage*.

13.2 The Checked Vowel /ɛ/

Articulation

The /ɛ/ phoneme is a mid-front monophthong in BE, varying from close (as in London) to open. Monophthongal open [ɛ] is the usual pronunciation in the American North and North Midland. An ingliding [ɛə], often rather close, predominates in the South and the South Midland, especially in such monosyllables as *bed, hen*. Before /g/, as in *egg, leg*, upgliding [ɛⁱ] is not uncommon in the South and in New England, particularly in folk speech.

Distribution

The phoneme /ɛ/ does not occur at the end of words and morphemes, or before vowels.

It appears before all consonants except /h, j, w/, as in *step, pepper, bet, petty, wretch, wretched, neck, reckon; ebb, rebel, bed, peddle, hedge, legible, leg, negate; deaf, heifer, death, method, less, lesson, flesh, special; heavy, leather, embezzle, pleasure; hem, blemish, hen, any, length, bell, yellow, berry, cherish*. It is rare before /z, ž, ŋ/.

Like other checked vowels, /ɛ/ occurs before /s, m, n, l/ clusters, as in *vesper, best, eschew, escort, hemp, embers, rent, bench, end, cleanse, help, belt, belch, elk, Elbe, elder, elf, else, delve*; also before /ft/, as in *left*, and before /zb/ in *Lesbian*.

Regionalisms

Regional differences in the incidence of /ɛ/ are rather rare. BE and some dialects of AE (New York, Pennsylvania, the Midwest) have /ɛ/ before /r ~ ə̯/, as in *fare, fair, Mary, dairy*, where other American dialects have /e/ or /æ/. AE has /ɛ/ in *esthete* and usually in *lever*, BE /i/; in *leisure* BE has /ɛ/, AE predominantly /i/; in *ate* BE has /ɛ/ (from ME /ę̄t/), AE predominantly /e/ (from the ME variant /āt/); in *economic* both BE and AE have /ɛ/ beside /i/.

Alternation

In some morphemes /ɛ/ alternates with /i/, as in *web ~ weave, led ~ lead, left ~ leave, depth ~ deep, health ~ heal, stealth ~ steal, theft ~ thief, wealth ~ weal, shepherd ~ sheep, cleanse ~ clean, pleasant ~ please, zealous ~ zeal, concept ~ conceive, prevalent ~ prevail, prejudice ~ prejudge*; in others with /ə/, as in *academic ~ academy, beneficent ~ benefit, lament ~ lamentable*. Alternation with /ɔ ~ ɒ/ occurs in *breadth ~ broad, querulous ~ quarrel*; with /æ/, in *many ~ manifold*; with /u/, in *web ~ woof*.

Homophones

The partial merging of the derivative of ME long /ę̄/ with that of ME short /e/ produced such homophones as *bread* n. = *bred* v., *lead* n. = *led* v., *let* (allow) = *let* (hinder), *red* adj. = *read* v., *wet* = BE *whet*. Other homophones are: *berry* = *bury*, regional AE *merry* = *marry*, *ferry* = *fairy*.

History

MnE /ɛ/ is chiefly derived from ME short /e/ and from ME long open /ę̄/ in checked position.

ME short /e/, from a variety of earlier sources, survives in *bed, better, west*, etc. (OE *e*); *seven, yellow* (OE *eo*); *bury, knell, merry* (Kentish *e*); *bless, brethren, kept, beckon, shepherd, errand*, etc. (OE *ē*); *friendship, devil, depth* (OE *ēo*); *cleanse, ever, health, wrestle*, etc. (OE *æ*); *left, bereft* (OE *ēa*); *jest, debt, gentle, cherry, relish*, etc. (OF *e*); *cell, memory, pregnant*, etc. (L *e*).

The early MnE free vowel /e/, from ME long open /ę̄/, was extensively replaced by checked /ɛ/ early in the 16. century, well before the first English settlements were established in America. Examples are: *tread, heaven, feather, wether, heavy*, etc. (OE *e, io*); *bread, death, threat, deaf* (OE *ēa*); *sweat, wet, dread, breath, weapon* (OE *æ*); *leaven, pleasant, measure, jealous*, BE *leisure* (OF *e, ei*). It should be noted that in other words MnE has /i/ from ME /ę̄/, as in *lead, read, beat*, etc. The incidence of /ɛ/ and /i/ in words of this group must have been settled by 1600, since AE is in full agreement with BE.

In words adopted from various languages in modern times, /ɛ/ renders short [ɛ ~ e] sounds, as in *bevel, celery, debut, menu, pell-mell, zest* (F); *credulous, despot, tense* adj., *veteran* (L); *telescope, tetrarchy, therapy* (Gr.).

BE and some dialects of AE derive /ɛ/ from earlier /e/ before a historical /r/, as in *care, fair, dairy, Mary*.

In some words, MnE /ɛ/ is derived from ME short /e/ that varied with other vowels, as in *many, Thames*, AE *again, against, ten, friend, feoff, jeopardy, leopard, Wednesday*.

Spelling

The usual spellings of checked /ɛ/ are *e* and *ea*: the former in words with ME short /e/, as in *bed, seven, blemish, jelly*, etc.; the latter in words with ME long open /ę̄/, as in *bread, sweat, deaf, feather, pleasant, zealous*, etc.

Deviations from this rule are uncommon. *e* instead of the expected *ea* appears in *shed* v., *shred, wet, wether*. The digraph *ea* for the expected *e* is written in the preterits *dealt, dreamt, leant, leapt, meant, read, spread*, in the derivatives *health, stealth, wealth, treadle, cleanse*, and in the compound *breakfast*.

Rare historical and foreign spellings are: *ai* in *said* and AE *again, against*; *ay* in *says*; *ei* in *heifer, Leister*, BE *leisure*; *a* in *many, any, Thames*, BE *ate*; *ie* in *friend, friendly, friendship*; *u* in *burial, bury*; *eo* in *feoff, feoffee, jeopardy, leopard*; *ae* in *aeronaut*, AE *aestival*; *ai, a* in *fair, fairy, care, Mary*, as pronounced in BE and some dialects of AE.

13.3 The Checked Vowel /æ/

In BE, the checked vowel /æ/ is a raised low-front monophthong, usually short. Prolongation occurs in monosyllables, especially before voiced consonants, as in *sad, bag, man*.

In America, the articulation of /æ/ varies regionally. In the North and the North Midland, /æ/ is monophthongal and usually prolonged before voiced consonants, as in *bad, ham, hand, salve, ladder*. The tongue is somewhat lower than in BE. However, in an area extending apparently from Metropolitan New York to Ohio, the younger generation often has an ingliding diphthong starting in raised position, at least in some words.

In the South and the South Midland, /æ/ is usually prolonged and diphthongal, except before voiceless stops. In most subareas of the South, ingliding [æ⁹] and upgliding [æᴵ] occur side by side, as in *bag, half, ashes, dance*, but with varying frequency. The initial tongue position is noticeably higher than in the North.

Distribution

The phoneme /æ/ does not occur at the end of words and morphemes or before vowels.

In AE, /æ/ is found before all final consonants, except /ð, z, ž, h, r, j, w/, as in *lap, hat, latch, lack*; *cab, sad, badge, bag*; *staff, bath, grass, lash*; *calve, salve*; *ham, fan, bang, pal* (friend); and before all medial consonants, except /ŋ, j, w/, as in *dapper, batter, satchel, tackle*; *abbot, ladder, majesty, haggard*; *raffle, mathematics, tassel, passion*; *slaver, lather, dazzle, casual*; *hammer, flannel, fallow, arrow*.

Finally and medially, /æ/ can be followed by clusters consisting of a resonant and an obstruent, as in *lamp, hamper, clamber, camphor*; *ant, antler, hand, candle, ranch, Manchu, flange, banjo, panther, lance, ransom*; *bank, rankle, dangle*; *scalp, halberd, alto, algae, alcove, algorism, alpha, salvage, halcyon*; and by the clusters of obstruents shown in *gasp, Caspar, fast, plaster, mask, basket, wax, adze*.

In BE, the incidence of /æ/ before fricatives and nasal clusters, as in *staff, bath, glass, rather* and *aunt, command, dance*, is greatly restricted, to some extent also in the dialect of eastern New England. In these positions, older /æ/ has been largely replaced by /ɑ/, especially in monosyllables. See the phoneme /ɑ/.

Regionalisms

For the occurrence of /ɑ/ instead of /æ/ in BE *staff, glass, can't*, etc., and in some varieties of coastal AE, see under the free vowel /ɑ/.

Before /r ~ ə̯/, as in *care, stairs*, /æ/ is common in the American South and in New England.

Azure has /e/ beside the more common /æ/. In America, /æ/ is heard beside the usual /e/ in *apricot*, and beside the usual /ɑ/ in *almond*. In BE, *garage* is pronounced /gǽrɑž/, in AE /gəráž, -áǧ/.

Alternation

For the alternation of /æ/ with /e/, see under /e/.

/æ/ alternates with /o/ in *gad-fly* ~ *goad*; with /ɔ/ in *draft* ~ *draw*; with /ɪ/ in *language* ~ *linguist*; with /ai/ in *band* ~ *bind*; and with /ə/ in *magic* ~ *magician, affix* n. ~ *affix* v., *abstinence* ~ *abstain, addict* n. ~ *addict* v., etc.

Homophones

Homophones, mostly of long standing, are: *bad* adj. = *bade* v., *bat* (implement) = *bat* (a mammal), *lap* n. = *lap* v., *mass* (bulk) = *mass* (ceremony), *wax* n. = *wax* v., AE *ant* = *aunt*, AE *last* n. = *last* adj. = *last* v.

History

The chief source of MnE /æ/ is ME short /a/, which in turn is largely derived from short OE *æ, a, ea,* ON *a,* OF *a,* or L *a* in closed syllables or before two unstressed syllables.

Examples are: *ash, nap, sat, thatch, black, glad, grass, gather, saddle, shadow* (OE *æ*); *flax, gallows, marrow, sparrow* (OE *ea*); *addle, adze, crack, man, hand, sang, stand, thank, hammer, answer, angle* (OE *a*); *anger, slaver* (ON *a*); *pass, bastard, haggard, chandler, anguish, language* (OF *a*); *add, altitude, family, masculine* (L *a*).

In a few words, ME short /a/, whence MnE /æ/, is derived from the OE long vowels *ǣ, ā* before a long consonant or a consonant cluster, as in *fat, blast, wrath, last* v. (OE *ǣ*) and *gasp, gadfly, hallow, last* n., *mash* n. (OE *ā*), or from OE *ēa,* as in *lather, lapwing.*

In words adopted from various languages in modern times, /æ/ takes the place of foreign [a]- like vowels, as in *aster, caste, fact, camp, harass, panic, salvage, bandit, bamboo, hammock, mustang, Hamburg.* This substitution is in part a spelling pronunciation, but may also be due to the fact that early MnE lacked an [a]- like vowel until the unrounding of ME /o/ to /a/, as in AE *lot.*

Before /r ~ ə/, as in *care, stairs,* earlier MnE /e/ has been lowered to /æ/ in parts of New England and in the greater part of the South.

Spelling

The usual spelling of the phoneme /æ/ is *a.* For examples see above.

Occasional spellings, reflecting various earlier pronunciations, are: *al* in *salmon* and in AE *calf, calve, half, salve, almond; au* in AE *aunt, Staunton, draught, laugh, laughter; ai* in *plaid, plait* (braid), and in *stairs, fair* as pronounced in New England and the South.

13.4 The American Checked Vowel /ɑ/

Articulation

The checked vowel /ɑ/ is current in most varieties of AE, but not in BE, which has /ɒ/. It is merged in the /ɔ/ phoneme in eastern New England, in western Pennsylvania, and apparently in parts of the Midwest and the Northwest. In Metropolitan New York and in the coastal South, areas in which postvocalic /r/ is lost as such, the checked vowel /ɑ/ of *hot* /hɑt/ is in contrast with the free vowel /ɒ/ of *far, heart* /fɒ, hɒt/.

Checked /ɑ/ is most commonly an unrounded low-central vowel, often prolonged before voiced consonants, as in *rob, nod, bother, calm, doll, far*. In the Lower South it is low-back and sometimes slightly rounded before /r/, also in eastern Pennsylvania.

Distribution

The vowel /ɑ/ does not occur at the end of words and morphemes, or before vowels. It appears before all consonants except /h, j, w, ž/, though rarely before /č, θ, š, ð/. Occurrence before /č, ǧ, f/ is limited to words from foreign languages. Examples illustrating the distribution of /ɑ/ are: *hop, proper, lot, totter, crotch, lock, rocket; knob, cobble, rod, fodder, lodge, cogitate, log, soggy; profit, brothel, blossom, wash, Joshua; hovel, providence, bother, gosling, closet, lozenge; bomb, calm, homage, honor, monogram, gong, mongrel; doll, follow, swallow, far, borrow.*

/ɑ/ occurs also before /m, n, l, r/ clusters, as in *pomp, sombre, font, fond, monster, bronze, longitude, longer, golf, harp, heart, park, harbor, hard, large, target, hearth, farce, harsh, starve, Mars, harm, barn, parlor;* and before /s/ clusters, as in *hospital, hostile, mosque,* though rarely.

Regionalisms

The checked vowel /ɑ/ occurs beside the free vowel /ɔ/ in such words as *log, fog, foggy, long; wash, water, swallow, swamp; orange, tomorrow; on; daughter, launch* v., *haunted, sausage, faucet.* The regional dissemination of these variants is highly complicated and inconsistent in the eastern United States, and presumably elsewhere.

Alternation

For the frequent alternation of /ɑ/ with /o/, see /o/; for alternation with /u/, see /u/.

/ɑ/ alternates with /o/ in *garfish* ∼ *gore, bonfire* ∼ *bone;* with /ɪ ∼ i/ in *starboard* ∼ *steer;* and with /ə/ in *produce* n. ∼ *produce* v., *progress* n. ∼ *progress* v.

Homophones

The following words are homophonous: *bomb* = *balm*, *heart* = *hart*, *profit* = *prophet*, *rock* n. = *rock* v., *park* n. = *park* v., *bark* (of tree) = *bark* (of dog); *carp* n. = *carp* v., *lock* (of hair) = *lock* v., *log* (timber) = *og* (nautical record), *hock* (a joint) = *hock* (a wine).

History

The chief sources of AE /ɑ/ are ME short /o/ and ME short /a/ before r, the latter only in dialects that preserve postvocalic /r/. These two vowels of ME must have been merged in some regional types of MnE before the first colonies were planted in America, otherwise this widespread striking feature of AE would be difficult to account for.

ME short /o/, chiefly in closed syllables, is the source of AE /ɑ/ in such words as the following: *fox, hop, knob, lot, lock, body, borrow, follow, mongrel*, etc. (OE *o*); *blossom, fodder, godfather, goshawk gosling, gospel, gossip* (OE *ō*)*; bonfire* (OE *ā*)*; lodge, rob, rock, closet, honor, profit*, etc. (OF *o*); *homily, hospital, longitude, pomp, providence*, etc. (L or OF *o*). BE has the checked vowel /ʋ/ in such words.

Note that before /f, θ, s, g, ŋ/, as in *off, moth, loss, dog, long*, ME /o/ remained rounded in AE, and became the vowel /ɔ/.

In words of the following type, AE /ɑ/ is derived from ME /a/ before tautosyllabic /r/: *barley, harm, sharp, starling, yarn*, etc. (OE *a, ea*); *garfish, garlic, lark* (OE *ā*); *bark* n., *carp* v. (ON *a*); *bargain, car, charm, parley, tardy*, etc. (OF *a*); *barn, far, heart, marsh, starch, starboad*, etc. (OE *e, ĕo*); *scar* (cliff), *tarn* (lake) (ON *e*)*; arbor, farm, harlot, parsley, parson, sergeant* (OF *e*). BE and some dialects of AE have the free vowel /ɑ/ instead of the sequence /ɑr/.

In monosyllabic *alms, balm, calm, palm, psalm, qualm*, AE /ɑ/ is derived from the lowered and backed allophone of /æ/ (ME /a/) before tautosyllabic /l/, the latter being lost c1600. Here BE and some varieties of coastal AE have /ɑ/. In American folk speech, /æ/ is sometimes preserved in *calm, palm* (of the hand). Note that in disyllabic *almond, salmon* the /æ/ survives also in cultivated English.

In words adopted from various languages in modern times, /ɑ/ is a spelling pronunciation of *o*, as in *hostile, homicide, nominal, popular, tonsure* (L.); *homonym, monarch* (Gr.); *hock* (a wine), *dollar* (Ger.); *hominy, toddy*. In words with the *a* spelling, the /ɑ/ renders foreign [a]-like sounds, as in *adagio, bazaar, bravado, Brahmin, garage, Kraal, massage, plaza, tomale, yacht*.

In exclamatory *ah, bah, hurrah*, in affective *Ma, ma'am, Pa*, and in a few recently adopted words, as *eclat, rajah, shah, pashah*, /ɑ/ appears in final position, which it never occupies in the normal older stock of words.

The French pronunciation is retained in *memoir* /mɛ́mwɑr/, *reservoir*, *soirée*; the French nasal vowel in *encore, entrée, ensemble* is replaced by the sequence /ɑn/.

Spelling

The spelling reflects rather consistently the two ME sources of AE /ɑ/. The spelling *o* continues that of ME /o/, as in *lot, rob, body, gospel, hospital*, etc.; the spelling *a* that of ME /a/, as in *barn, charm, marsh, parson*, etc. In words adopted in modern times, the foreign spellings *o* and *a* are retained.

Other spellings of /ɑ/ are infrequent. They reflect older or variant pronunciations in *alms, calm, palm*, in *heart, hearth, sergeant*, and in regional *haunt, launch* v. Foreign spellings are retained in *yacht, kraal, ensemble, entrée, memoir, soirée*, transliterations of other writing systems in *rajah, shah, pashah*. The spelling *ah* is introduced to represent /ɑ/ in the abnormal final position in *ah!, hurrah!, bah!*

13.5 The British Checked Vowel /ʋ/

Articulation

The checked phoneme /ʋ/ of BE is a short and slightly rounded mid-back vowel. It differs markedly from the free vowel /ɔ/ of *law, taught*, which is prolonged, well rounded, and articulated with considerable elevation of the back of the tongue. Since /ʋ/ it in contrast with /ɔ/ in *cot, tot* ≠ *caught, taught*, one cannot treat it as an allophone of /ɔ/.

In AE, words that have the phoneme /ʋ/ in BE have either /ɑ/ as in *lot*, or /ɔ/ as in *loss*.

Distribution

The BE phoneme /ʋ/ does not occur finally or before vowels. It appears before all consonants except /ž, h, j, w/, as in *hop, lot, crotch, rock*; *knob, rod, lodge, dog*; *cough, offer, moth, loss, blossom, wash*; *hovel, bother, closet*; *bomb, homage, honor, long*; *doll, jolly, swallow*; *borrow, orange*. It occurs also before the consonant clusters exemplified in *pomp, sombre, font, fond, monster, bronze, longitude, longer, golf, solve* and *hospital, hostile, mosque*.

Fluctuation

Before voiceless fricatives, as in *off, trough, loft, broth, moth, toss, cost*, both /ʋ/ and /ɔ/ are current; but words of more than one syllable, as *office, coffee, posse, jostle, hospital*, have only /ʋ/.

Hovel, hover have /ʌ/ beside the more usual /ʋ/.

Alternation

In some morphemes /ɒ/ alternates: with /o/, in *holiday* ~ *holy, dominate*
~ *domain*; with /e/ in *watch* ~ *wake*; with /u* ~ *ʊ/, in *gosling* ~ *goose,*
godfather ~ *good*; in others with /ə/, as in *próduct* ~ *prodúce.*

Homophones

The following words are homophonous: *hough* (a joint) = *hock* (a wine),
lock (of hair) = *lock* (on door), *log* (timber) = *log* (nautical record), *rock*
n. = *rock* v., *profit* = *prophet.*

History

In words already current in ME, BE /ɒ/ is largely derived from ME
short /o/. Examples are: *hop, lot, rock, knob, rod, lodge, fog; off, office,*
moth, loss, closet; homage, honor, long; solve, follow, sorrow.

In words adopted from Latin, Greek, and other languages in modern
times, /ɒ/ replaces short mid-back and low-back vowels, as in *hostile,*
popular, homonym, monarch, dollar, hock (a wine), *yacht, toddy.*

Another source of /ɒ/ is ME short /a/ after /w/, as in *wash, wallow,*
swamp, swallow.

Spelling

The spellings *o* and *a* of ME are retained, as in *hot, long, follow, borrow,*
etc., and in *wash, swallow,* respectively. The spellings of /ɒ/ in *yacht* /jɒt/
(from Dutch) is unique.

13.6 The Checked Vowel /ʌ/

Articulation

In BE, the phoneme /ʌ/ is an unrounded mid-back vowel, more or
less lowered and fronted. A similar phone, though somewhat higher than
in BE, is current in the American North and North Midland. In the
South and in the South Midland, the tongue has a noticeably higher
position and the lips are sometimes slightly rounded. Ingliding [ʌə ~ ʌ·ə]
is fairly common in these two areas.

Distribution

The checked vowel /ʌ/ occurs before all consonants except /h, ž, j, w/,
as in *cup, supper, nut, butter, much, duchy, buck, buckle; shrub, stubborn,*
bud, judge, hug; tough, nothing, bus, tussle, blush, Russian; love, hover,
mother, buzz, muzzle; come, summer, son, sunny, lung, hull, gully, BE *hurry,*
borough. It can be followed by clusters consisting of a resonant and a
plosive, as in *hump, hunt, punch, sunk; tumble, bundle, plunge, hunger;*

gulp, cult, mulch, bulk, bulb, indulge, promulgate; by /nθ, ls/, as in *month, pulse*; and by clusters consisting of /s/ and a plosive, as in *cusp, lust, husk*, or /f/ plus /t/, as in *tuft, mufti*.

Regionalisms

Regional differences in the incidence of /ʌ/ are few. BE has /ʌ/ before intersyllabic /r/, as in *hurry, worry, furrow*, where AE usually has /ɜ/. In the southern states, *soot* frequently has /ʌ/, *bulge, bulk*, on the other hand, /ʊ/.

Alternation

In some morphemes, /ʌ/ alternates with /au/, as in *southern ~ south, utmost ~ out, abundant ~ abound, fundament ~ foundation*; in others with /ə/, as in *prejúdge ~ préjudice, súbject ~ subjéct, cónduct ~ condúct*; in *punish ~ punitive*, with /u/.

Homophones

Merging of phonemes and the adoption of foreign words have produced homophones like *duck* (bird) = *duck* (cloth), *gull* n. = *gull* v., *must* v. = *must* n., *plum* = *plumb*, *pulse* (of heart) = *pulse* (beans, etc.), *rushes* n. = *rushes* v., *strut* n. = *strut* v., *stud* (horses) = *stud* (lumber), *sun* = *son*.

History

The MnE checked vowel /ʌ/ is mostly derived from the rounded short high-back vowel /u/ of ME, which was gradually unrounded and lowered in SBE during the latter part of the 16. century, except in certain positions (see under /ʊ/). Since AE is in substantial agreement with BE in the incidence of /ʌ/, this process must have been completed before the first American colonies were planted.

ME /u/, in turn, comes from various sources: OE /u/, as in *buck, nut, hundred, sun, son, love*; OE /y/, as in *blush, cudgel, much, puff, shut, worry*; OE /ū/, as in *dust, slumber, southern, husband, utmost*; OE /o/, as in *mongrel, oven, shovel*; OF /u, o/, as in *button, humble, plunge, supper*; OF /u, ui/, as in *duchess, judge, publish, usher*.

A second source of MnE /ʌ/ is late ME long /ū/, which was shortened in certain positions to /u/ in early MnE before the unrounding of earlier /u/ to /ʌ/ (see above). Examples are: *crumb, thumb, dove, rough, suck* (OE *ū*); *brother, mother, other, rudder, hover, month, Monday* and *blood, flood, stud, done, gums, glove, enough, tough* and *must, does* (OE *ō*, raised to /ū/ in late ME).

In Latin words taken into English in modern times, /u/ in closed syllables is regularly rendered by /ʌ/, as in *adult, custody, cult, fulminate, function, muscle, repulsive, rustic, ultimate*, presumably in accordance with the school pronunciation of Latin.

In words introduced from various languages since the Middle Ages, /ʌ/ has taken the place of various low or central vowels in checked position, as in *buffalo, buccaneer, curry* n., *gull* n., *hubbub, mufti, pundit.*

Spelling

The /ʌ/ phoneme is usually spelled *u* or *o*, but other spellings also occur.

The graph *u* appears in most words that had short /u/ in ME, as in *buck, shut, dust, supper, usher,* etc. It was introduced in a few words that had long /ū/ in late ME, as in *gums, must, rudder, studhorse.* Recently adopted words, such as *cult, buffalo, pundit,* also have the spelling *u.*

In ME, the phoneme /u/ was usually written *o* near *m, n, u* (= *v*), *uu* (= *w*), and this spelling has been retained in MnE, as in *come, son, money, love, govern, won, worry.*

The spellings *o, o-e* also appear in words that had long /ū/ from earlier /ọ̄/ in late ME, as in *brother, mother, other, glove, hover, month, Monday.*

Moreover, *o* is written in *color, dozen, none, nothing, one, once,* BE *borough, thorough.*

The French spelling *ou* of ME /u/ has been retained in *country, cousin, double, nourish, touch,* etc., and in the native words *southern, Southey, young.*

Chough, enough, rough, tough had long /ū/ in ME, spelled *ou.* Here the spelling *ou* has been retained despite the change to /ʌ/.

In *blood, flood* (but not in *stud*) the early MnE spelling of /u/ from earlier /ọ̄/ has survived.

13.7 The Checked Vowel /ʊ/

Articulation

In BE, /ʊ/ is a short, rounded, lowered high-back monophthong [ʊ]. This phonic type is also the usual one in the American North and North Midland. In the greater part of the South, /ʊ/ is an ingliding [ʊᵊ], often considerably fronted, occasionally even high-central.

Distribution

The distribution of /ʊ/ is severely restricted. It occurs before /d/ in *good, hood, stood, wood, could, should, would;* before /k/, as in *book, look, took;* before /š/ in *bush, bushel, cushion, push;* before /l/, as in *bull, full, pulley, pulpit, wolf.* It is rare before /t, č, s, z/, as in *foot, put, butcher, hussar, bosom.* Before labials, as in *hoop, roof, room,* it is restricted to certain dialects; also before /n/, as in *soon, spoon,* and before /r ~ ə̣/, as in *poor, sure.* /ʊ/ does not occur before /ǰ, v, θ, ð, ŋ/, nor before /g/, except in dialectal *goober* (peanut) and *coob* (a variant of *coop*).

Regionalisms

In some words, checked /ʊ/ occurs regionally before certain consonants, either alone or as a variant. Thus before /m/ in *broom, room,* both in England and in New England and Virginia; before /r ~ ə/, as in *poor, sure,* in BE and large parts of the American North and North Midland; in *bulge, bulk,* in the American South and South Midland; in *hoof, roof, coop, hoop, root, soot,* in various sections of America.

Homophones

Bull (animal) = *bull* (edict), *full* adj. = *full* v., *wood* = *would, moor* n. = *moor* v.

History

The chief source of MnE /ʊ/ is ME short /u/ between consonants that favor lip rounding, chiefly between a labial and /l, s/, as in *bull, full, pull, wolf, woman, wool, wood, worsted* (OE *u*); *bullion, pulley, ambush, bushel, push, butcher, cushion* (OF *ou, ui*); *bull* (edict), *full* v., *pulpit* (L *u*); *bulwark* (MDu. *o*). In words adopted in modern times, /ʊ/ renders foreign rounded high-back vowels in similar positions, as in *bouquet, boulevard, bullet, bulletin* (F) and *bully* (Du.), but also in *hussar* (Hungarian). It should be noted that words taken from Latin after 1400 have /ʌ/ in this position, as in *fulminate, repulse, vulgar.*

A second source of the MnE /ʊ/ is ME close long /ọ/, raised to /ū/ in the 15. century and shortened in the 17. century. This change took place regularly before /k/, as in *book, brook, shook, took,* sporadically or regionally before alveolars and labials, as in *could* (ME *coude* for earlier *couthe*), *good, hood, stood, foot, root, soot* and *hoop, hoof, roof, broom,* rarely before other consonants, as in *bosom,* BE *gooseberry.* ME /ū/ before labials (from OE *ū*), merged in /ū/ from Me /ọ/ in the 15. century, exhibits the same development in *coop, room.*

There are some isolated developments. In *should, would,* from ME *shulde, wulde,* /ul/ became /ū/, then /ʊ/ under weak stress (c1600); this is now the vowel in stressed *should, would.* In *sugar,* older /u/ became /ʊ/ in the 18. century. The suffix *-hood,* as in *childhood,* had close /ọ/ in late ME (earlier open /ǫ/ from OE *ā*); its later development parallels that in *good, hood.*

Some varieties of English have /ʊ/ before /r ~ ə/ from earlier /u/, as in *poor, moore, pure, sure.*

In early MnE, [ʊ] from ME /u/ was in complementary distribution with [ʌ], the former occurring only between labials and /l, s/, as in *pull, push, bull, bush, full,* the latter in other positions. The later substitution of [ʊ] for free /u/ (from ME close /ọ/), as before /k/ in *book, took, look,* raised the allophone [ʊ] to phonemic status, since it came to contrast with [ʌ] in this position, as in *book* /bʊk/ ≠ *buck* /bʌk/, *look* /lʊk/ ≠ *luck* /lʌk/, etc. Similarly, in some dialects, before other consonants, as in *roof* /rʊf/ ≠ *rough* /rʌf/, *room* /rʊm/ ≠ *rum* /rʌm/, *coop* /kʊp/ ≠ *cup* /kʌp/.

Spelling

The spelling of /ʊ/ largely reflects the two vowels of ME that were merged in it in the 17. century. In words that had short /u/ in ME, the spelling *u* has been retained, as in *full, pull, push, bushel, butcher, pulpit*. In words that had ME long /ọ/, *oo* is now written, as in *foot, good, book, roof, hoop*. The spelling *u* is also used in words adopted in modern times, as in *bullet, bully, hussar*.

Exceptional spellings are: *oo* in *wood, wool* (ME /u/); *o* in *wolf, woman, worsted* (ME /u/) and *bosom* (ME /ọ/); *ou* in *bouquet, boulevard* (modern French); *oul* in *should, would* (early MnE /ul/), secondarily also in *could*.

13.8 The Checked Vowel /ɵ/

Articulation and Incidence

The checked vowel /ɵ/, as in *coat, smoke, road, home, stone, whole*, occurs only in New England, and sporadically in the New England settlements along the Great Lakes. It is a slightly rounded mid-back vowel, always short and often ingliding. It contrasts with /ʌ/, as in *stone* ≠ *stun, whole* ≠ *hull*; and with /o/, as in *road* ≠ *rode, whole* ≠ *hole*.

In cultivated speech, checked /ɵ/ has been largely replaced by the free vowel /o/, especially in western New England and in the urbanized Boston area. In popular speech it is still widely used in northern New England, notably in such 'homely' expressions as *coat, road, folks, toadstool, smokestack, stonewall, whetstone, wishbone, at home, the whole thing*.

History

In standard BE and in all the American dialects spoken in the Midland and the South, the long open /ọ/ and the diphthong /ou/ of ME are completely merged in the free vowel /o/. New England, on the other hand, has preserved the old distinction in checked position, though rather sporadically, ME /ọ/ appearing as ingliding /ɵ/, ME /ou/ as upgliding /o/. New England shares this usage with the folk speech of the greater part of England.

7   Kurath, A Phonology and Prosody of Modern English

14. The Free Vowels

14.1 The Free Vowel /i/

Articulation

In BE, the free high-front vowel /i/ is articulated either as an upgliding [ij] or as a monophthongal [i·].

In America, these two variants also occur side by side, but with regionally varying frequency. In the Atlantic States, only northeastern New England and coastal South Carolina lack upgliding [ɪi ~ ij], the former having monophthongal [i· ~ i] in all positions, the latter [i· ~ i] in free position, as in *three*, but ingliding [iə] in checked position, as in *grease, eat*.

As in other free vowels, the regional phonic characteristics of /i/ are most marked in free position under full stress. Under half-stress and weak stress, as in *úpkèep* and *happý, détráct*, /i/ tends to be monophthongal everywhere, and more open.

In the folk speech of England, upgliding [ij] seems to be restricted to the eastern counties. The western counties have [i·], in checked position also ingliding [iə], which is paralleled by South Carolina usage.

In weakly stressed syllables, /i/ varies positionally. Finally, as in *bérrý, búsý, ládý, líbertý, wésterlý, emplóyèe*, it is pronounced either as a short upgliding diphthong [ɪi] or as a short monophthong [i ~ ɪ]. Before a stressed vowel, as in *gèógraphý, rèálitý*, it is sounded as a short [i ~ ɪ]. Before an unstressed vowel, as in *átheist, congénial, ódious*, it is articulated as [i ~ ɪ] or replaced by /j/.

When weakly stressed, the prefixes *be-, de-, e-, pre-, re-*, as in *bèfúddle, dèríde, dèódorant, èléct, prèfér, prèémpt, rèjéct, rèáct*, have the normal prosodic allophones of /i/; when unstressed, the /i/ may be replaced by /ə/, as commonly in AE *belíeve, prepáre*.

Whether the high-front vowel occurring before a stressed syllable, as in *èpidémic, ànticlimax, ántidòte, épilògue, hórticùlture* and AE *lègalizátion, mátrimòny*, etc., should be regarded as a positional allophone of the free vowel /i/ or of the checked vowel /ɪ/ is an open question. Phonically it is clearly closer to stressed /ɪ/; on the other hand, it ends morphemes.

Distribution

The vowel /i/ occurs (1) finally in words and morphemes, as in *see, three, pea, plumtree, behave, teacup, deity, react, preempt, detract, belittle, direct*; (2) before a vowel within a morpheme, as in *peon, real*; and (3) before all consonants except /b, h, j, w, ŋ/, as in *leap, beat, beech, seek; seed, siege, league; reef, wreath, peace, specious; reeve, seethe, ease, lesion; dream, bean, feel*, AE regional *fear* /fiə̯/.

The vowel /i/ is rare before /š, ž, g/, appearing here only in loan words. It can be followed by the clusters /ld/ and /st/, as in *field, east.*

Regionalisms

Before tautosyllabic or intersyllabic /r/, as in *here, ear, beard, experience,* or its derivative, unsyllabic /ǝ/, the free vowel /i/ has only limited currency.

In America it survives rather generally as a lowered long [i·] in areas where the /r/ has become /ǝ/—eastern New England, Metropolitan New York, and parts of the South. Elsewhere it has become checked /ɪ/ or hovers between free /i/ and /ɪ/. Parts of the South and the South Midland have the sequence /jǝ/ from earlier /iǝ ~ ɪr/, the Lower South not infrequently the unshifted mid-vowel /e/.

In BE, *here, ear, beard* now have the sequence /ɪǝ/ or /jǝ/. All variants of cultivated American and British English have their counterparts in English folk speech.

There are also some isolated differences in the incidence of /i/. In America, *creek* has /i/ in the South and the South Midland, but predominantly /ɪ/ farther north. *Negro* has /i/ in the North and the North Midland, /ɪ/ farther south, in BE only /i/. *Either* and *neither* have /i/ in America (occasionally /ai/, as in Boston, Manhattan, and Philadelphia), in BE usually /ai/. *Ego, egotist* commonly have /i/ in America, /ɛ/ in England. *Economical* has either the /i/ of *economy* or /ɛ/.

Alternation

The vowel /i/ alternates with /ɛ/ in a considerable number of morphemes, e.g. in *breathe ~ breath, bequeathe ~ bequest, sphere ~ spherical, beast ~ bestial, brief ~ brevity, redeem ~ redemption, appeal ~ appellant, repeat ~ repetitive, athlete ~ athletic.* In *lead ~ led, feed ~ fed, leave ~ left* this alternation has grammatical function. In *seat ~ sit* it alternates with /ɪ/.

/i/ varies with /u/ in *feed ~ food* and with /ʌ/ in *bleed ~ blood.* The alternation in *geese ~ goose, teeth ~ tooth, feet ~ foot* is grammatical.

Homophones

The merging of early MnE /e/ (from ME open /ē̦/) with /i/ (from ME close /ē̦/) produced such homophones as *beat = beet, beach = beech, heal = heel, leach = leech, leaf = lief, peace = piece, read = reed, steal = steel, weak = week.* Other homophones already existed in ME times, as *deer = dear, beer = bier, here = hear, steer* n. = *steer* v.

History

In the native vocabulary, MnE high-front /i/ is derived from two ME mid-front vowels, close long /ē̦/ and open long /ē̦/. The close /ē̦/ was raised to high position in late ME, open /ē̦/ much later.

ME close /ẹ/ is the source of MnE /i/ in such native words as *me, feet, seek, field, yield* (OE *ē); free, deep, freeze* (OE *ēo); deed, speech, sleep* (Anglian *ē*); *beetle, evil, week, weevil* (OE *i, io, y*).

ME open /ę/ is the source of MnE /i/ in such native words as *heat, lead, mean, reach, wreath* (OE *ǣ); bean, leaf, heap, stream* (OE *ēa); mead* (meadow) *meal* (as in *meal time*), *read* (WS *ǣ); eat, eaves, meat, even, fever, weir, beaver, keel* (OE *e, eo*).

In words taken from OF, ME close long /ẹ/ replaced OF close /e/ and /ie/, as in *agree, degree, brief, chief, niece, piece, ceiling*, and AF /ue/, as in *beef, people*. ME long open /ę/ took the place of OF open /e/ and /ai/, as in *cream, eagle, glean, peace, please, preach, treat, feast, regent, secret*. In such words the vowels shared the development of /ẹ/ and /ę/ in the native vocabulary.

In words taken from Latin, many of which entered English simultaneously by way of French, both /ē/ and /e/ were Anglicized as long /ẹ/ in the open syllable, as in *lesion, specious*, and later simply replaced by /i/ on the basis of the spelling, as in the case of *epoch, ether, ego, egoist*.

In more recent loans, /i/ takes the place of foreign high front vowels as in *breeze, veer, fatigue, machine, trio, hashish*.

Weakly stressed /i/ has, in part, the same sources as fully stressed /i/: ME close /ẹ/, as in *city, jelly, jury, liberty, piety*; open /ę/, as in *atheist, geometry, theology* and the prefixes illustrated in *deny, elect, prefer, rely*. But it has also a number of other sources: ME /ei ~ ai/, as in *abbey, money, palfrey*; ME /ĭ/ in the prefixes and suffixes of such words as *be-lieve, di-gest, di-rect, Anti-christ, demi-god*; and especially ME weakly stressed long /ī/ (which in fully stressed position became /ʌi/ in MnE), as in *barley, belly, daisy, forty, honey, ivy, lady*, and the numerous words with the suffixes *-y, -ly, -ary, -ery, -ory*, as *copy, happy, lovely, notary, bakery, illusory*.

In the Elizabethan period both undiphthongized and diphthongized derivatives of ME /ī/ were current under half-stress, so that Shakespeare could rime *warely* with *by*, *phantasies* with *eyes*, and, on the other hand, *amity* and *solemnly* with *be*.

Spelling

Four spellings of /i/ are common in stressed syllables: *ee* and *ie* in words with ME close /ẹ/, *ea* and *e* in those with ME open /ę/. In ME the close and the open vowel were not differentiated in the spelling. The modern spellings were introduced in the 16. century to distinguish the early MnE /i/ (ME /ẹ/) from the early MnE /e/ (ME /ę/). After the merging of these two phonemes in MnE /i/, these spellings were retained.

The digraph *ee* is now used in such words as *heel, see, week, freeze* and *agree, beef*; *ie* (a CF spelling), in *chief, niece, piece* and *belief, field, thief, yield*. The digraph *ea* appears in *eat, heal, leaf, weak*, etc., and in *cream, feast, peace, treat,* etc. The graph *e* occurs mostly in words taken from Latin, as *ether, legion, secret, specious,* but also in some English words, such as *even, evening, evil* and *he, me, we.*

Other spellings of stressed /i/ are: the split digraph *e-e,* as in *cede, compete, discrete;* the digraph *ei* (from OF), as in *deceive, deceit, conceive* and, secondarily, in *either, neither, ceiling* (earlier *ie*) and *weir* (earlier *ee, ea*); *ey* in *key; ay* in *quay; eo* in *people; ae* or *œ* in *aeon, aegis; e* or *oe* in *fetus, edema; e* or *œ* in *esthetic, medieval; eau* in *Beauchamp;* and *i* or *i-e* in late adoptions, such as *fatigue, liter, machine, police, suite, trio.*

In weakly stressed syllables the following spellings are current: *y,* as in *daisy, forty, happy, lady, lovely, ability, eulogy,* etc. (ME /ī/), and *city, jelly, piety,* etc. (ME /ē̜/); *i,* as in *happier, happiest, burial* and *dimension, direct; ie,* as in *cities, ladies, harried; ey,* as in *abbey, money* (ME /ei/) and *barley, honey, pulley* (ME /ī/); *e,* as in *atheist, theology* and the prefixes shown in *denounce, elect, prepare, repair* (ME /ē̜/); and *ee,* as in *lessee, employee, levee* (F *é*).

14.2 The Free Vowel /e/

Articulation

In BE, the free mid-front vowel /e/ is an upgliding diphthong [eɪ ~ ɛɪ], starting in mid-front position, close or open. This is also the most common articulation of /e/ in America, the variant [ɛɪ] being rather common in the Philadelphia area and the upper Ohio Valley, the variant [eɪ], with a closer beginning, everywhere else. Monophthongal [e· ~ e] and ingliding [eə], the latter in checked position, are a characteristic feature of the speech of coastal South Carolina. As in other vowels, the regional phonic characteristics of /e/ are most marked in free position, as in *todáy,* less so in checked position, as in *mistáke,* least under weaker stress, as in *níghtingàle, ínmàte, líberàte.*

Distribution

The vowel /e/ occurs at the end of words and morphemes, as in *day, daily, play, playing, gay, gaiety;* and before all consonants except /ŋ, j, w, h/, as in *tape, late, ache* (letter h), *make; able, aid, rage, plague; safe, faith, face, gracious; save, bathe, blaze,* AE *Asia; shame, rein; fail,* AE *fare, Mary.*

It is rare before /č, š, ž/. Before /r ~ ɚ/ its incidence is regional in AE and lacking in BE.

/e/ occurs also before the clusters /st, nǧ/, as in *haste, range.*

Regionalisms

In *again,* BE has predominantly /e/, AE almost universally /ɛ/. Only in some cities of the Atlantic States is /e/ current among a minority of the cultured. *Ate* usually has /e/ in America, but /ɛ/ in England. However, /ɛ/ is rather common in New England, New York State, on Chesapeake Bay, and in South Carolina.

Before /r ~ ə̞/, as in *fair, Mary*, the free vowel /e/ is common in New England and the South Atlantic States; elsewhere in America, as in BE, the checked /ɛ/ is widely current. Before the /ə̞/ of *ear, here*, etc., /e/ predominates in South Carolina and Georgia and occurs sporadically as far north as Chesapeake Bay (Baltimore), but is not found elsewhere in the Atlantic States.

Alternation

In some morphemes, /e/ alternates with /æ/, as in native *bathe* ~ *bath*, *glaze* ~ *glass*, *graze* ~ *grass*, *stave* ~ *staff*, *shade* ~ *shadow*, and in foreign *state* ~ *static*, *page* ~ *paginate*, *Spain* ~ *Spanish*, *nation* ~ *national*, *deprave* ~ *depravity*, *nature* ~ *natural*, *sagacious* ~ *sagacity*. It alternate with /ɛ/ in *say* ~ *says*, *break* ~ *breakfast*; with /ɔ/ in *freight* ~ *fraught* and with /ai/ in *bait* ~ *bite*. In *day* ~ *Monday*, /e/ alternates with weakly stressed /i/, in *native* ~ *nativity* with /ə/.

Homophones

Owing to the merging of ME /ai/ and /ā/ in early MnE, such words as the following became homophones: *ail* = *ale*, *hail* = *hale*, *pail* = *pale*, *pain* = *pane*, *sail* = *sale*, *seine* = *sane*, *steak* = *stake*, *tail* = *tale*, *eight* = AE *ate*. Other homophones are *rain* = *reign*, *way* = *weigh*, *wait* = *weight*, *nay* = *neigh*, *date* (time) = *date* (fruit), etc.

History

The two chief sources of MnE /e/ are ME /ā/ and /ai/.

ME /ā/, from OE short /a/ in the open syllable of disyllabics (c1200), is the source of /e/ in many native words, as *tale, bathe, shame, stave(s), whale(s), hazel, ladle, haven, acre, acorn*; and in words from OF, as *grace, fame, famous, table, haste*, and from Latin, as *dictate, dictation, tolerate*.

MnE /e/ from ME *ai* occurs in many words of native stock, as *day, say, fail, brain, maid(en), slain* (OE *æg*); *way, play, rain, sail, weigh* (OE *eg*); *clay, gray* (*grey*), *neigh, whey* (OE *ǣg*); *hay* (OE *ēg*). It is also found in many foreign words adopted in late OE or in ME times, as *bait, hail* (greet), *nay, raise, reindeer, they* (from ON); and *gay, array, plain, deign, reign, pain, pray* (from OF).

In a few native words, MnE /e/ comes from other sources, as in *break, great, bear, eight, weight, neighbor, raid*.

Spelling

The spelling of /e/ clearly reflects its two chief sources, ME /ā/ and /ai/, which were not merged until c1550. /e/ from ME /ā/ is represented

by the split digraph *a-e*, as in *tale, grace, dictate, cradle, able*; /e/ from
ME /ai/, largely by the digraphs *ai, ay*. But there are some deviations
from this rule. Though early ME /ei/ coalesced with /ai/ in ME, and is
now largely written *ai, ay*, as in *sail, play, pain, pray*, the spelling *ei,
ey* survives in some words taken from OF, as in *feint, rein, heinous,
convey, deign, reign*.

The spelling *eigh* for /e/ is found in *neigh, weigh, neighbor, eight, weight*.

The words in which ME open /ẹ/ survives as the mid-vowel /e/ have
the spelling *ea*: *break, great, steak, yea, bear, tear*.

Exceptional spellings occur in *thane*, for earlier *thein, thain* (since
c1575), in *waist*, for earlier *waste* (since c1750), apparently to distinguish
it from the homophone *waste* (desert), and in *gauge* beside *gage, gaol* beside
jail.

14.3 The Free Vowel /ai/

Articulation

In BE, the phoneme /ai/ is articulated as a diphthong starting in
low-front or low-central position and gliding to or toward high-back [ɪ].
Before the vowel /ə/, as in *society, fire*, the upglide is reduced or even
arrested. In the latter case, *fire, tired* become disyllabic [faˑə, taˑəd] or
monosyllabic [faˑ, taˑd], but remain phonemically distinct from *far,
tarred* /fɑ, tɑd/, in which the vowel is articulated farther back.

In AE, there is considerable variation in the articulation of the phoneme
/ai/. Variants corresponding closely to those of BE predominate in the
North and the North Midland, occurring in all positions. From Pennsylvania southward the situation is complicated. Finally and before
voiced consonants, as in *high, nine, ride*, all of the South, except coastal
South Carolina, and all of the South Midland have a 'slow' diphthong
[aˑᵋ ~ ɑˑᶾ] or [aˑᵊ], with only a brief upglide. Before voiceless consonants,
as in *twice, right*, Virginia and coastal South Carolina have striking allophones of /ai/, the former [əɪ], the latter [ʋɪ]. Thus Virginians say *nine*
[naˑᵋn] but *right* [rəɪt], South Carolinians [naɪn] but [rʋɪt]. In other
parts of the South and in the South Midland 'slow' [aᵋˑ ~ ɑˑᵊ] is used
in all positions.

In the West Midland, from western Pennsylvania to Georgia, *fire, tire,
wire* have the phoneme /ɑ/ of *far, tar*.

Distribution

The vowel /ai/ occurs (1) at the end of words and morphemes, as in
fly, lie, eye, high, higher, Friday, biped, science; (2) before vowels within
a morpheme, as in *fire, friar, viol, violet*; (3) before most of the consonants,
as in *ripe, bite, right, like*; *bribe, ride, oblige*; *life, ice, python*; *alive, writhe,*

rise; time, climb, nine, sign, mile; and (4) before some consonant clusters, as in *find, wild, Christ*.

/ai/ is not found before /č, š, ž, ŋ/ and only rarely before /θ, ǧ/.

Regionalisms

Regional differences in the incidence of /ai/ are rare. BE usually has /ai/ in *either, neither*, a pronunciation heard in America only in the seaboard cities from Boston to Baltimore. The suffixes *-ile*, as in *hostile, docile*, and *-ization*, as in *civilization*, have /ai/ in BE, /ɪ/ in AE. *Paradigm* has /ai/ in BE, /ɪ ~ ai/ in AE. The suffix *-ine*, as in *bromine, iodine*, varies between /aɪ/ and /ɪ ~ i/ both in England and in America.

Alternation

In some morphemes /ai/ alternates with /ɪ/, reflecting the ME alternation /ī ~ i/, as in *wise ~ wisdom, Christ ~ Christmas, bile ~ bileous, Bible ~ biblical, line ~ lineage, benign ~ benignant, sign ~ signal, transcribe ~ transcription, saline ~ salinity, Anglicize ~ Anglicism*. In others, stressed /ai/ alternates with weakly stressed or unstressed /i/, as in *variety ~ vary, satiety ~ satiate, bronchitis ~ bronchial*, or with unstressed /ɜ ~ ə/, as in *admire ~ admiration, shire ~ Berkshire*. In *sight ~ see* it alternates with /i/.

Homophones

The homophones *might = mite, plight* (pledge) *= plight* (predicament), *right = rite, sight = site, wright = rite* result from the merging of the sequence /ix/ with /ī/ in early MnE. Older homophones are: *die = dye, lie = lye, sty = stye, light* (illumination) *= light* (not heavy), *mine* n. *= mine* pron., *sleight = slight*.

History

The two chief sources of the phoneme /ai/ are the ME long high-front vowel /ī/ and the ME sequence *igh* /ix/.

ME /ī/, in turn, has a number of different antecedents, as in the following examples: *dike, life, rise* (OE /ī/); *child, climb, find*, (OE /ī/, from earlier /i/); *mile, wine* (OE /ī/, from L); *Viking* (ON /ī/); *fire, hide, mice* (OE /ȳ/); *kind, mind* (OE /ȳ/, from earlier /y/); *mire, sky* (ON /ȳ/); *Friday, nine, twice* (OE /ĭg/); *buy, dry, rye* (OE / y̆g/); *eye, fly, tie, high* (OA /ēg/); *bribe, cry, dime, guile, isle* (OF /i/); *define, diet, divine* (L /ĭ/ or OF /i/); *choir, entire, friar, umpire, dice* (late ME /ī/ for earlier /ę̄/, from OF /e, ie/).

ME *igh* /ix/, which merged with /ī/ c1500, also comes from several sources, as in *bright, knight, might* (OE /ih/); *light* adj., *tight* (OE /īh/); *flight, wright* (OE /yh/); *light* n., *height* (OA /ēh/); *sleight* (ON ǒg).

In the many words taken into English from Latin (or Greek) from the 16. century onward, /ai/ is a spelling pronunciation used in the teaching of Latin in England, as in *bile, bison, climax, idea, dilute, hypothesis, idyllic, kinetic, neophyte*, and in *fungi, alibi, a priori, vide*.

The foreign pronunciation (and spelling) is retained in some words adopted from various languages in recent times, as in *deictic, seismic, eiderdown, geyser, Heidelberg, Leyden, Cairo, Hawaii*.

Spelling

The spelling of /ai/ is *i, ie, i-e* or *y, ye, y-e*, except in words that had *igh* in ME. In ME and early MnE, *i* and *y* were used interchangeably in all positions, but *i* is now not written at the end of a word, except in such Latin expressions as *alibi, fungi* and in the pronoun *I*.

In detail, the modern spellings are: (1) *i*, as in *bind, child, climb, Friday, icicle, spider, friar, riot, science* and *drier, driest*; (2) the digraph *ie*, in final position and in inflected forms of words ending in /ai/, as in *die, lie, tie, vie* and *dies, died, skies*; (3) the split digraph *i-e*, as in *bite, dive, define, price, oblige, Bible*; (4) *y*, in most words ending in /ai/ and some derivatives, as in *by, why, dry, fly, sky* and *flying, trying*; also in words taken from Greek, as *dynamic, hydrogen, hyper-, hypo-*; (5) the digraph *ye*, as in *dye, lye, stye, good bye*, to distinguish them from *die, lie, sty, by*; but also in *rye*; (6) the split digraph *y-e*, only in words from Greek, as in *cycle, neophyte, type*; (7) *igh* (*eigh*) in words that had *igh* in ME, as in *high, nigh, sigh, thigh* and *flight, might, night, right, height, sleight*.

Exceptional and foreign spellings of /ai/ occur in the following words: *eye, aye, buy, either, neither* (BE), *eider, deictic, seismic, geyser, sign, malign, viscount, isle, island, aisle, choir, indict, Cairo, Hawaii*.

14.4 The Free Vowel /ɔi/

Articulation

The phoneme /ɔi/ is an upgliding diphthong starting in raised low-back position [ɔ] and gliding to or toward high-back [ɪ]. The lips are more or less rounded at the beginning. This is the usual pronunciation in BE and in AE. In most of the South and the South Midland of America, /ɔi/ is a 'slow' diphthong, [ɔ·ɛ], with but a brief upglide. In American folk speech it is frequently replaced by /ai/, as in *joint, poison*.

Distribution

The phoneme /ɔi/ occurs (1) at the end of words and morphemes, as in *boy, coy, joy, toy* and *buoyant, employer, royal, voyage*; and (2) before vowels, as in *foyer, oyez, Boyer* (surname). It is common before consonants articulated with the tip or blade of the tongue, as in *exploit, void, choice, foist, noise, join, point, boil, oil*. It does not occur before other consonants, except in *coif, boycott, troika*.

History

/ɔi/ is the only foreign vowel phoneme in English. It was introduced from OF during the ME period, rendering OF /ǫi/, as in *annoy, choice, coif, joy, noise*; CF /ǫi/ or NF /ui/, as in *boil, coin, join, poison, soil*; and CF /ǫi/ from earlier /ei/, as in *coy, exploit, royal*.

In early MnE /ɔi/ was in part replaced by /ai/, so that from c1550 to 1750 some poets rime *foil* with *file*, *oil* with *isle*, *point* with *pint*. After 1750, /ɔi/ was restored in cultivated use, presumably on the basis of the spelling, but /ai/ persists extensively in folk speech on both sides of the Atlantic. During this period of vacillation, /ɔi/ was introduced in *boil* (swelling), *groin* (part of the body), *hoist*, and *joist*, which earlier had /ai/ from ME /ī/.

In *doit, foist, loiter, toy*, introduced from Dutch into late ME or early MnE, /ɔi/ takes the place of Du. *ui, eu*. In *foyer, voile*, recently taken from French, /ɔi/ is a spelling pronunciation, as also in Russian *troika*. /ɔi/ occurs in the surnames *Floyd, Lloyd, Boyer* (Pa. Ger.), and in *boycott, doily*, which are derived from surnames. *Boy*, attested as early as 1300, corresponds to Frisian *boi*, but its exact provenance is not clear.

Spelling

The spelling *oi* is now used only before consonants, as in *join, soil, choice, cloister, poison*. At the end of words and morphemes, *oy*, is regularly written, as in *boy, boys, annoy, annoys, annoyed, employment, royal, voyage*; also before vowels, as in *foyer, oyer, oyez*. Before consonants, *oy* appears only in *oyster* and in such surnames as *Lloyd, Boycott*.

14.5 The Free Vowel /aʊ/

Articulation

In BE, the phoneme /aʊ/ starts in low-front or low-central position and glides to or toward high-back [ʊ]. Before /ə/, as in *flower, power*, the upglide is briefer or may be arrested.

In America, the North and the North Midland are in agreement with BE, and so is South Carolina with adjoining sections of the South Atlantic coast. Elsewhere in the South and the South Midland, the articulation of /aʊ/ is very different. Finally and before voiced consonants, as in *now, loud, down, houses*, the 'slow' diaphone [æ·ʊ] has general currency on all social levels. Before voiceless consonants, as in *out, south, house*, Viginia with adjoining parts of Maryland and North Carolina has a 'fast' allophone [əu], beginning in mid-central position; coastal South Carolina a somewhat less extreme [ʋu]; other sections of the South and all of the South Midland [æu ~ æ·ʋ].

Distribution

The phoneme /ʌu/ occurs at the end of words and morphemes, as in *now, bough, vow, allow, cowpen, bowing, prowess, allowance*, and before unstressed /ə ~ ɪ/ and /ɜ ~ ə/ in the morpheme words *bowel, towel, trowel, rowen* and *our, flower*. Before consonants its incidence is severly restricted. In the native vocabulary it occurs only before tip and blade consonants, as in *out, loud, mouth, mouths, house, houses, down, found, owl*. In words taken from French it appears in the same positions, as in *doubt, proud, oust, spouse, carouse, crown, counsel*, but also before /č, ǧ/, as in *couch, pouch, gouge*. AE *ouch!* and *grouch* (an affective variant of *grutch, grudge*), both recent, exhibit the sequence /ʌuč/ of words taken from French. In the surname *Cowper*, /ʌu/ beside /u/ is a spelling pronunciation.

Alternation

In some morphemes the phoneme /ʌu/ alternates with /ʌ/, as in *south ~ southern, out ~ utmost, utter, house ~ husband, found, foundation ~ fundament, abound ~ abundant*.

Homophones

Phonemic changes and adoption from foreign languages have produced such homophones as the following: *bow* v. = *bough*, *sow* n. = *sough* v., *foul* = *fowl*, *bound* n. = *bound* v., *count* n. = *count* v., *cow* n. = *cow* v., *down* (hill) = *down* (feather) = *down* adv., *hour* = *our*, *flower* = *flour*.

History

The phoneme /ʌu/ is largely derived from the ME long high-back vowel /ū/, usually spelled with the French digraph *ou* after 1300.

Examples from the native vocabulary are: *now, house, out, down, bound, hound* (OE /ū/); *down* (feathers) (ON /ū/); *bow* v., *sow* n., *fowl*, (OE /ŭg/); *cow* v. (ON /ūg/); *bow, plow, slough* (OE /ōg/); *bow* (of ship) (ON /ōg/).

ME /ū/ took the place of the French high-back vowel (which did not have phonemic length), as in *vow, allow, doubt, couch, spouse, power* (OF *ou*); *count, crown, counsel, round* (AF *ou* before *n*, corresponding to CF *o*); *crouch, oust, pouch* (AF *ou*).

It should be noted that ME /ū/ was not diphthongized to /au/ before labials and velars: hence the positional restrictions of /au/ in MnE.

In *drought* (*drouth*) and *doughty*, MnE /au/ is derived from the ME sequence *ugh* /ux/ before /t/. *Tit-mouse*, for earlier -*mose*, is blended with *mouse*. *Blouse, carouse, gouge*, adopted from French in modern times, and BE *acoustic* from Greek, have /au/ as a spelling pronunciation. The foreign pronunciation is retained in AE *gaucho* and *sauerkraut*.

Spelling

The spellings *ou* and *ow* of ME /ū/ have been retained for MnE /au/. Used interchangeably in ME and early MnE in all positions, *ou* is now written only before consonants, as in *foul, house, loud, south*. The spelling *ow* is now consistently used at the end of words and morphemes, as in *now, vow, cowshed*, and before vowels, as in *towel, allowance*; it is common before *n*, as in *brown, gown, town*, common before *l*, as in *fowl, howl, owl*, occasional before other consonants, as in *browse, crowd, dowdy*.

The spelling *ough* for /au/ is current in *drought* and *doughty*, which had the sequence /ux/ until c1500. *Bough, slough, sough*, and BE *plough* preserve the spelling of the ME uninflected form, though /au/ originated in the disyllabic inflected form, apparently to distinguish them from *bow, slow* and *sow*.

The foreign spelling is retained in *caoutchouc, gaucho*, and *sauerkraut*.

14.6 The Free Vowel /ɑ/

Articulation

In BE, the phoneme /ɑ/ is a rather long unrounded low-back vowel.

In America, where /ɑ/ is confined to dialects in which postvocalic /r/ is lost as such, its articulation varies regionally. In New England it ranges from low-front [a] to low-central [ɑ], in Metropolitan New York from low-central [ɑ] to low-back [ɑ]. In Virginia and South Carolina it is more often low-back than low-central, and along Chesapeake Bay (Baltimore to Norfolk) it is sometimes rounded to [ɒ] or a diphthong [ɑɒ]. All of these variants are relatively long.

Distribution

The phoneme /ɑ/ occurs at the end of words and morphemes, as in *car, far, shah* and *star-ling, star-fish*. It does not occur before vowels, since /r/ is preserved in this position, as in *starry, far out*.

/ɑ/ appears before all consonants, except /h, j, w, ŋ/, though rarely before /z, ž/. Examples are: *sharp, heart, larch, mark*; *barb, hard, large, bargain*; *scarf, staff, hearth, bath, farce, pass, marsh, mustache*; *carve, calve*.

farthing, father, raspberry, massage; *arm, alms, Brahmin, barn, starry, far out.*

/ɑ/ occurs also before the consonant clusters shown in *shaft, clasp, last, ask, sample, aunt, branch, command, dance.*

Regionalisms

The phoneme /ɑ/ occurs only in dialects in which /r/ in the ME sequence /ar/ was lost as such.

In America, /ɑ/ before voiceless fricatives, as in *staff, half, path, glass, father*, and before /n/-clusters, as in *aunt, dance, answer*, is largely restricted to New England. Even in that position it occurs in fewer words than in BE, and appears rather sporadically beside /æ/, except along the coast from Boston northeastward. Outside of New England, the phoneme /ɑ/ is rare in these positions. Some cultured speakers on the Atlantic seaboard prefer /ɑ/ to /æ/, but there is little consistency in their usage.

In BE, usage is unsettled in some words: *masque, sample, telegraph* and the prefix *trans-* have /æ/ beside the more common /ɑ/; *ant, contrast, graph, photograph, Mass* /ɑ/ beside the more usual /æ/; and *gauntlet, jaundice, launch, laundry* /ɑ/ beside the usual /ɔ/.

Alternation

The phoneme /ɑ/ alternates with /æ/ in such pairs as *pass* ~ *pass-age, class* ~ *class-ify.*

Homophones

England and New England have the homophones *arms* = *alms, carve* = *calve, arse* = *ass.*

History

The low free vowel /ɑ/ occurs only in BE and in some coastal dialects of AE. It is of rather recent date.

The most common source of /ɑ/ is the ME sequence /ar/ in preconsonantal and word-final position, as in *sharp, far.* In these positions, ME /ar/ changed to the sequence /ɑə/ in BE, and then became the new phoneme /ɑ/ in the latter part of the 18. century. Whether this change took place independently in certain seaports on the Atlantic coast of America (Boston, New York, Richmond, Charleston, but not Philadelphia) or was adopted from BE, is an open question. MnE /ɑ/ from ME /ar/ occurs before all consonants (see list above, under distribution) and word-finally, as in *star, far.* From word-final position, /ɑ/ has been extended analogically to derivatives, such as *starry* /stɑri/, *tarring* /tɑrɪŋ/, and to prevocalic position within phrases, as in *far out* /fɑr ʌut/, *tar it* /tɑr ɪt/. As a result of these analogical extensions, *star, tar, far*, etc., now have the positional allomorphs /stɑ ~ stɑr-i, fɑ ~ fɑr ʌut/, etc., which are consistently used in BE, in New England, and in Metropolitan New York, but not in the coastal south. That the allomorphs /stɑr, fɑr/ have analogical /ɑ/ is clear, since ME /a/ before intervocalic /r/ regularly became /æ/, as in *carry, marry, harrow*, etc.

It seems safe to assume that the free vowel /ɑ/ became established in BE by the fusion of the sequence /aǝ/, and that certain positional allophones of /æ/ from ME /a/ were aligned under /ɑ/ thereafter, as in *calm, fast, dance*.

In *alms, balm, calm, palm, psalm, qualm*, MnE /ɑ/ from ME /a/ had an allophone [a ~ ɑ] before /l/, which after the loss of /l/ was phonemicized as /ɑ/ in BE and in coastal AE. In *calf, calve, half, halve, salve* the same development took place in BE and to some extent in New England.

Before tautosyllabic fricatives, chiefly voiceless, as in *staff, bath, glass*, the phoneme /æ/ had a lowered and lengthened allophone [a· ~ ɑ·] in 18. century BE, which after the rise of free /ɑ/ was subsumed under it. This change was not observed, or approved, by English lexicographers and orthoepists until the last decades of the 18. century. In America, free /ɑ/ occurs in words of this type only in eastern New England, except for isolated instances in some of the larger cities (as New York, Philadelphia, Richmond).

Among the large number of words in which /ɑ/ is current in England, and to some extent in New England, are the following: *staff, laugh, bath, glass, draft, fast, gasp, ask, master, basket, father, rather, raspberry*.

As before /l/ and before fricatives, so also before the clusters /nt, nd, nč, ns, nz/, BE had a lowered allophone of /æ/ that became phonemized as /ɑ/ in the 18. century. Examples are: *aunt, grant, demand, slander, blanch, branch, chance, dance* and *a'nt* (am not), *can't, shan't, answer*. In America, /ɑ/ occurs in these positions to some extent in New England, especially in *aunt, can't*, and sporadically in Virginia and some of the coastal cities.

Before /m/ and /m/-clusters, /ɑ/ is exceptional. It occurs regularly in BE *example* and, beside /æ/, in *sample*. /ɑ/ beside /e/ in *amen* is church Latin; /ɑ/ beside /æ/ in *ma'am, mam* reflects French *madam*.

There are many irregularities and fluctuations in the incidence of /ɑ/ and /æ/ in words of the type of *staff, path, glass* and *aunt, dance*.

In words introduced from various languages in modern times, /ɑ/ takes the place of foreign [a]-like sounds, as in *Chicago, adagio, Brahmin, eclat, kraal, rajah, roulade, shah, soirée*; and of the foreign sequence /ar/, as in *bazaar, memoir, reservoir*.

Spelling

The two common spellings of BE /ɑ/ reflect its two chief ME sources, /ar/ and /a/, as in the following examples: (1) *sharp, hart, larch, barb*, *hard, large, scarf, parsley, harsh*; (2) *staff, bath, pass, fast, ask, pasture, father* and *chant, branch, demand, dance, translate.*

Other historical spellings are: (3) *al* in *alms, balm, calm, palm, psalm, qualm, calf, calve, half, halve* (ME /al/); (4) *au* in *aunt, gauntlet, jaundice, launch* and *laugh, laughter* (the ME spelling retained, though /ɑ/ is here derived from the ME variant /a/); (5) *ear, er* in *heart, hearth, sergeant* and BE *clerk, Derby, Hertford* (the spelling of the ME variants /ẹr, er/ of /ar/ retained).

Foreign spellings or transliterations of foreign graphs appear in *Brahmin, rajah, shah, bazaar, kraal, memoir, reservoir, soirée.* In *ah!, bah!, hurrah!* the digraph *ah* is used to suggest /ɑ/.

14.7 The Free Vowel /ɔ/

Articulation

The free low-to-mid back vowel /ɔ/ has rather marked regional diaphones.

In BE, /ɔ/ is a well rounded open mid-back vowel. It is prolonged unless followed by unsyllabic /ə̯/.

In America, well rounded long [ɔ·], somewhat lower than in BE, is current from Metropolitan New York southwestward to the Potomac River, in West Virginia, and in the coastal plain of South Carolina and Georgia, to some extent also in eastern Virginia.

Upgliding [ʋɔ] with progressive rounding is common in Virginia, North Carolina, and the southern Appalachians, presumably also to the west of these areas.

The greater part of the North and Pennsylvania west of the Susquehanna River have a rather weakly rounded long [ʋ·], and this articulation seems to predominate also in the Great Lakes area and to the west of it. In eastern New England and parts of western Pennsylvania, where the phoneme /ɔ/ occurs not only in *law, salt*, etc., but also in *rob, hot, rod, rock*, etc., short allophones [ʋ ~ ɑ] are common before plosives.

Distribution

The free vowel /ɔ/ occurs at the end of words and morphemes, as in *draw, law, lawyer, lawful*; and before all consonants except /ǧ, v, ð/, as in *pauper, caught, water, watch, hawk, talk*; *daub, laud, auger*, AE *dog*; *off, trough*, AE *office, author, moth, sauce, loss, caution, wash*; *cause*, AE *nausea*; *traumatic, dawn, gone*, AE *long*; *all, bawl, maul*; *aural;* and AE *for, war, borrow, quarrel.* It is rare before /p, b, č, ž, m/.

/ɔ/ appears both in AE and in BE before the clusters exemplified in *daunt, launch, jaundice, fault, salt, alder, cauldron, false.* In most varieties of AE, it occurs also before the clusters illustrated in *soft, cost, longer* and, following /w/, in *swamp, want, wander*. Moreover, in dialects of AE that preserve postvocalic /r/, the vowel is followed by /r/-clusters, as in *warp, corporal, thwart, short, orchard, fork, orbit, ward, order, orgy, organ, wharf, horse, north, swarm, form, corn*.

It should be pointed out that before /f, θ, s/, as in *off, moth, loss*, and in *gone, /ɒ/* is preferred to /ɔ/ in BE, and that *dog, fog, wash* have only /ɒ/ in BE.

Regionalisms

The chief regional differences in the incidence of the vowel /ɔ/ are pointed out below in the description of its various sources.

In America, the occurrence of /ɔ/ and /ɑ/ before /g/, after /w/, and before intervocalic /r/, as in *log, dog, wash, water, borrow, orange*, is highly erratic, varying not only regionally, but also from word to word.

Homophones

In BE and in the dialect of Metropolitan New York, *law = lore, flaw = floor, laud = lord, bawd = board, sauce = source, fought = fort, fourth = forth, hoarse = horse, mourning = morning, four = for* are homophonous; with some speakers of BE, also *pour = poor, shore = sure*.

In eastern New England, such pairs as the following are homophones: *caught = cot, taught = tot, wrought = rot, stalk = stock*.

History

The chief sources of MnE /ɔ/ are: (1) ME /au/ in all positions, (2) ME /a/ before /l/ and after /w/, and (3) ME /o/ before /r/, voiceless fricatives, and the voiced velars /g, ŋ/.

The ME diphthong /au/ became the monophthong /ɔ/, articulated as [ɔ· ~ ɒ·], in the 16. century. Examples are: *claw, raw, straw, thaw* (OE *aw, ēaw*); *draw, gnaw, maw, saw* n. (OE *ag*); *awe, law* (ON *ag*); *augur, laud, pauper* (L *au*); *cause, autumn, jaundice* (OF *au*); *daunt, launch, vaunt* (AF *au*); *brawn, fawn, pawn* (OF *ăo, ăou*); *auger, crawl, hawk, laundry* (from earlier /av/); *naught, ought, slaughter, taught* (OE *āh, ēah*).

ME /ou/ before the fricative /x/ merged with /au/ in this position c1500, and then shared its development, in *bought, brought, cough, daughter, thought, trough, wrought* (OE *ŏh*).

ME /a/ before tautosyllabic /l/ was diphthongized to /au/ shortly after 1500 and then became /ɔ/, as in *all, fall, salt, alder, chalk, walk* (OE); *call, auk* (ON); *appall, cauldron, false, fault, palsy* (OF).

After /w/, early MnE /æ/ from ME /a/ was backed and rounded and thus fell in with /ɔ/, as in *war, ward, thwart, wharf, swarm, squall*, and in AE *watch, wash, wander, quarrel*.

ME short /o/ before tautosyllabic /r/ remained a rounded open mid-back vowel in MnE, phonemically /ɔ/. In areas where postvocalic /r/ survives in AE, the phoneme /ɔ/ is rather short. When /r/ is lost as such, as in BE and in several coastal dialects of AE, /ɔ/ is long and sometimes followed by unsyllabic /ə/. Examples are: *for, corpse, short, torch, fork, morbid, order, gorge, organ, north, horse, northern, storm, corn*.

Before intersyllabic /r/, as in *borrow, coral, orange, tomorrow*, AE has /ɔ/ beside /ɑ/, BE /ʋ/.

In BE, the phoneme /ɔ/ occurs also in words with ME long back vowels before /r/, as in *boar, board, more* (ME /ọ̄/), *floor, whore* (ME /ọ̄/), and, beside /u ~ o/, in *moor, poor* (ME /ọ̄/), *pure, sure* (ME /iu/). These developments are rather recent and do not occur in AE.

In parts of England, ME short /o/ was lengthened before voiceless fricatives and (though less commonly) before the voiced velars /g, ŋ/, thus falling in with MnE /ɔ/ from ME /au/. In all types of AE that have contrastive /ɔ ≠ ɑ/, as in *laud ≠ rod*, /ɔ/ occurs regularly before tautosyllabic /f, θ, s/, as in *off, soft, broth, loss, frost, foster*; varies with /ɑ/ before intersyllabic /f, s/, as in *office, faucet*; and is more widespread than /ɑ/ before /g, ŋ/, as in *dog, fog, log, long, song, prong*. In BE, which has contrastive /ɔ ≠ ʋ/, the /ɔ/ phoneme is rather common beside /ʋ/ before voiceless fricatives, but does not appear before /g, ŋ/.

In eastern New England and in western Pennsylvania, ME /au/ and /o/ are completely merged in the phoneme /ɔ/, which in these regional dialects might better be represented by a different phonemic symbol, /ʋ/. Here this phoneme appears not only in *law, salt, corn, cough, loss, dog*, etc., but also in *hop, knob, knot, nod, lock*, etc., where other AE dialects have checked /ɑ/ and BE checked /ʋ/.

In *broad* and in AE *gone*, older /o/ from ME /ọ̄/ has been replaced by /ɔ/.

In modern times, /ɔ/ renders L and Gr. *au*, as in *august, autonomy, auxilliary, nautic, nausea, raucous* (in accord with the English school pronunciation of Latin); and [ʋ]-like sounds in words taken from American Indian languages, such as *squash* n., *squaw, Pawnee, Milwaukee*; and from various other languages, as *gauze, ricksha(w), shawl, Warsaw*, AE *boss* (manager). On the analogy of *dog, log*, AE has /ɔ/ in *catalogue, prologue*, words taken from Latin.

Spelling

The great variety of spellings of /ɔ/ in the several regional types of MnE reflects the numerous sources of /ɔ/. The most common graphs are *au, aw, a*, and *o*.

aw and *au* are written in words with ME /au/, as in *awe, draw, hawk, law, lawn, cause, sauce, launch, caution, pause*, and in words introduced in modern times from Latin and various other languages, as *cauliflower*, *pauper, gauze, shawl, squaw*. The spelling *augh* appears in words in which /au/ was followed by *ght* in ME, as *aught, caught, daughter, slaughter*.

The spelling *a* is retained in words in which ME /a/ is followed by /l/ or preceded by /w/, as in *fall, wall, bald, halt, false* and AE *war, ward, wharf, quart, wander, wash*. The spelling *al* was retained after the /l/ was lost in *chalk, talk, walk*, etc.; similarly, the *aul* in *caulk, haulm*.

The ME spelling *o* is retained before voiceless fricatives, as in *off, soft, moth, loss, cost*, before /g, ŋ/, as in AE *dog, long*, and before /r/ in AE *for, horn, horse, storm, orange*, etc.

The split digraph *o-e* appears in AE *gone, one*; the digraph *ou* before /f/ in *cough, trough*; the combination *ough* in *brought, ought, sought, thought, wrought*, where ME /ou/ was followed by /ght/.

The digraph *oa* in *broad* was retained when /o/ from ME /ǭ/ was replaced by /ɔ/.

Digraphs containing *r* occur in BE and in those regional dialects of AE in which ME postvocalic /r/ has been lost. The spelling *or* of the phoneme /ɔ/ appears in these regional types of MnE in words that had short /o/ in ME, as in *for, fork, north, horn, organ*; the spelling *ar*, as in *war, ward, wharf, quart*, where ME /a/ was preceded by /w/. In BE, where ME long back vowels and /ou/ plus /r/ also yielded /ɔ/ or /ɔə̯/, the following additional spellings occur: *oar*, as in *boar, board, roar*; *oor*, as in *door, floor, poor*; *our* in *four, pour*; *ore*, as in *core, more, whore*; *ure*, as in *pure, sure*.

In the prevocalic allomorphs of *for, war, door*, etc., and in the variant pronunciations of such words with unsyllabic /ə̯/ after the /ɔ/, *r* is of course not part of the graph for /ɔ/.

14.8 The Free Vowel /o/

Articulation

The articulation of the free mid-back vowel /o/ varies regionally. In BE it is an upgliding diphthong, starting in a more or less fronted mid-back position, moderately open and weakly rounded, and gliding toward high-back-round. In America, the /o/ is most widely pronounced as an upgliding [oʊ], starting mid-back-close and rather well rounded. The upglide is often very brief. A fronted and rather open beginning, similar to that in BE, has some currency in the Philadelphia area and the upper Ohio valley. Monophthongal [o· ~ o], with an allophonic ingliding [oə] in checked position, is a striking feature of the speech of coastal South Carolina. The regional phonic variants of /o/ are most pronounced in free position, less so in checked position, least under half-stress, as in *sáilbòat, nòtátion*.

Distribution

The free vowel /o/ occurs finally, as in *go, toe, flow, owe, dough, follow, bureau*, and before vowels, as in *going, poet, cooperate.*

It occurs before all consonants, except /ŋ, h, j, w/, as in *hope, boat, poach, oak, folk*; *robe, road, doge, rogue*; *loaf, both, post, notion*; *stove, loathe, nose, possess, erosion*; *home, own*; *hole, foal, roll*; AE *door, hoarse, mourn.*

/o/ is uncommon to rare before /b, ǧ, g, š, ž/, and in these positions confined to words taken from other languages. Before /r ~ ə̣/, as in *hoarse, mourn*, it occurs only in certain regional dialects.

Regionalisms

Regional differences in the incidence of /o/ before /r ~ ə̣/ are widespread. BE has /o/ beside /ɔ/ in *door, more*, etc., and beside /ʊ/ in *poor, sure*, etc. In America, /o/, usually with lowered tongue position, is regular in *door, more*, etc.; but *poor, sure* have /ʊ ~ u/, except in the South. In the New England settlements of the North and in the South, *hoarse, mourning* have /o/ contrasting with /ɔ/ in *horse, morning*; but in a wide belt extending from Metropolitan New York westward through Pennsylvania, this contrast does not exist.

BE usually has /o/ on *process, progress*, AE only /ɑ ~ ɒ/.

Alternation

In some morphemes, the phoneme /o/ alternated with /ɒ, ɑ/ as in *know ~ knowledge, holy ~ holiday, hole ~ hollow, joke ~ jocular, local ~ locative, mode ~ model, node ~ nodule, polite ~ polish, domain ~ dominate, tone ~ tonic, narcosis ~ narcotic, abdomen ~ abdominal, provoke ~ provocative, bureau ~ bureaucracy*; in some with /ai/, as in *abode ~ abide, drove ~ drive, stroke ~ strike.*

In others it alternates with /ɔ, ɒ/, as in *clothe ~ cloth*; with /æ/, as in *holy ~ hallow, clothe ~ clad*; with /ʌ/, as in *no ~ none, nothing*. In weakly stressed syllables it varies prosodically with /ə/, as in *obey, pronounce* and *follow, potato.*

Homophones

The merging of ME /ǭ/ and /ou/ in early MnE produced the homophones *no = know, doe = dough, groan = grown, soul = sole, toe = tow* v.

Lowering of /u ~ ʊ/ before /r ~ ə̣/ in some varieties of English results in homophonous *boor = boa   poor = pore, sure = shore.*

Other homophones, some ME and others recent, are: *hole = whole, road = rode, rose* n. = *rose* v., *moat = mote, loan = lone*, AE *loaf* n. = *loaf* v.

History

The three chief sources of MnE /o/ are ME long open /ǫ/, the ME diphthong /ou/, and ME short /o/ before /l/, as illustrated below.

(1) ME /ǫ/, from various sources: *go, toe, road, loaf, ghost, foam, lore, more* (OE *ā*); *old, cold, comb* (Anglian *ā*); *stove, stolen, foal, torn, before* (OE *o*); *note, poach, robe, pose, store, story, forge* (OF *o*).

(2) ME /ou/, from several sources: *know, snow* (OE *āw*); *owe, dough* (OE *āg*); *flow, grow* (OE *ōw*); *bow* (weapon), *tow* v. (OE *og*).

(3) ME /o/ before /l/, which in this position became a diphthong /ou/ in early MnE: *bowl* (dish), *knoll, mole* (animal), *colt, molten*; with later loss of /l/, *folk, yolk*.

Before /r ~ ǝ/, MnE /o/ is also derived from ME long close /ọ/, as in *floor, whore* and in regional *moor, poor*; and from the ME high-back vowels, as in regional *mourn, course, coarse, court, pour*.

The vowel /o/ also occurs in words adopted from various languages in modern times, as in *notion, doge, brogue, chorus*.

The merging of ME long open /ǫ/, as in *no*, and the ME diphthong /ou/, as in *know*, took place in the 16. century, well before Shakespeare's time and the planting of the first American colonies. On the evidence of the modern dialects of England, the merging was restricted to the London area (the Home Counties). Elsewhere, ME /ǫ/ and /ou/ usually remained distinct, the former represented by ingliding [oᵊ ~ uᵊ], the latter by upgliding [ou ~ ɔu ~ ʌu]. In America the two phonemes are generally merged, but in New England the old distinction survives to some extent, as in *stone* /stǝn/ ≠ *grown* /gron/. See the checked vowel /ɵ/.

Spelling

The most common spellings of /o/ are *o* ~ *o-e*, *oa*, and *ow*.

The digraph *ow* is used in native words that had the diphthong /ou/ in ME, as in *flow, grow, know, snow, snowing* and *follow, hollow*.

The digraph *oa*, replacing earlier *o* ~ *o-e* c1600 (to contrast it with *oo* /u/), occurs in some words that had /ǫ/ in ME, as in *foal, foam, road, hoarse* (native) and *coat, poach* (OF).

By far the most common spelling of /o/ from ME /ǫ/ is the split digraph *o-e*, as in *stone, stove, more* (native) and *note, robe, pose* (OF). A single *o* is written before consonant clusters, as in *old, ghost*, and before an inter-syllabic consonant, as in *stolen, story, posing*.

Spellings reflecting a variety of other sources of MnE /o/ appear in *knoll, colt*; *folk, yolk*; *door, floor* and regional *moor, poor*; and *course, mourn, pour*.

Rare spellings of /o/ appear in native *go, doe, toe, owe, dough, though*, BE *mould, moult*, and in foreign *mauve, chauvinism, chateau, bureau*.

14.9 The Free Vowel /u/

Articulation

In BE, the free rounded high-back vowel /u/ is articulated either as a monophthongal [u·] or as an upgliding [uw]. After /j/, as in *few, music, cube*, it is more or less fronted.

Monophthongal and upgliding variants of /u/ occur side by side in AE, the length of the monophthong and the extent of the upglide depending largely on prosodic factors. High-back [u· ~ ʊu ~ uw] is usual in the North, high-central [ʉ· ~ ʊʉ] in large parts of the South and the South Midland, an intermediate variety in the North Midland (as in Metropolitan New York and Philadelphia). In coastal South Carolina, ingliding [ʉə] varies with [ʉ·] in checked position, as in *noon, tooth.*

Under half-stress or weak stress, /u/ varies positionally. Finally, as in *argue, igloo, value, virtue, voodoo*, it is articulated either as a short upgliding diphthong or as a short monophthong; medially as a short [u ~ ʊ], as in *argument, valuable, usual*. When the syllable is unstressed it is replaced by /ə/, as in *argument, reputation*, before a vowel by /w/, as in *usually, visually.*

Distribution

The vowel /u/ occurs at the end of words and morphemes, as in *do, few, true, curfew, value, dual, visual*, and before all consonants, except /ŋ, j, w/, as in *droop, mute, mooch, duke; tube, food, huge, fugue; roof, tooth, goose, roost, douche; move, smooth, fuse, fusion, Hoosier; doom, soon, wound, cool, sure*. It is rare before /č, ǧ, g, š, ð/.

Regionalisms

In BE, there is little variation in the incidence of /u/ before consonants other than /m/. *Broom, room* have checked /ʊ/ more commonly than free /u/, *doom, bloom* regularly /u/.

In America, usage varies markedly in certain words before the labials /p, f, m/ and before /t/. Thus *coop, cooper, hoop* have predominantly /u/ in the North and the North Midland, but /ʊ/ in the South and the South Midland; *roof* usually has /u/, but /ʊ/ predominates in the North; *hoof*, on the other hand, has /ʊ/, except in Pennsylvania; *broom, room* have /u/, except for New England and Virginia. In *root*, /u/ predominates, but the North has also /ʊ/; in *soot*, on the other hand, /u/ is decidedly uncommon.

Before /r ~ ə̣/, as in *poor, sure*, the American North and North Midland have a high-back vowel, /u ~ ʊ/, the South and the South Midland usually the mid-back vowel /o/. In BE, /u/ does not occur in this position; there *poor, sure* end in /ʊə̣ ~ oə̣ ~ ɔə̣ ~ ɔ/.

AE has /u/ in *acoustic*, BE /au/. *Buoy, buoyancy, buoyant* sometimes have the sequence /ui/ in America, in England only /ɔi/.

Alternation

/u/ alternates with other vowels in a number of morphemes: with
/a ~ ʋ/ in *food* ~ *fodder*, *goose* ~ *gosling*, *bloom* ~ *blossom*, *good* ~ *god-
father*; with /ʌ/ in *punitive* ~ *punish*, *youth* ~ *young*; with /au/ in
dubious ~ *doubt*; with /ə/ in *repute* ~ *reputation*, *refute* ~ *refutation*,
luxurious ~ *luxury*, *argue* ~ *argument*. Besides, /w/ often takes the
place of /u/ in *usually*, *visually*, etc.

Homophones

The following words have been homophonous since ME times: *too*,
to = *two*, *boot* (profit) = *boot* (shoe), *blew* = *blue*, *dew* = *due*, *hew* = *hue*,
mew n. = *mew* v., *yew* = *ewe*. The homophones *boom* (of ship) = *boom* v.,
AE *stoop* (porch) = *stoop* v., *gnu* = *new* are more recent.

History

MnE /u/ has five ME sources: (1) The long close mid-back vowel /ọ̄/,
which was raised to high-back /u/ in the latter part of the 15. century.

(2) The decrescendo diphthong /iu/ (from earlier /iu, ęu/) in the native
vocabulary and as a substitute for the rounded high-front vowel /ǘ/
of OF. The diphthong /iu/ became the sequence /ju/ in early MnE. The
sequence /ju/ is preserved initially and after labials, velars, and /h/, as
in *yew*, *use*, *pure*, *bugle*, *few*, *mute*, *cure*, *argue*, *hue*. After /č, ǧ, l, r/, the
consonant /j/ is now generally lost, as in *chew*, *June*, *blue*, *true*; after
/t, d, n/, as in *Tuesday*, *dew*, *new*, also, in some sections of America.
See under /j/.

(3) ME /ęu/, which coalesced with ME /iu/ in early MnE and then
shared its development to /ju ~ u/.

/4/ The ME long high-back vowel /ū/ before labials and after /w/ and
/j/, which in other positions became MnE /au/.

(5) The ME sequence /ux/, only in *through*.

Examples of these sources are:

(1) ME /ọ̄/ stands back of MnE /u/ in such words as *cool*, *do*, *doom*,
goose, *moon*, *school*, *tooth* (OE ō); *boon*, *booth* (ON ō); *two*, *who*, *womb*
(OE ā after w); *choose*, *shoot* (OE ēo); *boot*, *fool*, *move*, *spool* (OF o after
labials).

(2) MnE /ju ~ u/ from ME /iu/ occur in such words as *hue*, *new*, *Tuesday*,
yew, *you*, *brew*, *chew*, *knew*, *true* (OE īw, ēow); *argue*, *blue*, *bugle*, *deuce*,
due, *fruit*, *June*, *sue*, *use*, *view* (OF u, ui, eu, ieu).

(3) ME /ęu/ is the source of MnE /ju ~ u/ in *ewe*, *spew*, *strew*, *dew*, *few*,
hew, *shrewd*, *mew* (gull), *lewd* (OE ēow, ēaw, ǣw).

(4) ME /ū/ survives as /u/ before labials, as in *room, stoop* (OE *ū*), *droop* (ON *ū*), *croup, whoop* (OF *ou*), *tomb* (AF *u*); after /w/ in *wound* (OE *ū*), *swoon, woo* (OE *ōg*); and after /j/ in *youth* (OE *ug*).

In words adopted in modern times, /u/ takes the place of foreign high-back vowels, as in *gruesome, uncouth* (Scottish); *group, rouge, routine, soup* (French); *boom, boor, groove, sloop,* AE *spook, stoop* (Dutch); *poodle* (German); *canoe, gnu, Hindu, igloo, loot, raccoon, taboo, typhoon, voodoo* (various languages).

In the suffix *-oon*, as in *balloon, buffoon, dragoon,* /un/ renders the French nasal vowel /õ/. AE *butte* /bjut/ is either a spelling pronunciation of French *butte* or else /ju/ was substituted for the French /y/ sound.

In words taken from Latin and Greek in modern times, /ju ~ u/ is a spelling pronunciation, as in *cube, enthusiasm, nutrition, tube, visual, feudal, neutral, Europe, Teutonic* (Latin); *eulogy, euphony, heuristic, neural, pneumatic* (Greek). This spelling pronunciation is also used in *manoeuver* (French), and perhaps in *cruise, cruiser* (Dutch or/and Spanish).

Spelling

The phoneme /u/ has a dozen different spellings. These fall into two groups: *o* or a digraph containing *o*; *u, w* or a digraph containing *u, w*.

The *o* spellings reflect ME /ō/ and /ū/, the former spelled *o, oo* in ME, the latter *ou*. The *u, w* spellings occur in words that had the diphthongs /iu/ or /eu/ in ME. It should be noted that the *u, w* spellings represent not only the vowel /u/ in MnE, but also the sequence /ju/, as in *ewe, few, hue, music*.

In detail, the spellings of MnE /u/ are:

(1) *oo* is written in the numerous words that had /ō/ in ME, as in *boon, boot, cool, fool, moon, soon, too, tooth*; in some words with unshifted ME /ū/, as *room, stoop, swoon, woo* (replacing *ou* by c1500); and in words adopted in modern times, as in *boom, loot, sloop, poodle, stoop, taboo, dragoon*.

(2) *o* appears in *do, to, two, who, womb* (ME /ō/), the split digraph *o-e* in *chose, lose, move, prove, approve* (ME /ō/), *oe* in *shoe* (ME /ō/) and *canoe* (c1600).

(3) *ou* occurs in *uncouth, wound, you, youth* (ME /ū/, written *ou*), and in some words taken from French in modern times, as *group, rouge, soup*.

(4) *ew* is written in words that had /iu/ or /eu/ in ME, usually so in native words, as *chew, few, hew, knew, yew, steward, lewd, shrewd*, but also in some words from OF, as *crew, Jew, pew, nephew, ewer, sewer, pewter*.

(5) *u, ue,* and *u-e* appear chiefly in words taken from OF, in which ME /iu/ took the place of various OF vowels and diphthongs. Examples are: *cruel, duty, ruin; blue, due, argue; bugle, duke, June, use*. This French

spelling replaced earlier *eu, ew* in some native words, as in *truth, ruthless, hue, rue, true, Tuesday, yule*. In words taken from Latin, the Latin *u* spelling is regularly retained, as in *cube, fluent, nutrition, visual*.

(6) Less common and occasional spellings are: *ui* in *fruit, nuisance, pursuit* (OF *ui*) and in *bruise, juice, recruit, sluice* (OF *u*); *ieu, iew* in *adieu, lieu,* AE *lieutenant, view* (OF *ieu*); *eu* in *deuce* (OF *eu*); *eau* in *beauty* (OF *eau*). In all these words, ME had /iu/.

(7) In words taken from Latin and Greek in modern times, the spelling *eu* is retained, as in *feudal, neuter, Europe, Teutonic* and *eulogy, neutral, pneumatic*. A Scottish spelling appears in *sleuth, sleuthhound* (ME /ọ̄/).

(8) Unique spellings of /u/ occur in *through* (which formerly ended in /ux/), and in *manoeuver* (French).

14.10 The Free Vowel /ɜ/

Articulation

In BE the phoneme /ɜ/, as in *fur, learn*, is articulated as a long unrounded mid-central vowel [ɜ·], without lateral constriction.

In America, the most widely used variant of /ɜ/ is a more or less 'constricted' mid-central [ɜʳ] sound, in which the tongue is withdrawn, humped up in the back, and laterally constricted. Not infrequently, there is an upglide with progressive constriction of the tongue. The tip of the tongue may be low or point at the gums.

Unconstricted /ɜ/ is used in America in several areas along the Atlantic coast and the Gulf of Mexico: eastern New England, Metropolitan New York, eastern Virginia, and an extensive belt extending from South Carolina westward as far as eastern Texas and up the Mississippi Valley into Tennessee and Arkansas. These areas contain about one third of the population of the United States.

In New England /ɜ/ is a fairly close mid-central vowel, not infrequently somewhat rounded. Metropolitan New York has a more open [ɜ·] sound beside diphthongal [ɜɪ]. Virginians usually retain weak constriction, but also use unconstricted [ɜ·]. From South Carolina westward diphthongal [ɜɪ] predominates, unconstricted and often slightly rounded.

Distribution

The phoneme /ɜ/ occurs at the end of words and morphemes, as in *fur, sir, wor-ship, mer-maid, pur-pose*. Before vowels it appears only in AE, as in *furry* /fɜ-i/, *stirring* /stɜ-ɪŋ/, *hurry* /hɜ-i/, *furrow* /fɜ-o/.

/ɜ/ occurs before all consonants except /h, ŋ, j, w/, though rarely before /ð, z, ž/, as in *chirp, dirt, church, work*; *herb, bird, urge, burgher*; *turf, earth, worse, assertion*; *curve, further, furze,* AE *aversion*; *worm, burn, earl*; BE *furry* /fɜri/, *stirring, stir it.*

/ɜ/ is found only before one cluster, /st/, as in *burst, thirst.*

Regionalisms

In addition to the regional differences in the articulation of the phoneme /ɜ/, there are some regional differences in its incidence.

Wherever constricted /ɜ/ is current in America, this phoneme occurs also in unstressed syllables, as in *father* /fáðə/, *further* /fɜ́ðə/, *perform* /pɜfórm/, *different* /dífɜ-ənt ~ dífrənt/. Here BE and the coastal varieties of AE have /ə/.

Except for the coastal dialects, AE has the phoneme /ɜ/ in *hurry, furrow, squirrel*, BE and coastal AE the sequences /ʌr, ɪr/.

BE has /jɜ/ as a variant of /ɪə/ in *fear, here*, some Southern and South Midland American dialects in *beard, ear, hear.*

Amateur, chauffeur usually end in stressed /ɜ/ in BE; Americans say /ǽməčur, -čɜ/ and /šófɜ, -ə/.

AE has /ɜ/ in *clerk, Berkshire, Derby*, where BE has /ɑ/.

Alternation

The alternations /ɜ ~ ɛr/, as in *érr ~ érr-or, de-tér ~ de-térr-ent*, and /ɜ ~ ər/, as in *pre-fér ~ pré-fer-ence, de-fér ~ déference*, occur in all types of English.

Alternation of /ɜ/ with /ɜr/, as in *fur ~ furr-y, stir ~ stirr-ing, prefer ~ prefer it* is regular in BE and some coastal dialects of AE. BE also has the alternation /ɜ ~ ʌr/, as in *in-cur ~ curr-ency, de-mur ~ de-murr-er* (objection).

BE and coastal AE have prosodic allomorphs in *her* /hɜ́ ~ hə/, *were* /wɜ́ ~ wə/ and positional allomorphs in *fur* /fɜ/ ~ *furry* /fɜr-i/, *stir* /stɜ/ ~ *stirring* /stɜr-ɪŋ/, etc. In all such cases, other varieties of AE have allophones of /ɜ/.

Homophones

The merging of the ME sequences /ir, ur, er/ in MnE /ɜ/ has produced some homophones, as *fir = fur, turn = tern, purr = per*, and the prefixes of *per-fume = pur-pose*, etc.

History

The phoneme /ɜ/ is derived from the sequence /ʌr/ in which the ME sequences /ir, ur, er/ had been merged in early MnE. The later change of /ʌr/ to /ɜ/ in preconsonantal and in phrase-final position, is parallel to the change of /ɑr/ via /ɑə/ to /ɑ/ in the same positions. It is important to note that the sequence /ɜr/ survives before vowels in BE and in coastal

AE, as in *furry, stirring*. The merging of ME /ir, ur, er/ in /ʌr/ took place
before Shakespeare's time, well before the first English colonies were
established in America.

In BE and in coastal AE, the early MnE sequence /ʌr/, passing through
the stage /ʌə/, became an unconstricted vowel /ɜ/. In other types of AE,
the articulation of the velarized /r/ was preserved and the preceding /ʌ/
more or less assimilated to it, so that the vowel is constricted. These
changes probably occurred in the latter part of the 18. century, and at
least to some extent independently in England and in America.

In detail, the sources of MnE /ɜ/ are as follows:

(1) ME /ur/, as in *curse, furlong, further, turf* (OE *ur*); *worm, worse*,
AE *worry* (OE *yr*); *work, world, worth* (OE *eor*); *curtain, courtesy, fur*,
journey, nourish, nurse, sirloin (OF *or, our, ur*).

(2) ME /ir/, as in *birch, chirp, church, churn, murky, swirl* (OE *ir*);
bird, dirt, third, thirty (OE *ri*); *burden, first, furze, hurdle, kernel, shirt*,
thirst (OE *yr*); *circuit, sir*, AE *squirrel* (OF *ir*); *circum-, dirge, firmament*,
virgin (L *ir*).

(3) ME /er/, as in *burn, burst, churl, earl, earnest, earth, herd, learn*,
yearn (OE *eor*); *dearth, early, heard*, unstressed *were* (OE *ēor, ǣr, ēr*);
certain, clergy, hearse, rehearse, herb, pearl (OF *er*); *determine, fervor* (L *er*).

In modern times, /ɜ/ or a preceding stage of its development was
introduced in words taken from Latin, as *averse, concern, deter, urban*,
urge, virgule; from French, as *burse, colonel, furniture* and BE *amateur*,
chauffeur; and from various other languages, as in *burgher, curl, Hamburg*,
Heidelberg, and AE *curry, hurricane*.

Spelling

The spelling reflects to some extent the three ME sources of the
phoneme /ɜ/.

(1) The spellings *ur, our, or* are current in words that had /ur/ in ME,
as in *curse, turf, fur, curtain, nurse, journey, nourish, work, worth*. After
the merging of ME /ir/ and /er/ with /ur/, the digraph *ur* replaced *ir*
in *burden, church, churn, furze, hurdle* and *er* in *burn, burst, churl*.

(2) The ME spelling *ir* survives in *bird, birch, birth, circuit, dirge, fir*,
firmament, first, thirst, etc., and has replaced *ur* in *sirloin*.

(3) The ME spelling *er* appears almost exclusively in words taken from
Old French and Latin, as in *clergy, concern, confer, determine, err, fervor*,
etc. Of native words, only *fern, herd, herdsman, were* seem to preserve
the *er* spelling. In *kernel, er* replaced earlier *ir, ur, or*.

In words adopted from European languages in modern times, the
foreign spelling is generally preserved, as in *urge, curl, circulate, virgule*,

averse, deter. In *colonel*, earlier also *coronel*, the spelling of one French variant and the pronunciation of the other are now in use.

15. The Unstressed Free Vowel /ə/

Articulation

In articulating the vowel /ə/, the relaxed tongue occupies a mid-central position, which varies somewhat with the adjoining phonemes.

Distribution

The vowel /ə/ occurs in checked as well as in free position, appearing initially, medially, and finally, but not before vowels. It is confined to unstressed syllables.

Initially, /ə/ occurs in *arise, again, account, apply, oppose*, etc.; finally, in *America, Martha, sulpha*, etc., in BE and coastal AE also in *father, offer*, etc. It is frequent before final and medial consonants, as in *abbot, kingdom, lonesome, human, atlas, stadium, bonus, real*, etc., and *alphabet, acrobat, regular, capable, possible, legacy*, etc.

Regionalism

The incidence of /ə/ before /s, z, t, d, ğ, č/ varies regionally in America, as in *menace, careless, kindness, princess, longest, houses, rises, bucket, bracelet, senate, minute, hated, village, sausage, spinach*. /ə/ is usual in the Midland (from Metropolitan New York westward through Pennsylvania and from there southward in the Appalachians), /ɪ/, articulated as a lowered high-central [ɨ], in New England and in the coastal South.

In all such cases, Standard BE has /ɪ/; but /ə/ is common in the present folk dialects of the southwest of England and of East Anglia.

In BE and those dialects of AE in which postvocalic /r/ is not preserved (see under /r/), /ə/ occurs also as the reflex of earlier /ər/, as in *father, tránsfer, fuller, doctor, nature, bitterness, liberty, energy, bastard, covert,* and unstressed *her, for, or.* When *father, nature, her*, etc., are followed in the same phrase by a vowel, as in *father and mother, the nature of man, her own opinion*, they end in /ər/. In all such words, those dialects of AE in which postvocalic /r/ survives, have the vowel /ɜ/, as in *further* /fɜ́ðɜ/.

Alternation

The vowel /ə/, confined to unstressed syllables, occurs as a prosodically conditioned alternant of all stressed vowels, with the possible exception of /ʌu/, as illustrated in the following examples: *vehícular* ~ *véhicle, académic* ~ *acádemy, plurálity* ~ *plúral, methódic* ~ *méthod, condúct* ~ *cónduct, full* ~ *fáithful*, AE *blasphéme* ~ *blásphemy*, AE *orátion* ~ *órator,*

repúte ~ *rèputátion, melódious* ~ *mélody, áuthor* ~ *authórity,* AE *óffice* ~
offícial, AE *transfér* ~ *tránsfer, admíre* ~ *àdmirátion.*

The first word of each pair has (or can have) /ə/, the second a stressed
full vowel. Vowel qualities intermediate between /ə/ and the several
full vowels are common under weak stress as distinct from unstress, as
in *rèpûtátion* ~ *rèputátion.* Numerous examples of /ə/ as a stress-conditioned alternate are given under the several stressed vowels.

In words adopted from OF, L, and Gr., /ə/ alternates with full vowels
in various prefixes, as in *accept* ~ *acceptation, addition* ~ *additive,*
analogy ~ *analogue, apply* ~ *applicable, catalysis* ~ *catalize, compress* v.
~ *compress* n., *conduct* v. ~ *conduct* n., *correct* ~ *corrigible, object* v. ~
object n., *oppose* ~ *opposite, perfect* v. ~ *perfect* adj., *produce* ~ *product,*
subject v. ~ *subject* n., *suspect* v. ~ *suspect* adj.

Words that are frequently unstressed in the sentence have /ə/ beside
the stressed full vowel, as the auxiliary verbs *can, could, must, should,*
would, have, has, had, was, do; the pronouns *him, them, us, you*; the
adverbs *as, than, so, just, up*; the prepositions *at, from, of, to, into*; and
the conjunctions *and, that.*

In some compounds, /ə/ appears as an alternant of a full vowel in the
unstressed final element, as in *Frenchman, woman, breakfast, Nottingham,*
Christmas, Plymouth, walnut, Washington.

Final /əl, ən/ vary prosodically with syllabic [ḷ, ṇ], as in *able, level,*
evil, vowel, careful and *chicken, seven, often, nation.* The variation /ən/ ~ [ṇ]
occurs also in the suffixes *-ance, -ant, -ence, -ent, -ment,* as in *assistance,*
pleasant, prudence, prudent, fragment, and in the final elements of *Boston,*
Johnson, motorman. Syllabic [ḷ] and [ṇ] are best treated as positional
variants of the resonants /l, n/.

When the sequences /əl, ən/ are followed by a vowel, as in *leveling,*
carefully, national, rationally, they may be reduced to the consonants /l, n/.
Similarly, the sequence /ər/ before a vowel, as in *average, different,*
victory, BE *dormitory, strawberry,* may be prosodically shortened to /r/.

History

MnE /ə/ is derived from nearly all the vowels, long and short, of ME,
including medial /ə/. In general, one can say that any vowel that came
to be unstressed either in ME or in MnE tended to be replaced by /ə/.

An exception to this general rule is found in the treatment of old
front vowels before /s, z, t, d, ǧ, č/, as in *careless, houses, closet, hated,*
cabbage, spinach, in BE and in some dialects of AE, where the unstressed
allophone of /ɪ/, is current. See above under regionalisms.

On the other hand, BE and those coastal dialects of AE in which /r/
is preserved only before vowels, have final and preconsonantal /ə/ from
early MnE /ər/, as in *mother, doctor, creature, liberty, perceive, forgive,*

pursue. Here the other AE dialects have the unstressed allophone of /ɜ/, as in *murder* /mə́dɜ/.

Spelling

Owing to the fact that MnE /ə/ is derived from a multiplicity of sources and occurs in alternation with nearly all the stressed vowels, most of the more common spellings of the stressed vowels are traditionally used to represent it.

Dialects in which the earlier unstressed sequence /ər/ yielded /ə/, except before vowels, have in addition the digraphs *er, ir, or, ur, ure* for /ə/, as in *mother, hibernate, perform, confirmation, doctor, Hertford, forget, nature, expurgate, pursuit, surpass.*

PROSODY

16. General Remarks

Prosody and syntax are complementary aspects of sentence structure. Conjointly they constitute the grammar of the sentence. Neither is subordinate to the other; if they clash, either one may outrank the other under certain conditions.

The prosodic features of intoning, stressing and timing are not correlated with the syntactic features of order and rank as such, but with the syntactic structure of the sentence as a whole. Their chief grammatical function is to signal the end, or the imminent end, of a segment of discourse. What is true of the sentence applies also to the prosodically signalled constituent phrases.

In the English sentence, intoning, stressing, and timing are interwoven in an intricate manner, and yet independently variable functional elements of prosodic structure. It is true that the grammatical pitch figure always starts with the heaviest stress of a sentence or of one of its constituent phrases. But the stress does not determine the kind of pitch figure that starts with it. On the other hand, a sentence may contain stresses, though of less force, that are not accompanied by pitch figures. Unless one is willing to treat the heaviest stress of a sentence as differing in kind from the lighter stresses, as some do, one must grant that stress is not an automatic reflex of intonation.

It is convenient, and appropriate, to call the prosodic complex consisting of a pitch figure and full stress the SENTENCE ACCENT, or simply the ACCENT. Its grammatical function is to signal the end of a sentence, as pointed out above. The sentence accent normally coincides with the end of the syntactic sentence. SYNTACTIC CLOSURE and the sentence accent thus conjointly segment the flow of speech.

The segmenting function of the sentence accent is often reinforced by the prosodic feature of timing, which is manifested by a retardation of the tempo of articulation on the full-stress syllable and/or pausing. Timing is effectively used in public speaking and to create suspense, but can be rather elusive in lively conversation. Though closely associated with the sentence accent, timing is nevertheless a separate prosodic feature of the English sentence and its constituent phrases.

Intonation and timing belong exclusively to the sentence and to its constituent parts. Words and syntactic phrases as such do not have these prosodic features. This is true despite the fact that they cannot be uttered without intonation and timing. Such expressions as ↓ *Cóme* and *Vèry* ↓ *góod* and ↑ *Now* are, of course, sentences and have the prosodic features of pitch and timing because they are sentences.

The prosodic feature of stressing belongs to the sentence as well as to the utterance phrase and the word. Words and phrases as such have inherent stress patterns, as *fáther, forgét, bláckbìrd* and *blàck bírd, gèt úp, nòt ríght.* The precise manifestation of these inherent patterns is determined by the prosodic structure of the sentence—the higher structural unit of speech. Under the sentence accent, the expressions illustrated above have the indicated stress patterns. In other positions the stress pattern is toned down, but not effaced. Thus *fáther* becomes *fàther*, *bláckbìrd* becomes *blàckbìrd*, and *blàck bírd* appears as *blâck bìrd*.

While the stress patterns of words and phrases are accommodated to the prosody of the sentence, the onset of the sentence accent is determined by the stress pattern of the inferior unit. Thus in the sentences *Hè's my* ↓ *fáther, Dòn't* ↓ *forgét, Sèe the* ↓ *bláckbìrd, Sèe that blàck* ↓ *bírd, Dòn't gèt* ↓ *úp, Thàt's nòt* ↓ *ríght* the accent starts on the inherently most heavily stressed syllable of the expression in question. This reciprocal relation between sentence stress and word or phrase stress is a characteristic feature of English prosody.

17. Grammatical Intonation

17.1 The Pitch Figures, their Relation to Full Stress, and their Grammatical Functions

English intonation is partly grammatical, partly referential. Before we can deal effectively with its expressive, attitudinal, and directive uses, which have reference to the speaker's feelings, to his attitude toward the content of his message and his audience, and to the effect he intends to produce upon the person(s) addressed, we must isolate, as best we can, all of its grammatical functions.

In its grammatical functions, intonation is primarily correlated with the syntax of the sentence, secondarily with its constituent phrases. Phrases and words as such have no grammatical intonation. Uttered in isolation, they are treated as if they were sentences of one kind or another.

The grammatical function of intonation is twofold: (1) It signals the end, or the imminent end, of a sentence or of one of its constituent phrases. (2) It serves to distinguish the 'yes-or-no' question from all other types of sentences.

The distinctive feature of the intonation of the sentence, or of one of its constituent phrases, is the behavior of the voice pitch on the full-stress syllable and the less stressed syllables that follow it before a pause. Here the pitch either falls or rises at the end of the sentence, and remains more or less level at the end of a non-final constituent phrase. We shall call the crucial fall ⟨↓⟩, rise ⟨↑⟩ and sustain ⟨→⟩ the GRAMMATICAL PITCH FIGURES of English, and write them as indicated, placing the proper symbol before the word (not the syllable) containing the full stress to which the onset of the pitch figure is invariably tied.

The occurrence and the placement of these three pitch figures will here be illustrated by a few examples.

The final fall ⟨↓⟩ occurs in statements, requests, and specific questions, which are differentiated from each other only by syntactic features.

Statements

He nòdded his ↓ héad ||
We hàd a gòod ↓ tíme ||
Màn is ↓ amázing ||
Yòu're sò ↓ góod to mè ||

Requests

↓ Lóok ||
Còme ↓ ín ||
Dòn't ↓ wórry ||
Dòn't ↓ forgét abòut it ||

Specific Questions

Whère does he ↓ líve ||
Whỳ are you ↓ láughing ||
Whò ↓ tóld you thàt ||
Whàt do you ↓ think of it ||

The final rise ⟨↑⟩ is peculiar to the question that calls for affirmation or denial. Such 'yes-or-no' questions are:

Wàs it ↑ trúe ||
Dò you plày ↑ brídge ||
↑ Díd yòu ||
Càn't you ↑ sée it ||
Shòuld I ↑ ásk him abòut it ||

As a grammatical pitch figure, the sustain ⟨→⟩ marks the end of a non-final constituent clause or phrase of a sentence. The sustain is less uniform in its manifestation than the final fall ⟨↓⟩ and rise ⟨↑⟩, and could be defined negatively as being neither a clear fall nor a clear rise.

Examples

Whìle there's → lífe | thère is ↓ hópe ||
Thère is → hópe | whìle there is ↓ lífe ||
I don't mèan to → sáy | that I ↓ regrét it ||
Thàt I → regrét it | gòes without ↓ sáying ||
It was → nót | I mùst → conféss | quìte ↓ cléar to mè ||

The pitch figures are realized on the full-stress syllable, if it is final, otherwise on the full-stress syllable and the following unstressed or less stressed syllable(s). When unstressed or less stressed syllables follow the full-stress, the pitch may glide down (or up) during the articulation of the full-stress syllable and then remain low (or high); or it may remain level on the full-stress syllable and then step down (or up). All such realizations of the several pitch figures are grammatically equivalent. Nor do the pitch intervals, large or small, have any grammatical relevance, whatever other meanings they may have.

The intonation of the part of the sentence or phrase preceding the pitch figure, which we may call the precontour, has no grammatical function. Hence it is not properly a part of structural prosody. The precontour varies regionally within the English-speaking world without affecting communication adversely. For instance, a relatively low beginning with little variation in pitch before the pitch figure is common in the American Midwest, whereas in Standard British English the precontour often starts rather high and descends by steps to the onset of the pitch figure. This difference in the pitch behavior of the precontour can be illustrated in sentences like the following:

I'm nòt so ↓ súre of it ||
Don't tàke it so ↓ hárd ||
What màkes you ↓ thínk so ||
Dòn't you ↑ thínk so ||

Such regional differences in non-grammatical intonation as the 'monotone' of the Midwesterner and the 'sing-song' of the Englishman are readily observable by a good ear and easily imitated. They must be acquired if one wishes to speak either of these dialects properly, just as one must adopt the regional allophones of shared phonemes when learning another dialect. Though important socially, such differences are nevertheless structurally irrelevant.

17.2 Deviations from Normal Grammatical Intonation

In normal speech, the sentence-final pitch figures are correlated with sentence types, the rise ⟨↑⟩ characterizing the syntactic 'yes-or-no' question, and the fall ⟨↓⟩ all other types of sentences. Deviation from the norm produces a clash between prosodic and syntactic features in which either one or the other dominates. In either case an emotive, attitudinal, or directive factor is superinduced in the utterance.

Replacing the fall ⟨↓⟩ by a sharp rise ⟨↑⟩ in a syntactic statement converts it into an emotionally charged question challenging the listener to affirm or deny the statement. Here the pitch figure overrides the syntax.

> *Hè's a ↑ póet //*
> *Whàles are ↑ mámmals //*
> *And yòu ↑ dený it //*
> *He dìd it ↑ agáin //*

Imposing a fall ⟨↓⟩ on a 'yes-no' question changes it to a request ranging in emotional overtones from mildness to harshness. Here again the syntax gives way to the prosody.

> *Wònt you ↓ hélp me //*
> *But hàs he the ↓ méans //*
> *Hè was ↓ rúde // ↓ Wásn't hè //*
> *Dò you ↓ dený it //*
> *→ Wíll yòu / or ↓ wónt yòu //*

Not infrequently a gentle rise ⟨↑⟩ replaces the normal fall ⟨↓⟩ in statements, requests, and specific questions in friendly or polite discourse, apparently more commonly in England than in America. This alteration of the normal pitch figure does not change these sentence types into 'yes-no' questions. Here the syntax dominates the prosody.

> *It ìsn't too ↑ bád //*
> *Yòu're so vèry ↑ kínd //*
> *Hàve a ↑ séat //*
> *Plèase ↑ help mè //*
> *Whỳ are you ↑ ángry //*
> *Whàt's the ↑ mátter //*

This 'intonation of politeness' may reflect a personal attitude of the moment or it may be habitual. Among certain social groups in Great Britain it is regarded as a mark of good breeding.

All of these deviant uses of the pitch figures are apt to be accompanied by a peculiar timbre of the voice reflecting the feeling or attitude of the speaker, ranging from the smoothness of the polite statement to the harshness of the question used as a threat. It is rather idle to speculate on the relative share of grammar and referential meaning in the intonation of such utterances. But there can be no doubt that structural uses of intonation are somehow involved, and that a description of the normal grammatical functions of the pitch figures in their relation to syntax must precede any treatment of such complicated utterances.

17.3 Emphasis With and Without Accent Shift

The special uses of pitch figures discussed above do not involve any shift in their location. The changed pitch figure remains where it is in normal grammatical intonation.

The prosodic phenomenon of emphasis is much more complicated in its manifestations. Emphasis is an effective device for directing the attention of the listener to a particular part of an utterance, driving home or shading a message, or giving vent to one's feelings. It pervades lively discourse and is deliberately used in careful exposition. Only some of its more striking uses can be treated here.

Heightened full-stress and/or increased intervals in the pitch figure are the characteristic features of emphatic utterance. Emphasis may be placed on the syllable that normally bears the sentence accent, i.e. the prosodic complex consisting of full stress and a pitch figure; or it may be put on any other element of the sentence, even on any part of a word, morpheme, or syllable that the speaker wishes to make prominent. In the latter case, the sentence accent is shifted away from its normal location. Since the normal accent is at or near the end of the sentence, forward shifts are the most frequent.

The shifted emphatic accent is of course more common on main words (nouns, adjectives, verbs, and certain adverbs) than on auxiliary words, and it is relatively rare on normally weakly stressed and unstressed syllables of words consisting of two or more syllables.

We shall write the emphatic accent with a double stroke over the vowel and indicate the accent shift by printing the word on which the accent falls in Roman, as in the examples given below.

Without Accent Shift

Thàt's ↓ grǎnd //
Àre you ↑ mǎd //
Còme and ↓ gĕt it //

With Shifted Accent

Normal Accent	Shifted Accent
Wìne tàstes ↓ bétter //	↓ *Wĭne tastes bètter //*
	Wìne ↓ tăstes bètter //
Hè's the ↓ óne //	↓ *Hĕ's the òne //*
Wè have ↓ séen it //	*Wè ↓ hăve sèen it //*
She wòre a rèd ↓ dréss /	*She wòre a ↓ rĕd drèss //*
Has Jòhn ↑ léft //	*Has ↑ Jŏhn lèft //*
↓ *Gìve it to hìm //*	*Gìve it to ↑ hĭm //*
It ìsn't that ↓ bád //	*It ìsn't ↓ thăt bàd //*
Nòt at ↓ áll //	↓ *Nŏt at àll //*
De ↓ líghted //	↓ *Dĕlìghted //*

For an even more drastic effect, the word bearing the shifted accent is itself shifted to an abnormal position in the sentence, or the syntactic structure of the sentence is changed in some other way.

Normal Accent	Shifted Accent
Yòu're in ↓ lúck //	In ↓ lúck you àre // ↓ Thát's whàt //
Nòw's the ↓ tíme //	↓ Nŏw's the tìme //
Wè ↓ sáw her //	↓ Shě's the òne we sàw //
Shè ↓ líkes this //	↓ Thĭs is whàt she lìkes //
I wànt to be ↓ thére //	↓ Thére's where I wànt to bè //
Òut you ↓ gó //	↓ Őut you gò //
He lìved on brèad and ↓ wáter //	On brèad and ↓ wăter he lìved //

It should be noted that the pitch figure does not lose its function as an end signal when it is shifted forward, since all that follows it up to the pause is part of it. This can easily be observed in such examples as

Wìne tâstes ↓ bétter //
Wìne ↓ tăstes bètter //
↓ Wĭne tâstes bètter //

or

Dòes he ↑ knów it //
Dòes ↑ hě know it //
But ↑ dŏes he knòw it //

Emotive-directive uses of intonation, as distinct from its grammatical functions, are innumerable, and they may overlay the grammatical intonation figures. Moreover, the relative intensity of emotion or purpose may be reflected in the pitch intervals. Hence, the precise notation of emotive-directive intonations is as complicated as the identification of the semantic range of words and morphemes. Both have referential meaning. They are correlated with the diversity of the 'real world', with the way the speaker reacts to it, and the impression he wishes to make upon his audience.

17.4 Some Special Cases

The grammatical pitch figures ⟨↓⟩ and ⟨↑⟩ function in one-word sentences and in fragmentary sentences exactly in the same way as in the full sentences illustrated above. Thus the one-word sentence *Cóme* normally has the fall ⟨↓⟩ of the request, but can be turned into a 'yes-or-no' question by the rise ⟨↑⟩. Similarly, the sentence fragment *Vèry góod* has the fall ⟨↓⟩ of a statement and can be changed into a question by the rise ⟨↑⟩. Such expressions can, of course, also have the full range of emotive-directive intonations that occur in full sentences.

Fragmentary sentences are very common in everyday conversation, and the rise ⟨↑⟩ and fall ⟨↓⟩ frequently are the only grammatical features conveying the speaker's intention, as in the following bit of dialogue:

A. *Lèt's ↓ gó ||*   B. *↑ Now ||*
A. *Rìght ↓ nów ||*   B. *Whỳ ↓ nót ||*

Although the sustain ⟨→⟩ normally signals the end of a phrase that is followed by an other phrase in the same sentence, it is sometimes used to link independent sentences of a discourse, as in the following examples:

I mày be → wróng || but I dònt' ↓ thínk sò ||
It ìsn't → hárd | Èven a ↓ chĭld can dò it ||
I lòoked at → hĭm || he lòoked at → mĕ || Nèither of us sàid a ↓ wŏrd ||
He wònt stây → hére || He ↓ hătes cìties ||

The speaker's intention may be to convey the connection in the subject matter of the successive sentences or to lead up to a conclusion or climax. Hence this use of the sustain ⟨→⟩ is referential rather than grammatical.

A pitch figure can span two clauses or comprise a clause and part of another, as in the following sentences:

Yòu're too ↓ slów you knòw ||
Àre you ↑ dóne she àsked ||
Nòt ↓ yét he replĭed ||
↓ Hèlp me plèase ||
Sùch → thíngs he sàid | ↓ wórried hìm ||
→ Nów he àsked | dò you ↑ sée ||
He tàlked without ↓ thínking as it wère ||

After a fall ⟨↓⟩, the appended or inserted clause remains low, after a rise ⟨↑⟩ it continues high, after a sustain ⟨→⟩ it is level in pitch. There is no separate pitch figure on *she àsked, he replĭed, he sàid, as it wère*. Even if a half-pause is introduced, as in *Nòt ↓ yét | he replĭed ||* and *Àre you ↑ dóne | she àsked ||*, the pitch figure spans both clauses.

A precontour may, of course, include more than one clause, as in

She sàid will you ↑ dó it ||
I sàid that I ↓ míght ||

Alternately, such sentences can be uttered with an intervening half-pause and have two pitch figures:

She → sáid | wìll you ↑ dó it ||
I → replĭed | that I pròbably ↓ wóuld ||

Reported Yes-or-No Questions

When reporting a 'yes-or-no' question directly, the rising pitch figure ⟨↑⟩ is retained along with the syntactic features, and the introductory clause is set off by a pause as in:

Hè → sáid | Dò you ↑ méan it ||
She → ásked | Are you còming ↑ alóng ||

Here the reporter mimics the speaker.

When reporting such a question indirectly with or without changes in syntax and/or morphology, the fall ⟨↓⟩ replaces the rise ⟨↑⟩:

He àsked dîd I ↓ méan it ||
He dìdn't sây ↓ máy I ||
She → inquíred | whèther I was còming ↓ alóng ||

Here the 'yes-or-no' question is prosodically treated as a statement and the introductory clause is usually not set off by a pause.

17.5 Concluding Remarks

In this discussion of English intonation, the attempt has been made to identify its normal grammatical uses; to treat its other grammatical functions as deviations from the norm; and to point out some of its emotive, attitudinal, and directive uses, which have nothing to do with the grammar of the sentence but are referentially meaningful. To what extent this approach to a complicated linguistic phenomenon has met with success, is left to the judgment of the reader.

17.6 Prosodically Analyzed Sample Texts

The interplay of the prosodic features of intoning, stressing, and timing has been pointed out above in connection with the discussion of their uses. The short texts that follow are intended to exhibit the many ways in which they function jointly and separately and to what extent they are correlated with syntactic units or clash with them.

The rendering presented here is not the only possible 'reading' of these texts, but one that is probable, one that seems to convey the intention of the authors.

The full pauses are represented by a double stroke, the half-pauses by a single one.

The crucial pitch figures, whether grammatical or emotive-directive, are represented by arrows: the fall by ⟨↓⟩, the rise by ⟨↑⟩, the sustain by ⟨→⟩. The extent of the falls and rises is not indicated. This could be done by writing dots on a staff of parallel lines above or below the text; or by writing numbers on a scale of 7 pitches (as some do); or schematically, on a scale of 4 (as others prefer). Since pitch intervals do not have grammatical function, they are omitted here.

Only full stress ⟨ ´ ⟩, half-stress ⟨ ˋ ⟩, and emphatic stress ⟨ ´´ ⟩ are indicated.

Shifted accents, i.e. combinations of pitch figures with full stress shifted away from their normal locations, are identified by printing the words on which they occur in Roman.

Conventional punctuation marks are, of course, omitted. They are a rather inadequate device to convey prosodic segmentation and syntactic structure to the reader. On the other hand, the capitalisation of sentence-initial letters, though not necessary, is retained.

Text I is an objective description containing rather long sentences; hence many instances of the sustain ⟨→⟩. There are no emphatic accents.

Text II.A contains a woman's emotional responses and outbursts, with shifted emphatic accents. In text II.B a doctor's reassuring comments to a worried young husband lead up to emphatic utterance at the end. The suspense-laden account of events in text II.C is characterized by the sentence-linking sustain ⟨→⟩, and at the end by the emphatic accents of impassioned outbursts.

Text III is a deeply moving reflective passage, characterized by frequent pausing, sentence-linking sustains ⟨→⟩, and emphatic accents; the last especially in the climactic evaluation of a friend's character.

In text IV, a young woman's persuasive argumentation, with its emphatic accents, stands out against the subdued responses of her friend.

Text V describes the meeting of a man with his former sweetheart, who shows the effects of an unhappy marriage. His distress is reflected in the emphatic accents toward the end of the passage.

A petulant woman's teasing of her sedate husband is portayed in text VI. There are many shifted emphatic accents and dramatic pauses.

Text I

The nàtion was stìll → séctional | in that the → Nórth | → Sóuth | → Wést | and the Pacìfic → Cóast | had èach its òwn → demánds | and tỳpes of ↓ lìfe || Bùt the frontìer had → góne | and the còuntry was fàst being ↓ integrated || Of the → ráilroad kìngs | for → exámple | Hàrriman rùled his Wèstern sỳstem from New → Yórk | Hìll hìs from → Minnesóta | and Hùntington hìs from ↓ Califórnia || The pròblem had becòme → nátional | as wèll as ↓ séctional || The mòst → préssing of thèse | was the → cónflict | nòt so mùch between càpital and → lábor | as between the òrdinary smàll → Américan | whèther → láborer | → fármer | or smàll → shòpkèeper |

and the new clàss of grèat → mágnates | who had còme to lòok upon the →
cóuntry | as their pèrsonal → próperty | to be rùn accòrding to their òwn
↓ idéas || Beyònd the first tèn or twènty → míllions | which they accùmulated
for → themsélves | they were nòt so much lùstful for → móney | as for pòwer
and → resóurces | with whìch to plày the ↓ gáme. || It was mùch the sàme
→ féeling | that màkes a bòy's hèart → thrób | as he ràces his càr with →
anóther | at hìghly illègal spèed and → rísk | and ↓ wins ||

From James T. Adams, *The Epic of America*

Text II.A

He. *Why → Wínnie | whàt's the ↓ mátter ||*
She. *↓ Nóthing ||*
He. *Has ànyone been ↑ cróss to yòu ||*
She. *↓ Nó || Whò ↓ wŏuld be cròss to me ||*
He. *Then whỳ are you ↓ crýing || There mùst be sòmething ↓ wróng ||*
↓ Téll me dèar ||
She. *There's ↓ ălways sòmething wròng | when yòu're not ↓ with me ||*
↑ Dŏn't go òut again || ↓ Dŏn't ||

II.B

Husband. *Do you thìnk she'll ↑ lìve ||*
Doctor. *↑ Líve || ↓ Lĭve || You'll be → lúcky | if she dòesn't ↓ outlíve*
you || Shè's → àll ríght | shè's ↓ ăll rìght my bòy || Màking ↓ fĭne prògress ||
↓ Dŏnt wòrry ||

II.C

The prìsoner was in the rèar → céll | awàiting his ↓ fáte || He hèard the
blòws on the → dóor | he hèard the dòor cràsh → dówn | he hèard the rùsh
into the → pássage | and he hèard → óaths | as the mòb trìed the → làst
dòor | and fòund that it fìrmly ↓ héld ||
Prisoner. *Gìve me a → chánce | you ↓ cŏwards |*
The Mob. *We'll gìve you the → săme chànce | you gàve ↓ ŏthers ||*

Adapted from Herbert Quick, *The Hawkeye*

Text III

Thìs is what I → mìss | whèn I look bàck upon Jìm's ↓ succéss || Whìle
there's → lífe | thère is → hópe || but thère is → fĕar | ↓ tŏo || I don't mèan
to → say | that I → regrĕt my àction || nòr will I → preténd | that I càn't
→ slĕep o'nìghts | in ↓ cónsequence || → Stíll | the idèa → obtrúdes itself |
that he màde so ↓ mŭch of his disgràce | whìle it is the guìlt ↓ alŏne that
màtters || Hè was → nŏt | if Ì may → sáy sò | ↓ cléar to mè || Hè was →
nŏt | ↓ cléar || And thère is a → suspícion | he was not → cléar | to →

himsĕlf | ↓ *ĕither* || *Thère were his fìne* → *sensibílities* | *his fìne* → *féelings* | *his fìne* → *lóngings* || *He* → *wás* | *if you will allòw me to* → *sáy so* | *vèry* ↓ *fĭne* || ↓*vĕry fìne* | *and* → *vĕry* | *unfŏrtunate* ||

Adapted from Joseph Conrad, Lord Jim

Text IV

Girl. *Pòor little* → *mé* | *I dòn't get as mùch as a* ↓ *lóok from yòu* || *Yòu'd* → *thínk* | *we dìd'nt* ↓ *knów each òther* ||

Boy. → *Wéll* | *I hàven't* ↓ *séen much òf you* || *Yòu're too* ↓ *déep you knòw* ||

Girl. *Òh* ↑ *yĕah* || *So* ↓ *thăt's what you thìnk* || *I'm nòt so* ↑ *déep* || → *Hŏnest* | *I'm prètty* ↓ *nĭce* || *If you're gòing to tàke me* → *hóme* | *lèt's* ↓ *stárt* ||

Boy. *Lòok* → *hére* | *I [interrupted].*

Girl. *You* ↓ *hăve to Òlly* || *I'm àll* ↓ *alŏne* || *Bìll lèft long* ↓ *agó* || *I'd be scàred to* → *dĕath* | *ùp through the* ↓ *pínes* || ↓ *Hŏnest I wòuld* ||

Boy. ↓ *Ăll rìght* || *Còme* ↓ *alóng then* ||

Adapted from Gladys H. Carroll, As the Earth Turns

Text V

This gàve them àll a chànce to → *láugh* | *and the air was* ↓ *cléared* || *It gave Àgnes* → *tíme* | *to* ↓ *recóver hersèlf* || ...... *Shè was* → *wórn* | *and* → *wásted* | ↓ *ìncrĕdibly* || *The blùe of her* → *éyes* | *seemed* ↓ *dímmed and fàded* || *and the scàrlet of her* → *líps* | *had been wàshed* ↓ *awáy* || *The sìnews of her* → *néck* | *shòwed* → *păinfully* | *when she tùrned her* ↓ *héad* ||

↓ *Pŏor gìrl* || *She* → *félt* | *that she was under* → *scrútiny* | *and her* → *eyes* | *felt hòt and* ↓ *réstless* || *She wìshed to rùn* → *awáy* | *but she* ↓ *dáred not* || *She* → *stáyed* | *while Wìll begàn to tèll her of his* ↓ *lífe* || ......

Once in a → *whíle* | *Àgnes* → *smíled* | *with just a* → *lĭttle flàsh* | *of the* → *ŏld-tìme* | ↓ *sŭnny tèmper* || *Bùt there was* → *nŏ dìmple* | *in the* → *chéek* | ↓ *nŏw* || *He was àlmost* → *réady* | *to tàke her in his* → *árms* | *and* ↓ *wĕep* ||

Adapted from Hamlin Garland, Main-Travelled Roads

Text VI

Wife. → *Dárling* | *do you knòw what's* ↑ *háppened* || ↓ *Guéss* || *You* ↓ *cŏuldn't gùess* || *Grèg wànts me to gò* → *báck* | *to* ↓ *wórk for him* || *I* → *wìll* | ↓ *nŏt* || *The* ↓ *idĕa* || *Màybe I* ↓ *wìll* || ↓ *Fĭring mè* || *the* → *bĕst* | → *cartŏonist* | *he'll èver* ↓ *gĕt* || → *Wéll* | *I guèss I was ràther* ↑ *bád* || *Màybe I'll be* ↓ *bétter nòw* || *Bùt I was a* → *prĕtty* | → *dărn* | → *gŏod* | → *cartŏonist* | *thèn* ↓ *tŏo* ||

Husband. ↓ *Whŏa* || *Whàt's all* ↑ *thìs* ||

She. ↓ Grég *called ùp* || *His nèw cartòonist has been* ↓ *dráfted* || *He sàys he could ùse a* → sýndicated *cartòonist* | *but he'd ràther kèep the lòcal* ↓ *tóuch* ||

He. *Do you* ↑ wănt *to dò this* ||

She. *For a* ↓ *while màybe* || →*Yés* | *I thìnk I* ↓ *dó* || *Wòuld you* ↑ *mínd* || ...

He. ↓ *Lóok Jìn* || *If thìs were a crìtical* → *wár jòb* | *I'd be* ↓ *glád* || *I'd mèrely be* → *wóndering* | *hòw I could* ↓ *help yòu* || *But [interrupted]*

She. *Dòn't* → *lóok* | *sò* → *ŭtterly* | ↓ *strĭcken* || *Of* ↓ *cŏurse I wòn't dò it* || *Fòul idèa* ↓ *ănywày* ||

Sinclair Lewis, *Cass Timberlane*

18. Stress patterns: Preliminary Remarks

The stress patterns of English sentences, phrases, and words can be adequately described in terms of five degrees of energy expended on articulation and phonation or of corresponding degrees of loudness, though, in actual speech, there is an infinite gradation of force and of resulting loudness.

The convention of describing stress patterns in terms of three, four, or five degrees of stress does not imply that these stresses are units comparable in their behavior to phonemes as units constituting morphemes. For one thing, phonemes are discrete and normally do not overlap phonically, whereas stresses overlap in their realization to such an extent that half-stress may actually be stronger and louder in some contexts than full-stress in other contexts. Secondly, and even more significantly, replacement of a single phoneme by another phoneme completely changes a morpheme in shape and meaning, as in *lip* ≠ *lap*. On the other hand, the replacement of one degree of stress by an other has no such consequences. For instance, *father* and *seaworthy* can have full-stress or half-stress, as in (*tèll*) *fáther* ∼ *fàther* (*knóws*) and (*nòt*) *séawòrthy* ∼ *sèawórthy* (*véssels*), without any change in meaning or in the inherent stress patterns. From this observation it should be clear that degrees of stress do not constitute a system comparable, say, to the system of checked vowels or fricative consonants. It is the stress patterns that contrast with each other, as in *inclíne* ≠ *íncline* or *blùe bírd* ≠ *blúebìrd*, and not the degrees of stress.

In what follows, the stress patterns of sentences, phrases, and words will usually be identified in terms of three degrees of stress: FULL STRESS, HALF-STRESS, and UNSTRESS. Full stress will be represented by the acute, half-stress by the grave, as in *híghwày*, and unstress will go unmarked. For certain purposes, reduced half-stress will be written with the circumflex, as in *ráilrôad brìdge*, and called WEAK STRESS. Heightened full stress, called EMPHATIC STRESS, will be represented by the double acute, as in *Yòu hǎve to dò it* or *She lĭkes tǎll mèn*.

19. Sentence Stress and Timing

As pointed out above (16 and 17.1), the English sentence and its prosodically marked phrases normally have the strongest stress at or near the end. Invariably accompanied by a pitch figure, this configuration of full stress and a pitch figure, called the sentence accent, signals the end of a segment of discourse.

For emotive-directive emphasis, the sentence accent can be shifted to other positions in the sentence (17.3). Ample illustrations of the sentence accent, both normal and shifted, will be found in the prosodically analysed texts (17.6).

The precise onset of the sentence accent is ultimately determined by the stress pattern of phrases or their constituent words.

Half-stresses and weak stresses in a sentence have no prosodic function. Their occurrence is determined by the stress patterns of the syntactic phrases contained in the sentence.

The prosodic feature of timing is closely associated with the sentence accent. It is manifested by retardation of utterance and the consequent prolongation of the phonemes of the accented syllable, especially of the vowel, and/or by pausing at the end of the pitch figure. Timing is rather variable. It is deliberately used in careful lecturing and for rhetorical effects. In lively conversation, on the other hand, it can be rather evanescent.

In the prosodically analysed texts (17.6), full pause at the end of sentences is represented by two slanting lines, half-pause by a single slant. This practice is a simplification of the actual manifestation of timing, which in any given case many ivolve retardation AND pausing, or only one of its aspects.

20. Phrase Stress

The English phrase normally has the heaviest stress at or near the end, irrespective of syntactic structure. The head of the phrase receives the heaviest stress only if it follows the modifier; if the modifier follows the head, the modifier bears the heaviest stress.

The following examples of noun, adjective, adverb, and verb phrases illustrate this important point.

(1) The head of the phrase follows the modifier and has the heaviest stress:

the wéather, a gòod stóry, a glàss dóor, a sèaside resórt, a rèd-and-white dréss, Jòhn's friends, in the gárden, òut in the cóuntry;
vèry góod, a lìttle tíred, blìssfully ígnorant, quite hàppily márried;
ràther slówly, mòst delíghtful, mùch too fást, fàr óut, stràight úp;
(he) nèver drínks, àlways láughs, èven protésted, òften thínks of yòu.

(2) The modifier follows the head of the phrase and bears the heaviest stress:

the attòrney géneral, a làbor of lóve, the Univèrsity of Míchigan, the màn in the móon, a wèek before Chrístmas;

gòod as góld, brìghter than the sún, wòrthy of respéct, drùnk as a lórd, glàd to hélp, too làte for the cóncert;

as quìckly as póssible, fàster than líghtning, nòt at áll;

thìnk cléarly, rùn fást, gèt úp ,wrìte létters, give Jàne a présent, càll him a fóol, jùmp to conclúsions, hòpe for the bést, lìke to réad.

The characteristic end-stress appears also when the phrase consists of two coordinate heads:

sòns and dáughters, dày or níght; blàck and blúe, for bètter or wórse; bàck and fórth, òver thére, nèver agáin; còme and gó, sìnk or swím.

Deviation from the rule that a modifier following the head word has the heaviest stress occurs in two constructions:

(1) When a verb is followed by one or two pronominal objects or by a prepositional phrase containing a pronoun, the stress is on the verb, as in: *(She) líkes mè, (John) knéw it, (Don't) sáy thàt, (She) tóld me thàt, (He) gáve it to mè, (I'll) wáit for yòu.*

(2) When a preposition is followed by a pronoun, the stress is on the preposition, as in: *(What) óf it, (John is) agáinst me, (We saw) thróugh him.* In addition, there are a number of other phrases that diverge from the rule, as *(I don't) thínk sò, (and) só fòrth.*

In all the examples given above, the stress patterns of the phrases are cited in the shape they assume under the sentence accent. In other contexts, (1) the stresses are proportionately reduced, thus preserving the pattern; or else (2) the stress pattern of the phrase is rhythmically reversed. Proportionate reduction is the rule, unless the phrase is immediately followed by the sentence accent.

The inherent stress pattern is preserved, though reduced, in the following examples: *In the gàrden (was a fóuntain)* vs. *(We sàt) in the gárden. The glàss dòor (was clósed)* vs. *(He òpened) the glàss dóor.*

Rhythmic reversal of the pattern before the sentence accent, i.e. a change of $\langle \acute{\ } \grave{\ } \rangle$ to $\langle \grave{\ } \acute{\ } \rangle$, is shown in the following instances: *(She wòre) a rèd-and-whìte (dréss)* vs. *(It was) rèd-and-whíte. A fàr-awáy (ísland)* vs. *(The ìsland was) fàr awáy.*

Aside from rhythmic alternation of the normal stress pattern of phrases, there are deviations for the sake of emotive or directive emphasis. These are illustrated in the section on intonation (17.3).

21. Word Stress

In English, words of more than one syllable, whether native or foreign, have an inherent stress pattern in that one and the same syllable always has stronger stress than any other. Although the stress pattern of words

is adapted to the prosody of the phrase and the sentence, it is not effaced
in the wider context, except under special conditions pointed out below.

In the context of the phrase or the sentence, the most heavily stressed
syllable of a plurisyllabic word may have full stress, half-stress, or even
weak stress. Thus under the sentence accent *fáther, Súnday, híghwày,
súmmertìme, ùnderstánd, fòresée, forgét, togéther* invariably have full stress
on the particular syllable so marked. In other contexts, the same syllable
has half-stress, as in *Sùnday mórning, the hìghwày to Bóston, to fòresèe a
dánger, forgèt a dáte,* and the other syllables are proportionately weakened.

When we call English a stress language, we have in mind the fact that
the stress patterns of words normally preserve their identity in the
context of the sentence and that the onset of the pitch figure of the
sentence is determined by the stress pattern of the word. In this
respect English differs, for instance, from French, where, aside from
special emphasis, only the sentence-final or phrase-final syllable is
dynamically prominent, and words as such have no stress patterns.

It is customary to indicate the stress patterns of words in the shape
they assume under the sentence accent, i.e. when they receive full stress
on the inherently most prominent syllable. But it must be clearly under-
stood that the whole pattern is downgraded in other contexts of the
sentence or phrase.

21.1 Monosyllabic Words

Words of one syllable have, of course, no stress pattern. Nor can they
be said to have, by themselves, one degree of stress rather than an other.
Their stressing, as that of plurisyllabic words, depends upon the syntax
and the prosody of the phrases and sentences of which they are constituent parts. The word *man*, for instance, can receive full stress, half-
stress, or weak stress, as in the phrases *the òld mán, the màn in the móon,
a màn to mân tálk*; and in compounds the morpheme *man* can be unstressed, as in *Frénchman*. The word *can* is often unstressed, but it may
receive half-stress or even full stress, as shown in the following sentences:
Nòw you can sée it. Càn you sée it? I cán.

Some word classes normally receive either full stress or half-stress in
the sentence, others are normally unstressed or half-stressed. To the
former group belong nouns, adjectives, main verbs, and descriptive
adverbs, which we may call main words; to the latter, auxiliary verbs,
pronouns, prepositions, conjunctions, and certain adverbs, which may
be called auxiliary words.

Main words have a rather stable phonemic shape, though the phonemes
of which they consist often have more or less marked prosodic allophones,
as *man, cold, rise, out*.

On the other hand, many auxiliary words have variable phonemic shapes in addition to very marked prosodic allophones, the full variant occurring under full stress or half-stress, the reduced variant(s) when the word is unstressed.

The prosodically conditioned variants of some of the auxiliary words are listed below.

Auxiliary verbs: *am* /ǽm ~ əm ~ m/, *is* /íz ~ z/, *are* /ár, ɐ ~ r, ə̣/, *was* /wáz, wɐz ~ wəz ~ wz/, *were* /wɜ́ ~ wɜ ~ wə/ and BE /wɛ́ə̣/, *have* /hǽv ~ həv ~ əv ~ v/, *had* /hǽd ~ həd ~ əd ~ d/, *can* /kǽn ~ kən ~ kŋ/, *could* /kúd ~ kəd/, *shall* /šǽl ~ šəl ~ šl/, *should* /šúd ~ šəd/, *will* /wíl ~ l/, *would* /wúd ~ wəd ~ d/.

Pronouns: *him* /hím ~ əm/, *her* /hɜ́ ~ ɜ, ə/, *them* /ðέm ~ ðəm/, *us* /ʌs ~ əs/, *you* /ju ~ jə/, *your* /júr, júə ~ jɜ, jə/, *the* /ðə, ði ~ ðí/, *a* /ə ~ é/.

Adverbs: *not* /nát, nɐt ~ nt/, *than* /ðǽn ~ ðən/, *as* /ǽz ~ əz/.

Prepositions: *but* /bʌt ~ bət/, *for* /fɔr, fɐ̣ ~ fɜ, fə/, *from* /frám, frɐm ~ frəm/, *of* /áv, ɐ́v ~ əv/, *to* /tú ~ tə/, *upon* /əpán, əpɐ́n ~ əpən/.

Conjunctions: *and* /ǽnd ~ ən ~ n/, *or* /ɔ́r, ɐ́ə ~ ɜ, ə/, *but* /bʌt ~ bət/, *that* /ðǽt ~ ðət/, *what* /hwɐ̀t, wɐt ~ wət/.

A few examples will suffice to illustrate the incidence of such prosodically conditioned allomorphs:

We've /v/ *nèver* ↓ *séen him* /əm/.
Hàve /hǽv/ *you àsked* ↑ *hĭm* /hím/.
I'd /d/ *ràther* ↓ *nót* /nát, nɐt/. *Wòuld* /wùd/ ↑ *yóu? I* ↓ *wóuldn't* /wúd nt/.
Hè's /z/ *the sòn of* /əv/ *a* ↓ *lórd. Whàt* ↓ *óf* /áv, ɐ́v/ *it?*

21.2 Complex Words

Native words with suffixes are stressed on the base morpheme, as the nouns *réader, chíldhòod, mótherhòod, gládness, lóveliness, fríendship, pénmanship, búrial, hóuses*; the adjectives *hármful, Énglish, cáreless, fátherless, gódlìke, fríendly, brótherly, lóathsome, ícy, lónger, lóngest*; and the verb forms *ríses, rísing, háted*. All of these formations thus have fore-stress.

Native words with prefixes are also stressed on the base morpheme, and hence have end-stress. The prefix may be unstressed, weakly stressed, or half-stressed-.

The pattern ⟨_ ⸍⟩ occurs in *arise, awaken* and, beside ⟨⸌ ⸍⟩, in *believe, belong, forgive, forbid, forget, forsake,* etc. The pattern ⟨⸌ ⸍⟩ is usual in *befriend, begin, behave, behold, beset, beseech, forbear, forgo, forswear, undo, unlock, untie*. Words with the prefixes illustrated below have the pattern ⟨⸌ ⸍⟩: *foreshadow, foretell, mislead, miswrite, outbid, outgrow, overdo, overreach, understand, underlie, uphold, uproot, withdraw, withstand*.

Nouns, adjectives, and adverbs derived from complex verbs retain the end-stress of the verb; thus *forgét, forgétful, forgétfulness*; *bêséech, bêséeching, bêséechingly*; *fôrbéar, fôrbéarance*; *ùnderstánd, ùnderstánding*.

These stress patterns are characteristic of verbs. Native nouns and adjectives with end-stress are infrequent. Among such nouns we may mention *bêlíef, bêhést, bêhávior, bêquést* (with which compare *bêlíeve, bêháve, bêquéath*) and *mìstáke, mìstrúst, mìsgívings*. Most of them, though not all, are derived from, or supported by, verbs.

Some complex verbs with end-stress are paralleled by nouns with fore-stress, as *òverflów ≠ óverflòw*; similarly, *overlook, overthrow, underline, upset*. Sometimes the corresponding noun has a suffix, as in the following examples: *fòresée ≠ fóresìght, fòreknów ≠ fóreknòwledge, òutgrów ≠ óutgròwth, òverdráw ≠ óverdràft, ùndertáke ≠ úndertàker, ùnderwríte ≠ únderwrìter*. In all such cases the verb underlies the noun.

Adjectives with the prefix *un-* have end-stress, as *ùnkínd, ùnbecóming, ùnbelíevable*. Under the sentence accent the stress pattern ⟨ ͜ ⟩ is regular in such adjectives; but immediately before the sentence accent the pattern is rhythmically inverted, unless unstressed syllables intervene. Thus *ùnkínd wórds*, but *únbelìevable nónsènse* (BE *nónsense*).

21.3 Compound Words

With the exception of certain types of asyntactic formations and phrase derivatives (decompounds), native words consisting of two or more free forms (bases) have fore-stress. In this respect, compounds differ sharply from the normally end-stressed phrases of English, as in the following examples: *a blúebìrd ≠ a blùe bírd, a glásshòuse ≠ a glàss dóor, a lády's-slìpper ≠ a làdy's slípper, évergrèen ≠ èver réady, a stándstìll ≠ stànd stíll, a bláck-òut ≠ blàck óut*.

Compound nouns of MnE, whatever their formation or history, have the heaviest stress on the first element, i.e., they have the stress pattern ⟨ ͜ ⟩.

Some consist of two nouns or noun stems, as *airport* (≠ *àir spéed*), *churchyard, dust storm, dining room, homestead* (≠ *hòme rúle*), *rainfall* (≠ *ràin fórest*), *newspaper, seashore, school teacher, sunrise, town house* (≠ *tòwn ófficer*), *wheatfield, woodcarver*; *lady's-slipper* (≠ *làdy's mán*), *Pittsburgh*. In some old compounds of this type the second member of the compound is now unstressed, as in *Christmas, England, fisherman, kinsman, neighbor*, BE *strawberry*, and in such names as *Charleston, Nottingham, Haverhill, Hampstead, Johnson*.

Others consist of an adjective and a noun, as *background* (≠ *bàck dóor*), *broadside, grandfather, general staff, highway, half-breed, midnight, numbskull, red-skin, white-caps*; *Main Street* (≠ *màin stréet*), *Newport, Longfellow Littlejohn*. With unstressed final member: *gentleman, highland, lowland*, BE *holiday* and *Newton, Oldham, Suffolk, Wessex*.

Some compound nouns are based on verb phrases, as *breakwater*, *dreadnought, playmate, scarecrow, skinflint, breakfast; black-out, breakdown, hold-up, lean-to, standin, stand-still*; with reversed order, *bypass, downpour, onset, output, overdraught, thoroughfare, shortcut, underwear, upkeep*.

Others again are based on various other phrases or sentence fragments, as *handful* (≠ *a hànd fúll of* . . .), *ne'er-do-well, forget-me-not, jack-o'-lantern, wherewithall*; or imitative words cast in pseudo-morphemes, as *killdeer, whippoorwill*.

Compound adjectives with fore-stress are infrequent. Most of them consist of a noun and a following adjective or participle, as *homesick, seasick, seaworthy, praiseworthy, steadfast, bed-ridden, homespun* (cp. *hòme-máde*), *lovelorn*; with now unstressed final member, *hopeful, careless, lovely*. From an adjective phrase, we have *evergreen*, from a verb phrase, *die-hard*, both also used as nouns.

Compound adverbs with fore-stress are rather numerous, chiefly derived from adverbial phrases. Examples are: *nowadays, piecemeal, headlong* (for earlier *headling*), *sideways, lengthwise, anyway, anyhow, anywhere, elsewhere, nowhere, somehow, somewhat, somewhere*; with unstressed final member, *homeward, northward, upward, afterward(s), forward, always*.

Several compound prepositions have fore-stress, as shown in the following phrases: *ìnto slávery, ínto it; ònto the rócks, ónto them; ùnto this dáy, ùnto Gód; ùp to a húndred, úp to it; òut of spíte, óut of it*.

Some compounds differ in their structure from the normal syntax of the phrase. Of these asyntactic compounds, some have a changed order of the morphemes in addition to fore-stress, as a *shórtcùt* ≠ *cùt shórt*, a *dównpòur* ≠ *pòur dówn, práisewòrthy* ≠ *wòrthy of práise, hómespùn* ≠ *spùn at hóme*.

Finally, some compounds with fore-stress contain morphemes that do not occur in free phrase construction or are no longer matched with free morphemes by speakers of MnE, as the first member of *cranberry, elderberry*, or the unstressed final members of such names as *Newton, Oldham, Greenwich*.

Some asyntactic compounds have end-stress, as the adjectives *lùkewárm, rèd-hót, ìce-cóld, skỳ-blúe*; the participles *èasy-góing, smòoth-rúnning, stìll-bórn, fùll-grówn, hòme-máde, fòredóomed, ìnbréd, òutspóken* (but cp. *hómespùn, súnbùrned, thúnder-strùck, dówncàst, báckswèpt, oútgòing*); the adverbs (also used as nouns) *bàck-stáge, dòwntówn, dòwnstréam, ìnsíde, òutdóor, òverséas, ùpstáirs*; and the numerals *thìrtéen, twènty-twó*.

Phrase derivatives (decompounds) in -ed are nearly always end-stressed, i.e. they retain the stress patttern of the noun phrase from which they are derived. Among the numerous instances are the following: *kìnd-héarted, hòt-témpered, òne-síded, wìld-éyed, òversízed, shòrt-síghted, bòw-légged, bùll-héaded, ràttle-bráined*.

Under the sentence accent, such compounds and decompounds regularly have end-stress, as in:

The tèa was lùkewárm, ìce-cóld.
Hè is òutspóken, èasy-góing, twènty-twó.
Hè is hòt-témpered, bùll-héaded.

When immediately followed by a syllable bearing the sentence accent, the stress pattern is rhythmically reversed, the first member bearing a heavier stress than the second, as in *lùkewârm wáter,* an *òutbôund véssel, ìce-côld téa,* a *fùll-grôwn éagle,* a *hòt-têmpered féllow, òutdôor spórts.* In this respect, such words exhibit the same rhythmic adjustment to the prosodic context as normally end-stressed phrases, e.g. *He was òut of tówn,* but *an òut of tôwn guést.*

End-stressed asyntactic compounds and decompounds like those exemplified above are often said to have 'level-stress', i.e. equal stress on the two members, and are so recorded in some dictionaries. But the facts are against such a conception of their stress pattern.

22. Historical Comments on the Stress Patterns of Native Words

With some modification, the stress patterns of Modern English words of native stock are inherited from Old English (ultimately from Proto-Germanic). Fore-stressed complex words like *bítten, bétter, wánder;* fore-stressed compound nouns and adjectives like *áppletrèe, híghwày, fóre-fàther* and *séawòrthy;* and end-stressed verbs with prefixes like *aríse, belíeve, forgét, ùnderstánd* were all current in Old and Middle English. On these models ,the stress patterns of words adopted from Old French and from Latin were reshaped to a large extent, as outlined below. Words taken from Old Norse and from Middle Dutch readily fell into the native patterns.

The chief changes in stress patterns from Middle English to Modern English times, some of them starting in later Middle English, can be briefly summarized.

(1) Most fore-stressed disyllabic words ending in an unstressed syllable became monosyllabic, as *bíte, bítes, sínned, wólves* (but *ríses, háted, búshes,* etc., preserve the older shape). As a result of this change, monosyllables vastly outnumber plurisyllables in Modern English texts.

(2) In many old compound nouns and complex nouns and adjectives, the pattern $\langle \perp \perp \rangle$ has been reduced to $\langle \perp \smile \rangle$, as in *séaman, híghland, Súnday, fréedom, bríghtness, hópeful, cáreless, lóvely.* This change is especially common in such compound names as *Bédford, Súffolk, Bírmingham, Néwton, Gréenwich, Jéfferson.*

(3) The older phrase stress ⟨ ˌ ˊ ⟩ has been replaced by ⟨ ˊ ˌ ⟩ or ⟨ ˊ ˍ ⟩ in *Lády Chàpel*, *lády's-slìpper*, *kínsman*, *Wédnesday*, etc., all of them originally genitive phrases.

The occurrence, in Modern English, of end-stressed phrases consisting of two nouns, such as *glàss dóor*, *mòrning páper*, by the side of fore-stressed compounds consisting of two nouns, such as *glásshòuse*, *mórning-glòry*, on the one hand; and the reversal of either of these normal stress patterns for contrastive or distinguishing emphasis, as in

a glǎss dòor | nòt a stěel dòor ||
the mǒrning pàper | nòt the ẹvening pàper ||

has produced a rather complicated situation. Under the circumstances, it is not surprising that usage sometimes differs regionally and even from person to person. Thus some Americans say *ìce créam*, others *íce crèam*.

Though the fore-stress of compound nouns consisting of two noun stems is inherited from Old English and would seem to be a sufficiently effective model for forming new compounds of this type, it is nevertheless probable that the use of emphatic distinguishing stress is a contributing factor in the creation of such compounds. For example, on the farm there is occasion to distinguish between the various crops: hence the frequent use of *whěat cròp, rȳe cròp, hǎy cròp, potáto cròp*, and thereafter the normal *whéat cròp, rýe cròp, háy cròp, potáto cròp*.

In place names originating as phrases, the phrase stress may survive, or fore-stress may come into use. Thus American *NèwYórk, Old Gréenwich, Ròcky Móuntains, Riversîde Dríve*, but *Líttle Ròck, Bád Lànds, Máin Strèet*.

23. The Adaptation of French and Latin Words to Native Stress Patterns

During the Middle English period a multitude of French and Latin words, or rather their stems, were taken into English. Since most English words, with the exception of verbs with prefixes, had fore-stress, and the stems of most foreign words had the heaviest stress on the last syllable of the stem, the foreign stress patterns were in sharp conflict with the native ones. Their adaptation to the native patterns was a complicated process that extended over several centuries.

The foreign stress patterns were doubtless retained for some time by those who knew Latin and spoke French as well as English. But when English gradually replaced French in the course of the fourteenth century and Latin words were used in the vernacular, adaptations to native patterns took place step by step. This process followed rather well defined prosodic rules, as outlined below.

End-stress was not unknown in the native word stock, but it was largely confined to verbs with prefixes, such as *aríse, belíeve, forgét, ùndó, ùnderstánd*. On the model of this stress pattern, Latin and Old French verbs with prefixes usually retained end-stress.

Among the hundreds of foreign verbs with the stress pattern ⟨_ ∠⟩ or ⟨⌣ ∠⟩ are the following: *abjure, acclaim, adapt, adjust, afflict, assure, collide, commit, compare, connect, consult, correct, deliver, dilute, disclose, evade, embark, enjoy, entertain, exalt, imply, include, intervene, observe, perform, prevail, provide, refer, submit, succumb, suffice, supervise, survive, transpose.*

Native nouns and adjectives had fore-stress in the ME parent forms of MnE *fáther, chíldhòod, háppy, cáreful, fátherly, cárelessness; dáylìght, híghwày, súmmertìme, físherman*. This pattern was gradually imposed on many foreign end-stressed nouns, adjectives, and participles.

In words of two syllables the full-stress was shifted onto the first syllable and the second syllable received half-stress or weak stress, which was later either retained or reduced to unstress. Half-stress or weak stress survives in *áccèss, cónvènt, énvòy, ímpùlse, prélùde, próvèrb, súbùrb*, BE *hóstìle*, etc.; it was reduced to unstress in *cíty, cóllege, cómfort, súrface, fátal, fámous*, AE *hóstile*, etc.

Among the many disyllabic nouns in which the full stress was shifted from the base morphemes to the prefix, or which were later shaped on this model, are the following: *access, assets, college, comfort, concord, conduit, convent, edict, envoy, expert, impulse, invoice, prefect, prelude, pretext, preface, prologue, proverb, substance, suburb, succor, surface, surtax, transept.*

As a result of the retention of end-stress in verbs of this type and the forward shift of full stress in nouns consisting of the same morphemes, MnE has the following words in which the pattern ⟨_ ∠⟩ of the verb contrasts with the pattern ⟨∠ _⟩ of the noun: *absent, abstract, accent, affix, attribute, combine, combat, commune, compact, compound, compress, concert, conduct, confine, conflict, consort, contest, contract, convict, convoy, digest, discount, discard, discourse, ensign, envelope, extract, exploit, export, impact, import, impress, imprint, incense, incline, increase, insert, interchange, interdict, interline, object, perfect, perfume, permit, pervert, prefix, present, preview, progress, project, protest, rebound, recess, record, refund, refuse, regress, reject, subject, suffix, survey, suspect, transfer, transform, transport.*

To this list may be added the following in which the noun has a suffix: *concéive ≠ cóncept, contáin ≠ cóntent, conscríbe ≠ cónscript, percéive ≠ pércept, prodúce ≠ próduct, subscríbe ≠ súbscript, transcríbe ≠ tránscript.*

In some nouns of this type, fore-stress is not yet fully established, in others it is beginning to intrude, as in *combine, concrete, conserve, decoy, descrease, discharge, egress, enclave, exchequer, recourse, recluse, redress, research, surmise, survey*. The adjectives *expert, extant* also waver.

On the other hand, in some nouns of this type the foreign end-stress has been retained, so that they are homophonous with the verb (except for final /f ~ v/ and /s ~ z/). Examples are: *abuse, accord, account, advise, affront, assault, assent, attack, attempt, attire, command, consent, concern, debauch, debate, decay, decline, disease, discomfort, disgrace, disguise, disgust, dishonor, dismay, dispatch, dispute, display, distrust, embrace, employ, enamel, endeavor, exchange, excuse, exhaust, exhibit, reform, regard, regret, relief, reproach, repeal, reply, report, repair, repose, reprieve, request, reserve, resort, result, revolt, reward, surprise, surrender.* Some of these end-stressed nouns are post-verbal, others not.

In some cases both noun and verb have end-stress, but differ in the shape of the base morpheme: *conceive—conceit, constrain—constraint, deceit—deceive, defense—defend, excess—exceed, expense—expend, success—succeed.*

There are also a few nouns with end-stress that are unpaired with cognate verbs: *distaste, example, remorse, renown, resources.*

Contrary to the general rule, some verbs of this structure have acquired fore-stress, some of them being post-nominal, others not. Thus: *comfort, comment, contact, conjure* (summon a spirit), *conquer, exile, implement, injure, premise* (also *premíse*), *presage* (also *preságe*), *profit, process, aroffer, promise, differ, offer, suffer, exit, succor, surfeit,* AE *accent* (beside *pccént*).

In stems of three or more syllables, the full stress was retracted to the third-last syllable (the antepenult) and the last syllable was given half-stress, which was either retained or further reduced at a later time. Final half-stress or weak stress survives in *návigàte, réconcìle, cólumbìne, ínfantìle, rélatìve, pácifìsm, véritŷ, prívacŷ,* etc.; reduction to unstress took place in *cónfidence, -ent, díssonance, -ant, géneral, génerous, délicate, végetable, ádmirable,* and in many other words with the suffixes illustrated here.

To the latter group also belong the many MnE words that after the retraction of the full stress ended in disyllabic *-iàl, -iànce, -iànt, -iènce, -iènt, -iòn, -iòus* in MnE, as *mártial, dálliance, váliant, pátience, -ient, nátion, précious.* Hence, though MnE *commércial, impátient, rotátion, precócious, senténtious,* etc., appear to contravene the rule that the third-last syllable received the highest stress, they really conformed to it in ME. The later loss of a syllable resulted from the change of the sequence /i-ə/ to /jə/ in late ME or in early MnE.

In stems of more than three syllables, the stressing of the syllables preceding the fully stressed antepenult is rhythmically determined. A syllable immediately before the full-stress is either unstressed or weakly stressed, a syllable once removed normally has half-stress, as in *advérbial, extrávagant, supérlative, ferócity, verácity* and *pèrpetúity, sùpernátural, hòmogéneous, hỳpercrítical, hòmosèxuálity,* respectively.

Some Special Cases

Trisyllabic verbs based on the stem of Latin participles in *-āt-um* now have full stress on the first syllable and half-stress on the last. They came into Middle English with the foreign end-stress.

Among the hundreds of such verbs with the ⟨́ _ ̀⟩ pattern are: *abrogate, accommodate, adulterate, aggravate, assimilate, castigate, concentrate, desecrate, dissipate, educate, eliminate, exhilarate, excavate, fascinate, immigrate, innovate, intercalate, liberate, obviate, obliterate, perforate, procreate, subjugate, suffocate, venerate.* Exceptions to the rule are: *incúlcàte, imprégnàte, adúmbràte* (beside *ádumbràte*).

The adaptation of Latin participles in *-āt-um* used only attributively is less consistent. The usual stress pattern of such adjectival participles is ⟨́ _ _⟩, as in *délicate.* We can safely assume that here the foreign pattern ⟨̀ _ ́⟩ first shifted to ⟨́ _ ̀⟩, as in the verb, and was then reduced to ⟨́ _ _⟩ before the more heavily stressed following noun. Examples are: *affectionate, delicate, deliberate, desperate, fortunate, inveterate, literate, obdurate, passionate, temperate,* and *reprobate* (beside *réprobàte*).

Disyllabic adjectival participles in *-āt-um* either preserve the foreign end-stress or shift it forward, and the other syllable receives half-stress. Thus: *sèdáte, ìráte ~ íràte, innàte ~ ìnnáte, òrnáte ~ órnàte.* It seems probable that some speakers use end-stress phrase-finally, fore-stress when a noun follows, e.g. *ràther órnáte ~ his òrnáte stýle.*

The partially divergent adaptations of the Latin participial stems in *-āt* in verbals and adjectivals has produced contrastive stress patterns in trisyllabic verbs and adjectives derived from the same stem. Retaining the half-stress, such verbs have the pattern ⟨́ _ ̀⟩, the corresponding adjectives (secondarily also such adjectives used as nouns) the pattern ⟨́ _ _⟩. The loss of the final half-stress has reduced the /e/ of the suffix to /ə ~ ɪ/ in the adjectival form.

Examples with ⟨́ _ ̀⟩ in the verb vs. ⟨́ _ _⟩ in the adjective and/or noun are fairly numerous. Thus *advocate, affiliate, aggregate, affricate, alternate, associate, confederate, conglomerate, coordinate, delegate, deliberate, desolate, elaborate, expatriate, moderate, precipitate, predicate, separate, subordinate, surrogate.*

With few exceptions, both verbs and adjectives from Latin participial stems in stressed *-ít, -āt* and unstressed *-it, -ut* now have fore-stress and end in half-stress, as the verbs *éxpedìte, éxecùte* and the adjectives *récondìte, ábsolùte, díssolùte, résolùte;* also the noun *áttribùte,* contrasting with the verb *attríbùte* in stress pattern. Exceptions to this rule are the verbs *attríbùte, distríbùte, contríbùte* and the adjectives *défìnite, explícit, implícit.* The Neo-Latin scientific terms *acetate, nitrate, sulphate,* etc., usually have half-stress on the final syllable in America, less commonly in England.

Latin stems in -ắri-, ǒri-, -ếri- taken into ME with full-stress on the suffix and half-stress two syllables before it, e.g. sècretắrie, nècessắrie, trànsitốrie, òratốrie, mònastếrie, were treated in a fashion parallel to that of stems ending in full-stress. The full stress was shifted forward and the suffix received half-stress, whence American English sécretàry, nécessàry, tránsitòry, óratòry, mónastèry. In British English, the reduction of the half-stress has produced nécessarŷ /nέsɪs(ə)rî/, óratorŷ /v́ret(ə)rî/, etc.

24. Cues to Word and Morpheme Boundaries

24.1 Preliminary Remarks

The native speaker of a language, whether literate or not, has practical mastery of its syntax and morphology. He can form new sentences and phrases on models he knows and form new words. As a listener, he can usually isolate words from the context of the utterance phrase and break complex words down into morphemes. He can perform this analysis— decode the message—without receiving overt cues; but in English he is often aided in this task by audible prosodic and/or phonotactic features of speech. This analysis of the flow of speech into meaningful units is essential to a proper understanding of what is being said. The listener is hardly aware of this habitual activity.

A speaker of English 'knows' that in the phrase whỳ lét 'er the phoneme sequence /létə/ consists of two words, but that in a fìne létter the same sequence, uttered in identical fashion, is a single word. Similarly, he takes the sequence /bítn/ in Hè was bítten as two morphemes, but the sequence /bátn/ in Pùsh that bútton as a single unit, although there is no phonic clue that one of these expressions is morphologically complex and the other simple.

There are no phonic clues to distinguish bi-morphemic bétt-er, lét 'er from monomorphemic létter, or wìnn-er from mínnow, gór-y from glóry, hígh-er from híre, húnt-er from wínter, gó-ing from rúin, tést 'er from Héster, a dóor from adóre, héel-ed from fíeld, hè-'d (knów) from nèed (móney). No overt clues indicate the morphological boundaries in the linked passages of the following sentences:

> Dòes⌣it shóck⌣you || Yès⌣it dóes ||
> I⌣can tèll⌣you àll⌣abóut⌣it ||
> Wìll⌣you hàve⌣anóther ||
> Dòn't màke⌣a fóol⌣of⌣'im ||
> I'm⌣agáinst⌣it ||

And yet, a speaker of English hearing such utterances will rarely be in doubt about any of the lexical units that enter into their formation.

Though not infrequently unmarked, word and morpheme boundaries within English utterance phrases are more often than not conveyed to the listener by perceptible features of speech.

Potentially perceptible clues to boundaries of the words of an utterance phrase and of the morphemes of a complex word arise (1) from the prosodic feature of stress and/or (2) from the rules governing the sequence of phonemes in morphemes and monomorphemic words. These clues are not separate functional units of speech, but automatic side-effects of English prosody and phonotactics, respectively.

Stress-conditioned prosodic boundary signals have nothing in common with phonotactic signals. Neither type depends upon the other, although the two may coincide in a given utterance phrase. To posit a 'phoneme of open juncture' comprising two radically different phenomena that happen to have the same potential function may seem 'convenient'. But such a fiction not only disregards the diverse nature of these phenomena, but treats them as separate entities when, in fact, they are automatic by-products of stress and of phonotactics. Any realistic account of boundary markers occurring within utterance phrases must keep prosodically and phonotactically conditioned signals apart.

24.2 Prosodic Cues

Stressed morphemes of English have a characteristic energy curve. The force of articulation rises sharply at the beginning, culminates in the syllabic, and tapers off towards the end. Hence consonants preceding the syllabic are articulated with greater force than those following it; the former are 'strong', the latter 'weak'. These prosodic allophones of the consonants can be easily observed in monosyllabic morphemes beginning and ending in identical consonants. Articulated with full stress, as if they had the sentence accent, such words as *peep, pup, coke, cook, gag, judge, fife, sauce, noon, nun, flail, lull,* AE *roar,* clearly start with 'strong' consonants and end in 'weak' ones. Stress-conditioned allophones are most striking in the voiceless plosives /p, t, k/ and the resonants /l/ and AE /r/, but are present in all consonants, as spectrographic research has demonstrated. Under half-stress the allophonic variation is reduced and may become imperceptible to the human ear. On the other hand, the speaker may enhance the prosodic allophones deliberately by using emphatic stress. For these reasons, prosodic boundary signals are potential rather than unfailing in connected discourse.

Within an utterance phrase, it is the morphological structure that determines the onset of stress. The onset of stress, in turn, strengthens the initial consonant or consonant cluster, which thus marks the beginning of a word or morpheme for the listener. This phonemenon is easily observed in such utterances as *sèll físh, shéll-fìsh* vs. *sèlf-ínterest, shélf-ìce*;

the stréet, twò stréets, Báy Strèet vs. *thìs tréat*; *ráce-tràck* vs. *làst ráck, tést rùn.* In each of these sets of expressions the consonant sequence between the syllabics is the same, but the breaks vary with the onset of stress as determined by morphological structure.

The same side-effect of stress occurs, when a single consonant intervenes between syllabics. Thus the 'strong' consonant in *mỳ cóat, hìgh nóon, a lóut* signals the beginning of a morpheme, while the weak intervocalic consonant in *lìke óats, fìne ápple, pìne-àpple, àll óut* signals the end. These stress-conditioned allophones are most easily observed in such minimally differentiated pairs as *a náme* vs. *an áim,* and in pairs containing the same vowels, as *nò dóubt* vs. *ròde óut.*

A few more examples will serve to illustrate the prosodic signaling of morpheme breaks. Strong allophones of consonants cue the beginning of morphemes in such cases as the following: *lòw tíde, bów tìe, gò báck, thrów-bàck, nò líght, tòo fást, be-líeve* and *hìll-tòp, wèll tóld.* Weak allophones signal the end in such instances as *gòad ón, pùll óut, mòve ín, tàil énd* and *hànd óut, bùild úp.* The effect of this process is most easily observed in pairs that differ little in their phonemic make-up, such as *téa cùp ≠ spèak úp, nò dóubt ≠ ròde óut, bùy tín ≠ bìte ín.*

Unstressed morphemes do not have a stress curve to produce perceptible allophones of the consonants. Hence their beginnings or ends are not prosodically cued in mid-phrase. The intervocalic consonants in *hìll-y* and *jélly,* in *mádd-er* and *ládder,* in *húnt-er* and *wínter,* etc., are phonically identical, although the first of each pair is bimorphemic, the second monomorphemic. *High-ly* and *wíl-y* have the same kind of /l/, although the /l/ begins a morpheme in the former and ends it in the latter. There is no prosodic clue to convey the fact that each of the following expressions begins with two words: *Shè's (níce). I've (séen it). Wè'll (dó it). Thèy'd (líke to). Tèll a (stóry). Nòt a (bít).*

In plurisyllabic foreign words, strong prevocalic consonants are not a safe guide to phonemic structure. Here strong consonants do indeed appear at the beginning of morphemes, as in *e-láte, di-láte, co-lláte, trans-láte, a-ttést, de-tést, con-tést, pro-tést, pre-ténd, dis-tráct, re-tráct, sub-tráct, in-fórm, per-fórm,* and in many other words with unstressed prefixes. But they also occur in positions where they do not start a morpheme, as in *petítion, equálity, ecónomy, polítical, América, canál, machíne, Chicágo, histórian.*

There are, finally, two points that should be mentioned. First, such expressions as *slówly, slýly, hígher* normally are prosodically identical with *hóly, wíly, híre,* respectively; but the morpheme-final vowels of *slów-ly, slý-ly, high-er* can be prolonged at will to cue the morphological break. Secondly, sometimes the stress-conditioned allophones are variable or ambiguous, as those of /n/ in *an óther* in such expressions as *gìve me an óther* and *hèlp one anóther.* Under such conditions a 'wrong' break may become established, as in *an ápron* for earlier *a nápron* and in *a nícknàme* for earlier *an ícknàme*.

24.3 Phonotactic Cues

Phonotactic cues to boundaries between the words of an utterance phrase and between the morphemes of a complex word result from limitations in the distribution of the phonemes in morphemes. Any deviation from the rules governing the sequences of phonemes in morphemes is a potential signal of a morphological break in the utterance.

Limitations in the positional distribution of phonemes are treated under the several phonemes. Rules governing the normal sequence of phonemes in morphemes and mono-morphemic words are described in the section devoted to phonotactics (see 3). The more common phonotactic phenomena that furnish potential clues to morpheme boundaries are pointed out below and illustrated by a few examples.

The consonants /h, j, w/ occur only before vowels, /ŋ, ž/ only after vowels. Hence, /h, j, w/ mark the beginning of morphemes, as in *knèe-hígh*, *tów-hèad*, *sèe wéll*, *séa-wày*, *Nèw Yórk*, *láw-yer*; and /ŋ, ž/ the end, as in *hàng úp*, *síng-er*, *masságe it*. The fact that in a few foreign words /h, j, w, z/ occur also between vowels within a morpheme, as in *Sahára*, *Máya*, *Hìawátha*, does not obscure their function as potential boundary markers.

The vowels illustrated in *pin*, *pen*, *pan*, *hot*, *hut*, *foot* do not occur at the end of morphemes. Hence any single consonant following one of these 'checked' vowels in a sequence vowel + consonant + vowel must belong to the same morpheme as the vowel, as in *pìck úp*, *ègg ón*, *lòck óut* and *thíck-er*, *páss-age*, *wóol-en*. When the second syllable of such an expression is unstressed, the listener must have other information to tell that *thíck-er*, *wóol-en*, etc., consist of two morphemes, and *dícker*, *súllen*, etc., only of one.

In the native vocabulary of English, vowels do not occur in sequence within a morpheme. Hence successive vowels can cue a break between native words and morphemes, as in *twò éggs*, *gò ín*, *séa ùrchin*, *láw òffice*, *blów-ing*, *slów-er*, *gráy-ish*. In the foreign vocabulary this type of break is common enough, as in *rè-áct*, *cò-éval*, *dù-ét*, *dú-al*; but it is not without exception. Disyllabic *rúin*, *vówel*, *póet*, *pòét(ic)* are clearly monomorphemic.

The sequence of consonants before and after the syllabic of a morpheme is rather definitely regulated. Any sequence of consonants in an utterance phrase that does not occur ('is not permitted') in morphemes is therefore a potential clue to a morphological break. The chief types of such incongruous consonant sequences are pointed out below and illustrated by a few examples. The potentially cued breaks between words are indicated by spacing, those between morphemes by hyphens. These graphic devices

do not represent a 'phoneme of juncture'; they merely indicate the
secondary effects of deviations from phonotactic rules.

The following types of incongruous consonant sequences can cue
morphological breaks:

(a) A consonant followed by its like: *night-tìme, rìght tíme, it tóre,
gráss-sèed, hòme-máde, táil-lìght.*

(b) A stop followed by an other stop, or a fricative by an other fricative:
hát-pìn, báck-gròund, hóuse-hòld, gìve thánks, líve thère and *kép-t, bégg-ed,
láugh-s, lív-es, fíf-th.*

(c) An obstruent followed by any other obstruent (except /s/-clusters
and /-ft/): *mád-hòuse, lìke fún, hélp-fùl, púsh-càrt, stìff pénalty, wís-dom.*

(d) A nasal followed by another nasal: *còme néar, màn-máde, háng-man,
cálm-ness.*

(e) Any obstruent, except /s/, followed by a nasal: *càtch míce, hàlf-
móon, égg-nòg, rásh-ness.*

(f) Various other incongruous sequences: *óut-lèt, bráin-less, hóme-ward,
úp-ward, ráil-ròad, hòme rúle.*

It might also be pointed out that the syllabic division regularly falls
between two incongruous intersyllabic consonants, thus coinciding with
the morphological break. But this is fortuitous, since the syllabic division
also falls between congruous intersyllabic consonants, as in *hélp ùs,
hánd-òut.*

24.4 Sample Sentences and Text

The relative frequency of potential boundary signals within utterance
phrases and of unmarked morphological breaks is illustrated below in a
number of unconnected sentences and in a short text. Prosodically cued
breaks are indicated above the line, phonotactic ones below it. Uncued
breaks are not pointed out, but should be obvious to the reader.

In the short text, approximately two thirds of the actual morpheme
boundaries within the utterance phrases are potentially signaled, the
remaining third not. The ends of the phrases obviously coincide with
morpheme boundaries, so that more than two thirds of the morpheme
breaks have a definite or a potential boundary signal.

This brief text is fairly representative of simple conversational English.
In learned and technical discourse containing numerous plurisyllabic
foreign words, the percentage of unsignaled breaks is somewhat higher.

Sample Sentences

Clàss wĭll téll.

Gŏ́ tó ĭt.

Sŏ you wĭll not hắve ĭt. Sŏ whắt.

He wŏuldn't dó ĭt.

Why wàste thĕ móney?

Get hòmĕ éarly. I'll sĭt úp for you.

Perhàps there ̆ĭsn't àny such ̆rùle.

Ĭ càn't téll you.

Shê̆'s a hĭgh-clắss ̆gírl. Why dŏn't you invíte hèr?

Dòes ĭt ̆shóck you? Yès ĭt ̆dŏes.

Yòu ̆sắid ĭt.

Hè hít 'ĭm.

I can ̆tèll you àll abóut ĭt.

Sample Text

A. *I'm ̆súre | you hàd a wònderful tíme ||*

B. *Whý | Yès Ĭ ̆díd. ||*

A. *Dìd you enjòy hòlding hánds | in the ̆móonlĭght ||*

B. *Enjòyed ĭt vèry múch || Espécially |*

   as Ĭ wòn't have anòther ̆chánce ||

A. *Sŏ you ̆dòn't ̆thínk | yòu'll ̆sée her agàin ||*

   Yòu're not ̆màking a ̆fóol of yoursèlf | áre yòu ||

   . . . I was just ̆tẽasing you abòut thĭs ̆gìrl ||

   Ĭ knów | you'd ̆nèver fắll for hèr | whoềver she ̆ĭs ||

Adapted from Sinclair Lewis, *Cass Timberlane*

25. Syllabification

The syllable is a directly observable datum of speech. Whether listening to utterances of a language one knows or to an unfamiliar language, one observes peaks of loudness and can make a rough count of such peaks. The perception of peaks is of course influenced by one's speech habits. Thus a speaker of English or of German may count the sequence /ai/ of Italian *mai* as a single peak; and vice versa, a speaker of Italian may take the English diphthong in *my* as two peaks. But such exceptions do not contradict the observation that, by and large, peaks of loudness are directly observable.

To the listener, the English syllable is a wave of loudness. Its peak is normally formed by a voiced open sound (a vowel), as in *hat, egg, tea*; less often by a voiced resonant, as in the second syllable of *nation, table*. The syllabic peak may be followed by less sonorous sounds (consonants), as in *egg, old*; preceded by consonants, as in *do, true*; or flanked by consonants, as in *hat, man, blank, frost*. Only rarely does the syllabic stand alone, as in *I* and the exclamations *ah!, oh!*

The acoustic-auditory shape of the syllable results from the natural sonority of the several types of phonemes. Voiced open sounds (vowels) and the voiced resonants /m, n, l/, having the greatest sonority, form the peaks, and less sonorous phonemes (consonants) the margins. When two consonants precede or follow the peak, those of greater sonority (the resonants) adjoin it and those of less sonority (the obstruents) form the margin(s), as in *blue, fry, elk, aunt, blank*, AE *dwarf*. When two obstruents follow a vowel, the fricative precedes the less sonorous plosive, as in *soft, guest, ask*. Exceptions to these rules are the /s/-clusters, as in *fox, lapse, spin, stop, skin*.

It will be observed that the acoustic shapes of English syllables are often identical with the normal phonemic shapes of English morphemes as described in section 3.

Syllable boundaries frequently coincide with word boundaries and morpheme boundaries, as pointed out below. But they can also be independent of morphological boundaries or run counter to them. Thus (1) monomorphemic *letter, bitter, dicker, simmer, little, battle, fellow, berry* consist of two syllables, having a boundary in the intervocalic consonant. (2) In bimorphemic *bett-er, thick-er, funn-y, legg-y, swell-ing, rott-en*, the syllable boundary is in the intervocalic consonant, the morpheme boundary after the consonant. (3) Discrepancy between the syllable division and the break between morphemes occurs also in such cases as *hunt-er, sulk-ing, fast-er*, where the syllabic boundary falls between the two consonants and the morpheme boundary follows them. (4) Such words as *ruin, cruel, vowel, fire* are mono-morphemic, but consist of two syllables.

(5) A single syllable often consists of two morphemes, as *leng-th*, *build-s*, *kep-t*; or of two words, as *we-'ll* (*do it*), *it-'s* (*good*), *we-'ve* (*seen it*), (*he*) *can-'t*.

Inspection of syllable boundaries that deviate from morpheme boundaries shows that they occur at points of least sonority: in a consonant separating vowels (examples 1 and 2), or in the transition from consonant to consonant (examples 3 and 4). They show further that syllable divisions do not occur unless there is a more or less marked increase in sonority after a syllabic peak (examples 5).

The principle of relative sonority that produces the peaks and the boundaries of syllables also obtains when the syllable boundaries coincide with word or morpheme boundaries.

Morphological boundaries are signaled by stress-conditioned allophones and/or by incongruous sequences of phonemes (see 24). In *dáy-tìme*, *mỳ fáce*, the strong allophones of /t/ and /f/ signal the beginning of a morpheme; in *báke-òven*, *tàke óver*, the weak allophone of /k/ cues the end of a morpheme. Since the beginning of a new syllable is heard whenever sonority increases, the syllable division here automatically coincides with the break between morphemes.

In *bréak-fast*, *húsband*, the break between morphemes is signaled by incongruous consonant clusters. Here the syllable division coincides with the morphological break, since in accordance with the principle of sonority the syllabic division falls into the transition from consonant to consonant, if the cluster is flanked by vowels.

In *mán-pòwer*, *grèat lóve*, where the morphological break is cued both prosodically and phonotactically, the syllable division naturally coincides with the breaks, for the reasons stated above.

Though in part an automatic correlate of the shapes of morphemes and their boundaries, the syllable, with its peak and margins, is an independent entity in the flow of speech, an acoustic-auditory unit of utterance based on the natural sonority of the phonemes as modified by stress. It is not a part of the phonemic, the morphological, or the prosodic structure of English, but rather an aspect of the mechanics of utterance.

Since, to the listener, syllabification depends upon perceptible variation in sonority, it varies with changes in sonority induced by the tempo of utterance or by the prosody. Thus the phrase *hìgher and hígher* can have from three to five syllabic peaks, depending upon tempo and prosodic context; after a stressed free vowel, the syllable division may be before a following consonant or in it, as in *mùch láter* (with prolonged emphatic vowel) vs. *làter ón*, respectively; under emphatic stress the syllable division may be shifted, as in the phrase AE *nòt at ↓ áll*, with normal syllable divisions in the two /t/ sounds, but with division before the /t/ sounds in emphatic → *nŏt | àt ↓ áll*.

The fact that syllable divisions vary with tempo and prosody accounts for such shifts in morphological boundaries as those appearing in *an apron* for earlier *a napron*, and in *a newt* for earlier *an ewt*.

In conclusion, it should be pointed out that there are some regional differences in syllabification. (1) After the stressed checked vowels of such words as *middle, leather, ladder, bother, sunny*, the syllable division regularly occurs in the consonant in British English and in some varieties of American English. But in types of American English in which the checked vowels are markedly prolonged or ingliding, as in parts of the South, the division comes before the consonant. (2) *Squirrel, towel* are largely monosyllabic in AE, but disyllabic in some coastal areas. (3) Under emphatic stress, such words as *fear, fair, four, poor* are often disyllabic in those coastal dialects of AE that lack post-vocalic /r/.